AF505918

# STATES OF PASSION

# States of Passion

## Law, Identity, and the Social Construction of Desire

YVONNE ZYLAN

OXFORD
UNIVERSITY PRESS

OXFORD
UNIVERSITY PRESS

*Oxford University Press, Inc., publishes works that further Oxford University's objective of excellence in research, scholarship, and education.*

Oxford   New York
Auckland   Cape Town   Dar es Salaam   Hong Kong   Karachi   Kuala
Lumpur   Madrid   Melbourne   Mexico City   Nairobi   New Delhi   Shanghai   Taipei   Toronto

With offices in
Argentina   Austria   Brazil   Chile   Czech Republic   France   Greece   Guatemala   Hungary
Italy   Japan   Poland   Portugal   Singapore   South Korea   Switzerland   Thailand   Turkey
Ukraine   Vietnam



Library of Congress Cataloging-in-Publication Data
Zylan, Yvonne.
  States of passion : law, identity, and the social construction of desire / Yvonne Zylan.
     p. cm.
  Includes bibliographical references and index.
  ISBN 978-0-19-973508-2 ((hardback): alk. paper)
  1. Sex and law—United States. 2.  Sociological jurisprudence. 3.  Homosexuality—Law
and legislation—United States.  I. Title.
   KF9325.Z85 2011
   342.7308'7—dc22                                                          2010053149

1 2 3 4 5 6 7 8 9

Printed in the United States of America on acid-free paper

**Note to Readers**
This publication is designed to provide accurate and authoritative information in regard to the subject matter covered. It is based upon sources believed to be accurate and reliable and is intended to be current as of the time it was written. It is sold with the understanding that the publisher is not engaged in rendering legal, accounting, or other professional services. If legal advice or other expert assistance is required, the services of a competent professional person should be sought. Also, to confirm that the information has not been affected or changed by recent developments, traditional legal research techniques should be used, including checking primary sources where appropriate.

*(Based on the Declaration of Principles jointly adopted by a Committee of the
American Bar Association and a Committee of Publishers and Associations.)*

You may order this or any other Oxford University Press publication by
visiting the Oxford University Press website at www.oup.com

# Contents

# Acknowledgments

To my chagrin, this book has been several years in the making. It has traveled with me (first in my head, and then increasingly on paper) from San Diego to upstate New York, to Atlanta, back to New York, to Albuquerque, and back to New York again. It has even spent some time in British Columbia. Not surprisingly, then, many people have made contributions to it along the way—each indispensable to (but not responsible for) the version that appears here. Many have offered constructive advice and criticism to written and presented portions of the manuscript, including: Lynn C. Jones, Anna-Marie Marshall, Scott Barclay, Steven Boutcher, Sandra Levitsky, Julie Nice, Heidi M. Hurd, Jessica Mitchell, Jason Weinstein, Morgan Stewart, Eric Schmale, Sara Hess, Kay Aschenbeck, three anonymous external reviewers solicited by Oxford University Press, and readers and audiences at: the Law and Society Association Annual Meetings in Berlin (2007) and Denver (2009); the University of Toronto; the University of California - Irvine; the University of New Mexico; and Hamilton College. Lynn Jones, Scott Barclay and Anna-Marie Marshall have been especially important to the process of completing this project, both for their substantive feedback and for being so welcoming of me as I have sought to reinvent myself as a Law & Society scholar.

I am exceptionally lucky to be a member of the faculty of Hamilton College, a liberal arts institution of the best sort: one that genuinely embraces its liberal arts mission, and which supports a diversity of scholarly endeavors. What it lacks in congenial weather, Hamilton more than makes up for in exceptionally smart students and faculty, a gifted and dedicated staff, and an unswerving institutional commitment to helping everyone do their best work. (Also, you should try the cider donuts in town.)

I wish to specially thank my colleagues in the Department of Sociology at Hamilton. Jenny Irons, Stephen Ellingson, Daniel Chambliss, and Dennis Gilbert have all read and commented on portions of the manuscript and have provided important feedback and support along the way. Dennis and Steve gave detailed comments on earlier drafts, and Dennis offered some very useful advice ("more stories!") at a critical moment in the writing. Jenny Irons is not only a colleague whom I admire greatly, but also one of my closest friends, as well as the person perhaps most responsible for my return to academe after my stint in legal practice. She certainly is responsible for my being at Hamilton, and for that I will always be grateful. Along with Jenny, many other friends and colleagues at Hamilton, including (but not limited to) Julio Videras, Michelle LeMasurier, George Hobor, and Tina Hall, have created a nurturing and intellectually stimulating community for me in Clinton. They are all talented scholars, gifted teachers, and funny, funny people.

A portion of the early part of the research for this project was undertaken pursuant to a generous understanding of the concept of "business development" held by my former colleagues at Pillsbury Winthrop Shaw Pittman LLP, and I learned a great deal about the practice of law from them during my time at the firm. PWSP was also where I met C.J. Martin, who has become a brother to me, and who has been an enthusiastic supporter of this project since its inception. C.J. provided a writing retreat for me (and my dog) during the earliest stages of the research, and has offered both material and emotional support throughout. Along with Kate Nyce, C.J. is also one of my favorite (ex)lawyers in the world.

I also wish to thank my editors at Oxford University Press: Chris Collins (who began the process with me) and Michelle Lipinski (who ended it), as well as Jessica Picone (also of OUP), who was understanding and encouraging throughout. I thank as well the *Michigan Journal of Gender & Law* and the *University of Michigan Journal of Law Reform*, both of which graciously granted permission to reprint portions of articles that they had previously published.

Others who contributed include: Martha Fineman, who was both kind and generous to me during my time in Atlanta, making me feel personally welcome in her home and providing me with space and resources at the Feminism and Legal Theory Project at Emory University; Robin Vanderwall, who has been an engaged and gentle interlocutor throughout the writing of the book, as well as a friend, a cheerleader, and an administrative genius; my colleagues in the Department of Sociology at the University of New Mexico, who invited me to join them and thus gave me the opportunity to spend a productive and memorable year in Albuquerque; Luke Maher, who provided last minute (and frankly brilliant) cite-checking assistance; and the many Hamilton students who have informed this work along the way through challenging and inspiring discussions held in classes, seminars, and the occasional random chat at the Fitness Center. Also, while I know it's a ridiculously late modern, bourgeois thing to do, I have to acknowledge my dog, Oliver, who was with me—literally—as I wrote virtually every page of this book.

Finally, I wish to thank my family. My partner in all things, Laura Spitz, has read more versions of this manuscript than either of us cares to count or remember, and it is my pure, dumb luck that she happens to be a brilliant lawyer and scholar, a closet sociologist, and a whip-smart editor. She has also encouraged me, cajoled me, flattered me, and probably hoodwinked me along the way—whatever it took to help me finish this project. But this hardly begins to describe all of the ways in which she has been important to the writing of this book and—more importantly—to me. I could not have written it without her. Nor would I have wanted to.

Our son Oakley has evinced very un-teenager-like levels of understanding as weekends and vacations were nibbled away at (and sometimes consumed) by the demands of deadlines and workloads. He and Laura (and Oliver, and Maple) have had to hear the phrase "when the book is done" more often than anyone ever should, and yet their patience has never wavered. I dedicate this book to them. h/t: my family.

# 1

# Introduction



*"The law is a department of sociology."*

—JAMES C. CARTER
*"The Ideal and the Actual in the Law"*
*Annual Address to the American Bar Association*
*Aug. 21, 1890*[1]

What is sexual identity without sexual desire?
What if hatred and desire are not antithetical?
What if love and marriage are?

In contemporary American society, these are questions not for philosophers, but for lawyers. Seemingly in spite of its reputation as a site of rational discourse,[2] law is a set of institutional practices increasingly preoccupied with giving shape and definition to various forms of passion. Desire, love, fear, loathing, and hatred figure prominently in many of the most contentious and significant jurisprudential developments of late capitalist American society. They are also—and this is not a coincidence—central concepts at play in the equally contentious cultural and social debates over the nature of modern identity and selfhood.

1. As quoted in Tamanaha 2006: 17.

2. The idea that law is dispassionate is of long standing, going back at least to Aristotle's claim that "law is reason, free from passion" (Aristotle 1962: Book IV, xvi). *See generally* Bandes 1999.

As French social theorist Michel Foucault observed nearly 30 years ago, sexuality, the body, and authoritative discourses of the self are crucial, interlinked features of Western modernity. Not only are discourses of sexuality fundamental to postmetaphysical regimes of personal "truth," he contended, but sexuality also operates as "an especially dense transfer point for relations of power."[3] Sex is knowledge, so the saying goes, and knowledge is power.[4]

While Foucault focused primarily on medical and religious discourses of sexuality in his *History of Sexuality*, his genealogy of modernity plainly implicated law as well.[5] Indeed, if, as he argued, one of the central mechanisms by which the self is constituted in the modern West is the creation and invocation of disciplinary regimes of truth,[6] we would be surprised *not* to find that law plays an important role in articulating normative conceptions of self, identity, and sexuality. Similarly, Foucault's claim (though it hardly originates with him)[7] that sexuality is

3. Foucault 1990: 23, 58–63, 103.

4. Foucault 1990; Foucault and Gordon 1980.

5. Obviously, Foucault had been interested in law—especially penal law—throughout his career. See, for example, Foucault 1995. However, perhaps because of his interest in decentering the state as a locus of power, law was not the focus of his *History of Sexuality*.

6. *See* Butler 2005: 22.

7. Within sociology, the concept of "social construction" well precedes Foucault's *History of Sexuality*. Berger and Luckmann's <u>The Social Construction of Reality</u> (first published in 1966) articulated an explicitly social scientific version of the concept, and Howard Garfinkel's (1967) study of a male-to-female transsexual he called "Agnes" elaborated upon the interactional and symbolic qualities of gender. West and Zimmerman (1987), drawing upon Garfinkel, produced the canonical essay within the discipline on the performative nature of gender, which has informed the work of numerous scholars of sexuality, including Joshua Gamson (1998), Stephen Seidman (1993, 1996), Cindy Patton (1993), Michael Warner (1993, 1999), and many others. David Greenberg (1988) was one of the earliest sociological proponents of the idea that same-sex sexuality is variably experienced and understood

*socially constructed*—that it is variable, performative, mutable and shaped by social, political, historical and economic forces—would seem to point toward the significance of law as a set of structuring discourses and institutions.

In short, if law is an important institutional setting for the negotiation of modern notions of identity, and sexuality is a key feature of identity that is subject to social forces that shape and inform its meaning, then it makes sense to examine law as an important site of sexuality's construction. In fact, a number of extant studies do examine the intersection of law and sexuality. This research is primarily focused on (1) theoretical and empirical examinations of sexuality as a basis of citizenship rights, and (2) empirical studies of the legal tactics and strategies of lesbian/gay/bisexual (LGB) social movements. To a significant degree, both sets of literatures have been fundamentally concerned with the utility and puissance of identity-based legal *rights* claims. That is, they have been concerned with whether and how legalism does or does not "work for" political subjects identified as gay, lesbian, bisexual and, to a lesser extent, heterosexual.[8]

This is an important research question, and addressing it advances both normative and descriptive scholarly and political programs. Yet in fundamental ways, examining the issue in this

over time and across space. Similar arguments abound in history, philosophy, psychology, and cultural studies. Beyond the discipline of sociology, Judith Butler's influence cannot be overstated. *See* Butler 1990.

8. *See, for example*, MacKinnon 1989; Kennedy 1993; Hyde 1997; Eskridge 1999; Phelan 2001; Stychin and Herman 2001; Armstrong 2002; Stychin 1998; 2003; Bernstein and Schaffner 2005; Halley 2006; Pinello 2003, 2006; Andersen 2006; Yoshino 2006; Cossman 2007; Fetner 2008; Fineman, et. al. 2009; Barclay, et al., 2009; Nussbaum 2010. There is also an extensive literature produced in law reviews focusing on doctrinal questions. I discuss this in greater detail below so will note here only that such research also tends to privilege questions of political efficacy. *See, for example*, Franke 2004: 1404 (examining the doctrinal contours of *Lawrence v. Texas* in an effort to determine "whether [articulation of] a different kind of right might have opened up different possibilities for future legal and political action" for LGB people.)

way brackets some of the essential questions posed by constructionist theories of identity and sexuality. Among such theories,
perhaps the most influential is Judith Butler's account of the
performative qualities of gender and sexuality[9]—a study that,
more than any other, marks an anti-foundationalist[10] turn in
the field. Drawing upon Lacanian, Foucaultian, and Derridian
epistemologies, Butler redirected social constructionist accounts
of gender, the body, and sexuality away from their foundational
allegiances and toward poststructural notions of decentered and
destabilized identificatory *processes*. Yet much extant research
on law and sexuality, while frequently referring to Foucaultian
and Butlerian conceptions of sexuality and identity, instead treats
sexual and gendered subjects as prediscursive and coherent—
as existing prior to their imbrication with legal doctrine and
institutions.

Moreover, sexuality appears in many of these studies as fundamentally binary in nature, embedded in a matrix of discrete,
categorical conceptions of emotion, identity, and status. This is
true even where these binaries are criticized as problematic. And
while scholars sometimes contend that sexuality and sexual
identity are constructed by law, further analysis is needed to
demonstrate *how* sexuality is installed or reinscribed by law as
part of the conceptual and empirical grid that maps particular
conceptions of desire, love, animus, and fear in relation to one
another; and posits specifically anchored social relationships

9. Butler 1990.

10. There are many ways to describe the array of contemporary theories of sexuality,
gender, and identity. Alternately referred to as postmodern, poststructural, and
anti-foundationalist, these theories are tethered to one another by their rejection of
structural and material determinism and (more generally) foundationalism: the
notion that identity and social action are grounded in the intentional, autonomous,
self-conscious action of prediscursive social agents. *See* Namaste 1996. I explore
these distinctions in greater detail in Chapter 3.

between oppositional or affined social, emotional, and political personae. Attention to such processes permits us more fully to understand the productive effects of law as a discursive regime.

In *States of Passion*, I explore the discursive effects of law on the constitution of sexual experience, expression, and identities. In doing so, I take seriously the notion that law may profitably be read as a series of texts that serve to socially construct sex, gender, and the desiring body. However, like many poststructuralists, I resist the suggestion that such texts exist in some imagined free-floating linguistic space. Rather, I contend that they are always embedded within specific institutions and, as such, are shaped, constrained, and enabled by the organizational features, mandates, and resources that serve to make up those institutions. And, like other constitutive theorists of law, I argue that law not only speaks to us or for us but also helps to constitute us in the first instance as social beings with distinct identities and passions. I seek to improve upon existing scholarship on the constitutive power of law by incorporating the insights of poststructural theorists and some social movements scholars, and contextualizing the discursive production of subjectivity within specific institutional dynamics. In short, I seek to bring to the study of sexuality law a poststructural, yet institutionally grounded, "sociological imagination". In adopting a sociological imagination, I seek to situate individual lives and life experiences within their sociologically meaningful context.[11] This approach is familiar—even canonical—to sociologists.

It may seem odd or oxymoronic to refer to a poststructural institutionalism. However, I do not view poststructural theory as dispensing with social structure entirely. While it rejects the notion that "deep" social structures are foundational to human

11. Mills 1959.

action, poststructural theory is not antistructural. Instead, post-structuralism posits social structure as the product of iterative social action. Social structures exist in provisional, dynamic form, but they are sufficiently concrete and ontologically "real" to constrain and shape further social action. Accordingly, my perspective is poststructural in that it eschews reliance upon notions of the deep, fixed, material foundations of social identity. But it remains institutionalist in its attention to the importance of relatively stable and semiautonomous institutional features of what I have elsewhere termed "preexisting policy environments," including temporally prior discursive streams, organizational practices, and institutional mandates.[12]

## I. Contextualizing Doctrine

As Foucault and the generation of scholars influenced by his work have demonstrated, discursive effects and objects are embodied in texts produced within and around social institutions.[13] With respect to law, this means we should be interested in the legal opinions, law review articles, briefs, and transcripts that are the stuff of judicial practice, itself characterized by multiple layers of rules, procedures, and patterned social action. Unpacking and identifying the juridical discursive effects constituting the sexual thus requires that law be examined as a set of texts—that we consider the precise doctrinal formulations of the dimensions of sexual experience, expression, and identity announced in legal texts. It also means, however, that we

12. Zylan 2000: 612. *See also* Zylan 1996.

13. *See, for example,* Smith 1990.

consider the institutional features of the judiciary, broadly con-ceived, that serve to shape, enable, and constrain doctrine.

As a general matter, prior research on sexuality law typically emphasizes one or the other of these dimensions but not both. Sociologists of law—particularly those who examine law and LGB movements—have constructed sophisticated, nuanced accounts of how movement activists and organizations mount challenges to the polity, articulate new social problems as targets of legislative intervention, and deploy identity constructs in efforts to win legal recognition or constituent benefits.[14] Some of these studies examine doctrine, but few do so in a way that destabilizes or interrogates the normative conceptions of identity and sexuality that are positioned as instruments of contentious politics.[15]

At the same time, legal scholars interested in jurisprudence and doctrine operate largely outside of broader sociological literatures on the social construction of identity, the nature of social institutions, the origins and strategies of collective action, and state/society relations.[16] To some extent, this is the result of disciplinary allegiances; students of doctrine and jurisprudence work primarily within the legal academy, while sociologists of law pursue their research in social science departments.[17] Also, it

14. *See, for example*, Pinello 2006, Bernstein 1997, Jenness and Broad 1997, Jenness and Grattet 2004.

15. To some extent, this may reflect a more general tendency within social move-ments scholarship to view identity as a social fact established and claimed prior to engagement in collective action. *See* Melucci 1996.

16. A number of philosophers and historians of law do place legal doctrine and jurisprudence within broader philosophical and historical frameworks, moving back and forth between specific doctrinal analysis and larger questions of normativity/morality and historiography. Curiously, however, there have yet to appear similar sorts of studies blending detailed analysis of doctrine and a sociological perspective on law and sexual identity.

17. *See generally* Hunt 1993.

is unrealistic (and probably a bad idea) to ask every scholar to do and be every thing as they undertake a study of sexuality and law; often, the bracketing of these complex questions of identity construction operates as a useful or necessary heuristic device. To a significant extent, however, the failure to simultaneously interrogate the constructed nature of both doctrine and the social context within which it is created, amended, and deployed may reflect a set of epistemological assumptions about the nature of the law/society relationship.

## A. Rethinking Law "and" Society: Beyond Rights, Duties, and Arenas

Implicit in much research on law and sexual identity is a fundamental conception of law and social change that views law as standing outside of social relationships. A group's social status is viewed as deriving from its relative position along a predetermined path of "progress" or "equality." This conception of status, in turn, rests on a notion of law as a bundle of rights, obligations, duties, and entitlements: one achieves greater or equal status by virtue of gaining a certain share and mixture of the available rights, obligations, duties, and entitlements enjoyed by others. If I have to pay my taxes, for example, but am not allowed to marry the partner of my choosing, then my legal status is inferior to that of someone who also pays taxes but does have the right to marry a partner of his or her choosing.[18] Here, the "right to marry" is conceived as a concrete benefit, granted by the state and wielded by the rights-bearing citizen as a tool in securing happiness, social status, financial security, and a host of other goods. One would place it in the "plus" column of a kind of legal

18. *See, for example*, Sullivan 1996.

ledger, to be measured against items in the "minus" column such as the duty to pay taxes and the obligation not to assault or steal from one's neighbors. Taken together, the balance of rights and duties is thought to create an overall experience of relative *liberty* or *freedom*.

This quasi-arithmetic[19] approach to understanding legal status is intuitively appealing and, in a sense, partly accurate. Law does, indeed, convey a variety of rights, obligations, duties, and benefits upon those subject to its jurisdiction. And law's subjects are often acutely, if inaccurately, aware of the ways in which legal rules and sanctions constrain and enable their behavior through this pattern of give and take. Yet law does much more than this. Law speaks to us about ourselves—ever more so in a society self-consciously engaged in the contentious politics of identity. If we want to know what it means to be a parent, a family court will tell us. If we wonder what drives one person to commit unspeakable violence against another of a different race or religion, a Lexis® or Westlaw® search will provide answers. On a daily basis, law answers questions that range from the ridiculous to the sublime, from the mundane to the metaphysical. And every day, it seems, we ask it to do more.

That law operates symbolically is hardly a new or controversial insight. Yet most accounts of law's symbolic dimension are grounded in what legal scholar Brian Tamanaha refers to as the "mirror thesis": the idea that law merely reflects back society's

---

19. I refer to it as "quasi" -arithmetic because social status is not simply a function of adding or subtracting rights and duties to or from one another. Marriage, for example, is itself a bundle of benefits and obligations such that "the right to marry" is in many ways a dangerously seductive misnomer. As I discuss in greater detail in Chapter 6, one does not necessarily achieve a net gain of liberty when one is permitted entrance into state-sanctioned marriage. However, what is important here is not the empirical facticity of the arithmetic model of legal status but, rather, its discursive contour. This is how law is often *seen* and *described* by those who would use it in instrumental ways to pursue social change.

underlying norms, values, and structures.[20] On this view, law is a social institution that may act to enhance social integration, solve social problems, or enforce social control, but—for good or for ill—it does so by *aggregating* or *processing* actors, resources, and interests. It does not constitute them in the first instance. As in the materialist view of instrumentalism, law is conceived by those embracing this expressivist view as standing outside of social relations. That is, regardless of whether they focus on the ways in which social actors engage the law for material or for symbolic purposes, these models begin with the assumption that law exists beyond the political and social subject—in short, that subjects possess identities, interests, and statuses prior to their engagement with law and legal institutions.

Similarly, if subjects stand on one side of the law/society divide in these accounts, "the law" usually stands on the other. Indeed, a de facto division of labor has sprung up within research on the relationship between law and society: while social scientists examine how actors attempt to change law or how law reflects, reinforces, or modifies social norms and political or economic structures,[21] legal academics and—to a lesser extent— philosophers and historians have focused on the internal nuances of doctrine and jurisprudence.[22] Yet the analysis of doctrine is important not just for what it tells us about the possibilities of law as a set of ideas or concepts, but also for what it tells us about how, as a set of dynamic discourses, it shapes and produces the social objects it purports to regulate.

An example may help to help flesh out this distinction. In Chapter 4, I discuss the drive to enact and enforce hate crime

20. Tamanaha 2001.

21. Hunt 1993: 2–3.

22. *See generally* Dworkin 1977; Sunstein 1990; Tamanaha 2001.

legislation that specifically includes LGB people within its protective ambit. One could think about hate crime legislation in at least two different ways. First, one could believe that a criminal law prohibiting anti-gay hate crimes merely punishes hate crimes that already exist, in a knowable and identifiable form, "out there" in the world. Alternatively, one might assert that the law must first *create* hate crimes—via specific doctrinal and statutory moves—as particular objects or targets of state intervention. Most social movement scholars and activists would likely subscribe to the former view, though some might modify it and say that the law labels and circumscribes some subset of actual, objective hate crimes in order to render them subject to regulation.[23] I contend, however, that law does not merely identify, but actually produces, a discretely specified object we call an "anti-gay hate crime." It does this discursively and textually, in a complex interaction between movement actors and institutional actors that takes place within a defined set of institutional constraints. Moreover, in identifying what a hate crime is, the law draws lines around sexual desire, animus, fear, and vulnerability. It also links these emotions in determinate relations to specific identity constructs: gay and straight, male and female, subject and object. In so doing, law helps to construct the binary matrix of sexuality and gender that forms the basis of sexual identity as well as the ground of its social and political regulation. Similar dynamics can be discerned in legal proceedings addressing same-sex marriage and sexual harassment.

In examining anti-gay hate crime law, same-sex harassment jurisprudence, and the current litigation effort surrounding

---

23. An example of this view would be Jenness and Grattet's volume on hate crimes. They argue persuasively that hate crimes were identified as a social problem by social movements who were able to convince many state legislatures and Congress that there was an "epidemic" of anti-gay hate crime observable in American society. Jenness and Grattet 2004.

same-sex marriage, I seek to demonstrate how contemporary sexual subjectivity is being produced by a process best conceived as discursive in nature. I argue that law is a crucial institution engaged in the social construction of sexuality, a dimension of subjectivity that many theorists, following Foucault's lead, see as centrally important to contemporary social life.

## B. Decentering Legal and Political Instrumentalism

My position is incompatible in many ways with the conventional wisdom that stresses the instrumental dimension of legalism—whether it emphasizes material or symbolic ends. Nor does it cohere particularly well with much of the prevailing sociological research on the outcomes and objectives of social movements and collective actors. While there are a number of competing perspectives on social movements, the leading models emphasize social movement activism as a form of political action; movement actors and organizations contend for inclusion in the polity or to obtain material benefits and/or symbolic recognition from the state.[24] Here, again, social actors and organizations are viewed as being possessed of interests and identities prior to their interaction with state institutions.[25] Moreover, while some social movement scholars examine discourse as a significant dimension of movement activism, few attempt to do so outside of an instrumental conception of collective action, in which discourse

24. *See generally* McAdam, et al, 1996. My own prior research emerged from one segment of this tradition: state-centered (or institutionalist) political mediation theory. *See* Amenta, Carruthers and Zylan 1992; Zylan 1995; Soule and Zylan 1997; Zylan 2000.

25. A significant exception to this tendency within social movements research is the work of Alberto Melucci. Melucci's theorizing of "new" social movements emphasizes the ways in which collective identities are created *through* collective action. *See* Melucci et al. 1989; Melucci 1996.

is a resource that might be used strategically or tactically to achieve certain ends.[26]

Conventional wisdom is usually conventional for a reason. In this case, it offers a perfectly reasonable image of how contentious politics, legalism, and social change are related to one another. If I reject this view, what image do I offer in its stead? Whereas the conventional view depicts already-constituted subjects deploying discourses (legal and cultural arguments, for example) that more or less reflect their aims, objectives, and interests in achieving social equality, I believe a more accurate account of this process emphasizes the contingency and indeterminacy of political subjectivity. On this view, normative and empirical frameworks are unpacked, interpreted, and reinscribed via the interplay of institutionally situated discourses.

In this account, courts indeed operate—as James C. Carter averred in his 1890 address to the American Bar Association—as "department[s] of sociology." Striving to describe and predict human behavior, courts render judgments that can productively be read as a kind of amateur social science. Most notably, they regularly and necessarily attribute causation to patterned social action and establish discursive boundaries between social structure and human agency. Although they do not appear to be so, social, legal, and political identities are always, in this process, provisional—subject to an intentional, self-consciously positivistic effort at something quite close to Weberian interpretive sociology.

At the same time, however, the process by which sexuality is constructed by law is not unbounded. Law is not an "empty

26. The lion's share of research emphasizing discourse construction within social movement activism—especially work in the "law and social movements" literature—descends from "framing" analysis. *See* Cress and Snow 2000; McAdam, et al. 1996: 261–356.

vessel," open to any and all articulation or rearticulation of its contents.[27] Instead, legal doctrine, institutional processes and characteristics, and extant social norms profoundly constrain the discursive construction of sexuality as a legal, political, and social identity and experience. In other words, I do not contend that the conventional wisdom about how law and sexual identity intersect is entirely wrong; rather, I contend that it is incomplete, overly deterministic, and needlessly mechanical. The relationship between law and social change is more complex and dynamic than either instrumental or expressivist accounts suggest.

## II. The Law of Homosex

This book is an effort to flesh out this model of social action, a form of what Alain Touraine has called the "self-production of society"[28] by focusing attention on the contemporary drive to create, amend, and shape what I will term the law of homosex. The word "homosex" may be a bit perplexing; such a facially inelegant phrase requires an explanation and probably a defense. Words—particularly nominatives—are consequential. In examining laws and policies designed to describe conduct and status defined by a specifically sexual relationship between men or between women, one might be expected to use the more common phrasing of "gay and lesbian," "homosexual," or even "queer" to denote the domain of intervention. But there are difficulties with each and all of these choices. First, using any of the three would situate the analysis within a specific political position: "gay and lesbian" connotes a specifically late-modern liberal

27. Tamanaha 2006.
28. Touraine 1977.

political allegiance,[29] "queer" connotes a conflicted, purportedly postmodern political allegiance (more on this, later), and "homosexual" would locate the point of reference somewhere in the first half of the twentieth century and/or in a critical stance toward the morality and normalcy of same-sex desire. None of these will do.

More importantly, however, each of these terms connotes status—a "being" rather than a "doing" of sexual practice and identification—while the term homosex elides that very distinction. In its slippage between action and identity, homosex suggests precisely the sort of provisional concept I contend law is wrestling with and against as it seeks to pin down and contain same-sex and opposite-sex passions. It is, indeed, inelegant and jarring, but that is at least partly the point.

Substantively, I will be examining the content of jurisprudential contests over the following domains within the contemporary American law of homosex: anti-gay hate crimes, same-sex sexual harassment, and same-sex marriage. I am interested in a number of questions. First, what do these contests tell us about how we understand and ought to experience desire? Hatred? Sexuality? Love? How do they codify and institutionalize these conceptions in ways that structure performances of identity and selfhood? Do efforts to change the law of homosex inure to the benefit of sexual "freedom," or do they contribute, rather, to a normative[30] regime that channels sexual expression and replicates social divisions predicated upon sexual "identity"?

29. As such, I use the term "gay and lesbian" or "gay, lesbian and bisexual" (LGB) throughout the book to refer to specifically constituted political and social movement actors.

30. I should note here that my use of the word "normative" is intended in its sociological, not moral or philosophical, sense. That is, while much of the analysis that follows suggests certain "ought" statements about what social actors and organizations might do with respect to the law of homosex, I am not attempting to construct

In short, by examining the discursive products of the law of homosex, I will be attempting to illustrate one of the central ways in which sexuality is socially constructed in contemporary American society: through the engagement and production of legal discourses. In so doing, I hope to make visible some of the ways in which sexuality is simultaneously disciplined and produced by legal discourses and institutions.

## III. Get Out the Map[31]

This book proceeds as follows: in Chapters 2 and 3, I undertake a more systematic and rigorous analysis of the extant literatures on law, the social, and sexuality. I critique and synthesize works in jurisprudence, political sociology, and social theory in an effort to derive a framework for understanding how law discursively constructs a binary matrix of gender and sexuality. I then use this framework to examine three substantive topics: anti-gay hate crime laws, same-sex sexual harassment laws, and same-sex marriage. Each topic implicates broader themes of passion. In Chapter 4, I explore hatred, especially as it is juxtaposed to loathing, disgust, and desire. In Chapter 5, sexual desire is foregrounded, but loathing, disgust, and hatred are never far from view. Finally, in Chapter 6, romantic love takes center stage, with sexual desire and parental love playing vital contextual roles.

This survey of substantive topics is not intended to be exhaustive but, rather, suggestive of the ways in which law instantiates and inscribes matrices of gender, sexuality, and the sexed body

a normative argument. Rather, I am attempting to construct a descriptive account of a normative framework.

31. Salier and Ray (The Indigo Girls) 1997.

via juridical discourses of passion. I hope merely to demonstrate some of the ways in which law's power to authorize specific discourses and practices of love, desire, hatred, fear, and vulnerability remains grounded in the equally powerful discourses and institutional practices that mark law as dispassionate, cerebral, and fundamentally procedural. Put simply, *States of Passion* contends that those states of passion we experience in our daily lives as particularly significant—to our sense of self, to our collective and social identities, and to our ideas about the body and its dictates—have as much to do with the state as they do about passion.

# 2

# Desiring the Discipline of Law

## I. Some of the Many Appealing Qualities of Homosex

There are at least two reasons why we ought to be interested in homosex and, therefore, the *law* of homosex. First, sexuality is centrally implicated in contemporary Western discourses of the self. Eve Sedgwick contended that Western culture—premodern, modern, and postmodern alike—is fundamentally unintelligible unless considered in light of the homo/hetero divide.[1] Michel Foucault argued that sexuality represents the locus of discourses of personal truth.[2] And Anthony Giddens observed that late capitalist society is deeply and uniquely marked by the unmooring of intimacy, love, and sexuality from kinship and procreation.[3] If it is not the hallmark of a postmodern notion of the self, the articulation of homosex is nonetheless an important feature signaling its arrival.[4]

Second, many of the most contentious and dynamic jurisprudential debates in contemporary American law circulate around the definition and regulation of passions organized by sexuality,

1. Sedgwick, Eve Kosofsky. 1990. *Epistemology of the closet.* Berkeley: University of California Press.

2. Foucault 1990.

3. Giddens 1992.

4. Not coincidentally, it may also portend a nostalgic longing for the reconfinement of sexuality within a stable and predictable—if expanded—familial form. *See* Chapter 6, *infra.*

gender, and the sexed body. Reproductive autonomy, sexual expression and identification, and marriage predictably and repetitively appear in the "hard" cases that increasingly define the contours of larger social, legal, and political questions.[5] As a specific domain within this jurisprudential space, the law of homosex repeatedly provokes (and invokes) lingering uncertainty about how to understand the nature of public vs. private, state vs. society, self vs. other, and adjudication vs. legislation. Examining it promises to tell us about much more than whether or not LGB people are likely, someday, to be included within the hegemonic institution of marriage or whether "Don't Ask, Don't Tell" has any long-term future (although these are important and interesting questions in their own right). In this book, I argue that, because certain social discourses not only describe but *constitute* the body and the self, examining the law of homosex also promises to offer analytical purchase on understanding the elusive nature of law's participation in the social construction of sexuality as a materially and symbolically resonant category of identity and experience.

How, then, shall we go about understanding law's construction of sexuality and sexual identity? First, it appears evident that we need a sociological theory of law—one that helps us connect social categories, legal categories, institutions, institutional actors, structure, agency, and meaning. Of course, no single theoretical perspective predominates within this field of research. Indeed, while empirical sociological research on law abounds with increasing depth, reach, and complexity, jurisprudence—the theory of law—appears to have received declining attention from

5. *See, for example, Roe v. Wade,* 410 U.S. 113 (1973), *Lawrence v. Texas,* 539 U.S. 558 (2003), *Perry v. Schwarzenegger* 704 F. Supp. 2d 921 (N.D. Cal. 2010), *Griswold v. Connecticut,* 381 U.S. 479 (1965).

sociologists.[6] Nonetheless, we can identify the contours of a contemporary sociological theory of law that has moved from deeply structural to increasingly autonomous, conceiving of law in the latter instance as an institution and an interpretive process. In fact, sociological theories of law may productively be explored as instances of broader trends within social theory; both have wrestled with similar questions concerning determinism, instrumentalism, materialism, and symbolism.[7]

Second, we need a sociological theory of gender, sexuality, and the body. Again, while sociologists have been, and continue to be, engaged in important empirical work examining the ways in which gender, sexuality, and the body are experienced and deployed in an array of social settings,[8] most influential theoretical work on these topics has lately emerged from other disciplines, especially philosophy, psychoanalytic theory, law, and cultural studies. Most of this work is feminist in orientation,[9] although some of it moves beyond (or works around) feminist frameworks.[10] Building upon this literature, in Chapter 3 I propose a framework for understanding how law—as an inscriptive institutional project—serves, in part, to constitute embodied, engendered, desiring subjects. I embrace the position advanced by poststructural theorists that sex, gender, and the body are produced discursively, through processes that link the intrapsychic, the social, and the cultural to one another. On this view,

6. Seron and Munger. 1996; Hunt 1993: 43–47.

7. *See* Sarat and Simon 2001; Stryker 2007.

8. *See, for example,* Gamson 1998; Rubin 2003; Hill Collins 2004; Bernstein 2007; Pascoe 2007; Kimmel 2007; Kimmel and Messner 2007.

9. *See, for example,* Irigaray 1985; Benjamin 1988; MacKinnon 1989; Butler 1990, 2004; Wittig 1992; Braidotti 1994; Grosz 1994a, 1994b; De Lauretis 1994; De Lauretis and White 2007.

10. *See, for example,* Foucault 1990; Bersani 1995; Hyde 1997; Halley 2006.

discourse matters not because it reflects a preconstituted material reality that might be termed "anatomical sex," or "gender," or "sexuality," but because it creates the set of relational forces, experiences, identifications, and effects that are experienced as reality. Thus, it is important to examine the law of homosex not (merely) as a set of regulative mechanisms that constrain or enable the expression of sexual freedom but as an array of discursive objects that constitute the very substance of sexual subjectivity. In order to enable such an examination, in this chapter I first synthesize constitutive and neoinstitutional theories of law.

## II. Theorizing Law and Society

Where does the law stand with respect to social and political life? Does law simply mirror social relations, reflecting back a more or less mimetic image of things as they are and thus reinforcing social and cultural norms? Does it provide an institutional arena within which organized social groups may pursue their interests through rational argumentation and contestation? Is it a functional tool of state power, designed to perpetuate and extend hegemonic relations of class, gender, race, or sexual privilege? Might it instead be a crucial instrument of resistance, providing opportunities for relatively marginal social groups to pursue innovative and progressive social policies when the other institutions of democratic influence remain deaf to their numerically weak voices? Or is this notion of law as an arena or instrument—whether conceived in terms of social change or the reproduction of systems of power—misguided to the extent that it imagines law to exist *outside* of social life, rather than to be constitutive of it?

In truth, no single model of the law/society relationship prevails in sociolegal research. Indeed, like social theory broadly conceived and (more precisely) sociological theory concerning the state/society[11] relationship, sociological theories of law and society have an epistemological history that evinces a shift in emphasis from deterministic, structural accounts to approaches that allow for more or less autonomy for law, legal institutions, and legal doctrine.[12] Yet, while a notion of law's autonomy has gained increased acceptance over time, there remains (within this latter body of scholarship) a persistent tension turning on the question of whether it makes sense to envision legal doctrine, argument, and institutions as primarily *instrumental* in nature or, alternatively, as a set of objects and practices that *constitute* social and legal subjectivity and identity.[13]

How one answers this question is important for many reasons, including the fact that instrumental and constitutive accounts of the law/society relationship approach legal doctrine and argument in divergent ways. Instrumental accounts conceive of doctrine as a tool or resource, more or less broadly consonant with the "frames"[14] or "interests" of dominant and/or marginal extralegal social groups. Meaning-based accounts of law attend very carefully to the nuances of legal doctrine, seeing in them the

11. One way of thinking about sociolegal scholarship is as a subset of state/society scholarship. *See* Stryker 2007. Certainly, law as a set of adjudicatory practices and institutions implicates—but does not exhaust—the state/society relationship. Because different models of "the state" will suggest different positions for law within those models, I bracket the question of how important adjudication is relative to other operations of the state, though I recognize that a focus on law as adjudication is necessarily limited and partial.

12. *See generally* Sarat and Simon 2001, Stryker 2007. *See also* Suchman and Edelman 1996; Hunt 1993.

13. *Ibid. See also* Tamanaha 2006, Conley and O'Barr 2005; Brigham 1996.

14. *See generally* McAdam, et al 1996; Cress and Snow 2000; Barclay, et al 2009.

essence of law as a constitutive set of social practices.[15] I will argue—in line with constitutive theories of law—that the creation and announcement of doctrine does, indeed, participate in the social construction of identity and experience. That is, the content of doctrine does not merely reflect or codify a prediscursive social reality (understood as identities, bodies, actions, statuses, and interests) but, rather, serves in part to constitute it. At the same time, however, the content, meaning, and signifying import of doctrine can only be understood by adopting an equally attentive and nuanced posture toward the institutional features of law as a dynamic, yet durable, set of organizational practices, rules, procedures, and professional habits. Thus, in what follows, I outline a theoretical framework for understanding the law/society relationship that highlights the importance of doctrine and argument—conceived as a set of discursive objects—but which establishes as equally important the array of institutional practices and features within which such objects are produced, attain legitimacy, and become constitutive of social life.

## A. Law and Social Theory: Mimesis and Autonomy

As others have noted,[16] the founding fathers[17] of sociology—including iconic figures Marx, Weber, and Durkheim—were profoundly influenced by law as an intellectual and practical enterprise. Many (including Marx and Weber) were first trained

---

15. *See* Merry 1990; Hunt 1993; Ewick and Silbey 1998; Conley and O'Barr 2005; Sarat and Simon 2001; Brigham 1996. John Brigham describes the constitutive theory of law as an approach that falls between legal formalism and legal realism: it addresses how "groups seeking to influence the law are themselves influenced by the way they understand" various "forms" of law. Brigham 1996: x.

16. *See* Calhoun1989. *See generally* Deflem 2008.

17. Gendered nominative intended.

as lawyers, and law figured centrally in their understanding of social life. For Marx and Durkheim, law was largely emblematic of the underlying logic or logics governing social life and social change.[18] Each suggested more or less *functional* notions of law's position and operation—a posture that reflected the anchoring of their theories in the deep structures of political economy and social order, respectively.[19] Contemporary systems theory follows a similar line of inquiry.[20] Nicholas Luhmann contends that social systems are autopoietic; communicative processes (including those issuing from legal subsystems) effectively stabilize social behavior, rendering it predictable and (again) functional. Luhmann's theory is relatively agnostic as to the substance of law. Autopoiesis ensures that systems stabilize, regardless of the validity, verifiability, or truth value of specific claims made within legal systems. Rather, what is important in this account is that law sufficiently cohere with its environment and manage

18. *See, for example*, Cotterrell 1999: chs. 1–3.

19. For Marxist theory, law operates as a legitimating and enabling structure for the principal engine of social, political, and economic life: capitalism. In Marx's work, the state, including law, was envisioned as epiphenomenal of capitalism as a structural form; on this view, the shape, content, and implementation of legislation predictably correspond with the dictates of accumulation, reproduction, coordination, and/or consumption. *See* Jessop 1990: chapter 1. Subsequent Marxist theorists elaborated on the concept of law as a repressive and legitimating institution, describing legal doctrine and practice as performing vital coordinating, appeasing, and ideological functions for capital—perhaps in the form of a "semi-autonomous" state apparatus. *See* Miliband 1969; Poulantzas 1969, 1978; Block 1987; Althusser 2001: 85–126; Hunt 1993. Durkheim posited changes in the form of legal authority as societies moved from mechanical to organic bonds. Taking this argument to its extreme, Durkheim contended that law might serve as an "index" of the underlying moral structure of a society. *See* Cotterrell 1999; Durkheim 1982; Durkheim and Halls 1984. In a similar vein, some Durkheimian social control theorists, such as Donald Black, have argued that social norms become legal norms only as long as, and to the extent that, they serve to replicate structures of social inequality. Black 1976.

20. *See generally* Elder-Vass 2008; Pickel 2007.

problems as they arise—in short, that it effectively reduce social uncertainty.[21]

Thus, for Durkheim, Marx, and systems theorists, law is (selectively) mimetic of an underlying structure of social order with respect to both its normative and its material dimensions. These sorts of deterministic accounts of law's relationship to social structure have declined in influence in recent years.[22] This is perhaps because they appear inadequate to the task of explaining nonfunctional legal outcomes. For example, many empirical studies produced by law and social movement scholars demonstrate that legislative and adjudicative outcomes often fail to faithfully reproduce class-, race-, gender-, or sexuality-based forms of inequality.[23] Law appears to move, at least in part, according to an internal logic that cannot always be neatly mapped onto existing social or political hierarchies. Sometimes law seems to rebel.

21. *See* Luhmann and Albrow 1985; Luhmann, et al 2004. Dave Elder-Vass and others are highly critical of the determinism of Luhmann's version of systems theory, contending that there is room in the theory for human agency. Elder-Vass posits an "emergentist" systems theory that shifts the angle of focus from the level of the system or "whole" to the emergent properties of groups and institutions: "Wholes are emergent when they possess emergent properties, and properties of wholes are emergent if they would not be possessed by their parts, were those parts not organized into such a whole." Elder-Vass 2008. While emergentism plainly introduces a kind of dynamism and uncertainty that is lacking from Luhmann's account, it is not clear how this shift permits a greater role for human agency. For example, Elder-Vass compares the emergent properties of social structures to a dog's emergent power to bark. *Ibid.* It is the organization of the dog's vocal cords, windpipe, lungs, etc., he contends, that gives the dog the capacity to bark. The parts on their own have no power except and until they are brought into simultaneous connection to/with one another. Similarly, Elder-Vass says, social relations, normative institutions, and human behavior each have "causal power" only when conceived as emergent properties or structures relating to a whole system. If human behavior is rendered meaningful and efficacious only to the extent that it can be read as indicative of a system-level logic, emergentism appears to replicate much of the functionalist cast of Luhmann's autopoietic theory. *See also* Pickel 2007.

22. *See* Seron and Munger 1996.

23. *See, for example,* McCann 1994; Marshall 2005; Barclay, et al 2009.

As a consequence, recent sociolegal scholarship has increasingly emphasized the autonomy, or relative autonomy, of law from social structural loci of power and control.[24] Such an approach is not new: it may also be traced to classical sociological theory. Max Weber posited an autonomous position for legal institutions vis-à-vis social structures. Indeed, for Weber, it was precisely this independent institutional quality that defined law *as* law:

> An order will be called law if it is externally guaranteed by the probability that coercion (physical or psychological), to bring about conformity or avenge violation, will be applied by a staff of people holding themselves *specially ready for that purpose*.[25]

For Weber, the existence and codification of a coercive institutional mandate—in the form of the predictable presence of a staff dedicated to the enforcement of the rules—established a legal order. Weber thus paralleled Marx and Durkheim in adopting a fundamentally structural view of law, but for Weber, legal orders may or may not serve important integrative and coordinating functions. The embodiment of law in a social institution leads law to develop as all Western social institutions do in a Weberian world: it differentiates, rationalizes, and bureaucratizes.[26] Over time, the rules, procedures, and practices that make up a legal system develop logics of their own, which operate in ways that may be functional for specific economic, political, and social configurations. But they may not be. Or, at least,

24. Stryker 2007.

25. Weber 1954: 5 (emphasis added).

26. 26 *See, for example*, Weber 1978: 217–226, 809–899.

these logics may open up spaces within which law becomes permeable to other imperatives—beyond those derived from the demands of capitalism or social integration.

Weber's account of law permits theorists of law and society to consider at least two additional possibilities concerning law's relationship to the social. First, Weber's description of the autonomous (or semiautonomous)[27] development of legal systems creates the space for a focus on aspects of law's influence or importance that are not directly derived from the deep structures (economic and social orders) that serve as the focus of much classical social theory. To the contrary: for Weber, law's semiautonomous development as a rationalizing and internally rational set of institutions is crucial to its ability to shore up system legitimacy in the face of growing social differentiation and inequality.[28]

Sociolegal scholars working within a "new institutionalist" framework have taken up this suggestion from Weberian sociology, developing a rich and expansive body of scholarship that examines law as a set of organizational practices, routines, sites, and cognitive/normative frameworks.[29] As Mark Suchman and Lauren Edelman observe, there are many aspects of neoinstitutionalism for sociolegal scholars to find appealing: "[it] takes rule systems seriously; it acknowledges and even exalts the causal

---

27. As noted earlier, some Marxist theorists see law as part of a semiautonomous state apparatus. In that sense, law is not merely epiphenomenal of capitalist relations but stands somewhat apart from them in order to ensure that coordination and regulation can be accomplished effectively (which sometimes requires the taking of actions that appear in the short run to be antithetical to capital's interests). *See* Block 1987 (especially chapter 3). This is distinguishable from Weber's conception of law's autonomy, however, in that the Marxist account retains its overall functionalist cast, while Weber's version of law's autonomy allows for outcomes that may genuinely conflict with capitalism's imperatives.

28. Weber 1954: 225.

29. Suchman and Edelman. 1996.

force of normative beliefs; and it thoroughly embraces the kinds of cognitive and constitutive effects that play an increasingly large role in sociolegal theory."[30] New institutionalists offer sophisticated accounts of how institutions structure "choice opportunities" for problem solving and decision-making[31]; how they create, and then operate within, "taken-for-granted" cognitive frameworks[32]; and how they interact with other organizations, institutions, and environments.[33] They thus contribute a variety of tools and insights that have clear applicability to the study of law and society, for law is decidedly rule oriented and institutionally embedded.

At the same time, as Suchman and Edelman note, neoinstitutionalism can embrace a kind of abstract formalism with respect to the *substance* of institutional rules, practices, and outputs[34] and so foreclose the sort of interpretive approach to legal doctrine that represents the second area of inquiry opened up by Weber's notion of law's autonomy. While hardly constituting a precocious postmodernism, Weber's interpretive sociology nonetheless prefigured a future course of theorizing on law, the state, and society that would come to value analysis of law's cultural, social, and symbolic dimensions. Constitutive and cultural theories of law pursue such analyses, viewing substantive law as "seamlessly part of the social construction of identities, understandings, problem definitions and the like."[35] In scholarship

30. *Ibid*: 904.

31. Cohen, et al. 1972: 16–17.

32. Powell and DiMaggio. 1991: chapters 2, 4. See also March and Olsen 1984.

33. Suchman and Edelman. 1996: 918–28.

34. *Ibid*: 928 (for some new institutionalists, "laws mean what they say, and do what they mean").

35. Stryker 2007. *See also* Sarat and Simon. 2001.

adopting a constitutive or cultural approach, law does not merely reflect the interests and identities of social groups and actors who come into contact with legal institutions. Rather, law shapes understanding and identity—in part by constituting a sense of consciousness born of legal categories.[36] In spite of their increased importance in sociolegal scholarship, however, constitutive and cultural approaches remain overshadowed by the pervasive instrumentalism that characterizes the field.

## B. Law as Arena . . . and Instrument

Once conceived as an autonomous or semiautonomous set of organizations or practices, legal institutions readily cohere with the notion that they, like legislative institutions, constitute arenas of contestation. Indeed, the idea that the American legal system operates as a kind of forum, within which different actors vie for ascendancy with respect to their interpretive claims is simultaneously commonsensical and controversial. On the one hand, this image of law coheres with what is often viewed as the essence of American law: its adversarial nature.[37] This adversarialism—built into the system's procedures, rules, and institutional structures—relies upon, and consistently demands, a fundamentally contentious legal process. The adversarial system confidently assumes that the "truth" that law seeks to discover (factual or doctrinal) will emerge from the back-and-forth between unabashedly partisan advocates. The judge acts as a purportedly neutral arbiter, ensuring the rules are followed. It is this combination of features—partisan adversaries presenting

36. *See generally* Gabel 1980; Merry 1990; Brigham 1996, especially chapter 1; Ewick and Silbey 1998; Barclay and Marshall 2003; Marshall 2005.

37. Landsman 1984; Friedman 2005.

cases within a frame of neutral and objective rule enforcement—that is said to produce a just and legitimate outcome.[38]

Yet this sort of partisanship is deemed legitimate only as long as it remains formally and structurally confined. So, for example, judges who depart from absolute neutrality (variously defined) may be deemed illegitimately "activist" in their work[39]; lawyers who step over the line from vigorous advocacy to naked instrumentalism in their selection and deployment of precedent and doctrine may be accused of injecting "politics" into the judicial arena; and the filing of too many amicus curiae briefs (especially by social movement organizations) can lead to the claim that political interest groups are compromising the "rule of law."[40]

These are all normative claims. But they point to an empirical question about how law does, or does not, operate as an arena.[41] If law is best conceived as a semiautonomous or autonomous set of institutions, does it make sense to think of the legal system as primarily a public forum within which extralegal disputes between social actors or groups are settled? And, if so, do legal

38. Shaman 1996; Landsman 1984. *See generally* Lind and Tyler 1988; Johnson, et al 2006; Ewick and Silbey 1999.

39. President Barack Obama stirred controversy in 2009 when he suggested that "empathy" would be one of the characteristics he would be seeking in a replacement for retiring Supreme Court Justice David Souter. Critics of the president roundly denounced "empathy" as a coded reference to partiality in favor of the socially disadvantaged. *See* The New York Times 2009; Lithwick 2009. *See generally* Kmiec 2004.

40. Tamanaha 2006; Glendon 1991, 1994.

41. *See* Hunt 1993: chapter 5. Hunt's advocacy of the notion of law as an arena is somewhat perplexing, given his desire to point the way toward a constitutive theory of law. He contends that the arena concept "rejects any instrumentalist theory of law, which presents law as being available to any particular class or dominant group as an instrument or means of effecting their will or furthering their interests" and as "rejecting a general politics of law," but it's not clear how the arena concept achieves either objective. In fact, it seems to me that the notion that law is an "arena of struggle" embodies *both* a notion of legal instrumentalism (though not necessarily the classical Marxist version) *and* a law-as-politics thematic.

doctrine, argument, and precedent function as instruments, to be wielded intentionally and strategically by actors within and outside legal fora, toward the achievement of social or political objectives? In other words, is there not only a conceptual distinction to be drawn between social life and the legal practices that shape and define it, but also an objective, empirical separation between the two? To return to the claims of constitutive theorists of law, does law merely codify social reality, or does it create it?

Legal scholars[42] have advanced both positive and negative evaluations of the notion of law-as-politics. Critical legal scholarship (CLS), critical race theory (CRT), and feminist legal theory (FLT) all contend that the very idea that law is and ought to be "impartial" or "neutral" (and thus "apolitical") is endemic to its hegemonic power to reproduce class-, race-, gender-, and sexuality-based inequality.[43] For example, CRT and CLS scholars frequently advocate a process of "unmasking" and deconstructing the power relations that are embedded within legal institutions and which structure social relations through law.[44]

Arguing the matter from the other direction, Brian Tamanaha finds the trend toward an instrumental use and conception of law deeply troubling.[45] For Tamanaha, law is increasingly an

42. Social scientists tend to bracket these kinds of normative evaluations, while legal scholars often engage them directly. The difference in approach may be the result of differences between the two disciplines with respect to training, institutional imperatives, and professional norms and practices.

43. *See, for example*, MacKinnon 1987, 1989, 1993;Fineman 1991; Fineman and Thomadsen 1991; Crenshaw 1991, 1995; Weisberg 1993; Kennedy 1993; Kennedy and Carrington 2004; Kairys 1998; Delgado and Stefancic 2000, 2001; Levit and Verchick 2006.

44. Kairys 1998; Crenshaw, et al 1995; Williams 1991; Delgado and Stefancic 2000; Yoshino 2006.

45. Tamanaha 2006.

"empty vessel," susceptible to being deployed in the service of almost any social or political objective.[46] Developments in jurisprudence, legal education, and the growth of social movements embracing legalistic strategies have combined, he argues, to create a legal system that has been unhitched from any underlying moral or social justificatory order. This, he contends, is to be contrasted with earlier notions of law as either the codification of imminent social reality (natural law) or as the embodiment of social custom (customary law).[47] For Tamanaha, the movement from a formal toward an instrumental view of law is particularly troubling because the ends to which law might be applied remain unspecified.[48] In the absence of such clearly articulated "public goods," he argues, interest groups have stepped into the judicial arena in an effort to determine the direction of law's intervention, rendering the judiciary virtually indistinguishable from the legislature and threatening law's very foundation.[49]

Yet Tamanaha's claim that doctrine, rules, procedures, and other features of law function as truly "empty" vehicles for social and political activism can be persuasive only if it discounts the specificity of law's institutional location. Neoinstitutionalism

46. *Ibid*: 4.

47. One can readily imagine why critical and progressive legal scholarship does not find a return to "customary" or "natural" law quite as appealing as Tamanaha perhaps does.

48. *Ibid*: 72.

49. *Ibid*: 83, 215. According to Tamanaha, "a few centuries ago," law was "widely understood to possess a necessary content and integrity that was, in some sense, given or predetermined. Law was the right ordering of society binding on all . . . Law was thought to consist of rules or principles immanent within the customs or culture of the society, or of God-given principles disclosed by revelation or discoverable through the application of reason, or of principles dictated by human nature, or of the logically necessary requirements of objective legal concepts." Today, however, "law is widely viewed as an empty vessel to be filled as desired, and to be manipulated, invoked, and utilized in the furtherance of ends." *Ibid*.

suggests that law is produced and practiced within richly textured organizational and inter-organizational settings.[50] Lauren Edelman contends that "the meaning of law is determined largely within (rather than outside of) the social arena that it seeks to regulate."[51] Neoinstitutionalists expressly reject the means-ends or "market" rationality suggested by the Weberian ideal-typical bureaucratic legal system and impliedly critiqued by Tamanaha.[52] At the same time, neoinstitutionalism complicates the critical legal view of law as an instrument of hegemonic or amoral power. Instead, neoinstitutionalists point toward a conception of law that is attentive to the *limitations* on legal instrumentalism—whether it emerges in the service of political power or market efficiency—which are imposed by the institutional features of legal practice.

## III. Law and Identity Politics

A similar sort of instrumentalism also runs through research on law and collective action. A great deal of extant research in this field, while recognizing law's power to construct social reality, at the same time presumes or rests on an implied instrumentalism. In part, this can be traced to the situation of law and social movements scholarship within broader political sociology scholarship examining the state/society relationship.[53] To a significant

50. *See* Heimer 1996, 2001; Powell 1996; Suchman and Edelman 1996; Sutton 1996; Edelman 2002.

51. Edelman 2002: 192.

52. *Ibid.*

53. *See, for example*, Amenta, et al 1992.

extent, current research on American social movements works within political process and political opportunity models of movement activism.[54] These models conceive of social movements as a species of contentious politics; social movement organizations seek to extract benefits and recognition from the state much like other organized constituencies do. Because of their numerical weakness and/or position on the social margins, however, social movements must work creatively and assiduously to extract even the most basic concessions from state institutions. One such concession may be legal recognition—of the existence of the group, its members' identity construct(s), or its status as a rights-bearing or -claiming constituency.[55] These dimensions of legal recognition are often perceived by social movement organizations (SMOs) as threshold rights, which may then be used strategically to achieve deeper or broader rights or benefits, or as a ticket to routinized participation in state decision making.

This sort of instrumentalism is particularly evident in research on those social movements, such as the movement for LGB equality, which assert identity-based claims. Identity-based social movement organizations are described by researchers–and assert themselves to be–*representational* entities that aggregate and operationalize the interests of constituencies defined by one or another social metric.[56] Such entities are then depicted as using the criminal and civil law (or changes therein) as tools or resources for creating "extralegal" social change.[57] By most accounts, the juridification of identity politics has produced

54. Tarrow 1998; McAdam, et al 2001; Meyer 2004.

55. *See generally* Gamson 1990; Amenta, et al 2010; Bernstein 2005. For a nuanced account of this process with respect to the LGB movement, *see* Bernstein 1997.

56. *See* Touraine 1981; Melucci 1996; Melucci, Keane, and Mier 1989.

57. Brown and Halley 2002.

mixed results. Certainly, activists have achieved some notable legal victories. One would be hard pressed, for example, to contend that the United States Supreme Court's voiding of state laws criminalizing homosexual conduct in *Lawrence v. Texas*[58] was anything other than a victory for the movement for gay, lesbian, and bisexual equality. Activists and scholars remain divided, however, over whether legalism as a strategy has been "good" for progressive social movements or "bad" for them, framing this discussion as a question of whether legal strategies are sufficiently transformative and/or whether they short-circuit other, more radical strategies for achieving social change.[59]

But posing the question in this way is limiting in crucial respects. As Alberto Melucci has argued, such accounts of social movement effects assume a pre-constituted, unified social movement "subject."[60] This subject is a fiction, according to Melucci. Instead,

> Whatever unity exists [in a social movement] should be considered the result and not the starting point, a fact to be explained rather than assumed. When actors produce their collective action they define both themselves and their environment (other actors, available resources, opportunities and obstacles). Such definitions are not linear but are produced by interaction, negotiation and conflict.[61]

---

58. 539 U.S. 558 (2003).

59. On the limits of liberal legalism, *see* Rosenberg 1991; Handler 1990; Kairys 1998. On social movements and "cause lawyering," *see* Scheingold and Sarat 1998; Barclay and Marshall 2005; Sarat and Scheingold 2006.

60. Melucci, et al 1989: 28–29.

61. *Ibid*: 26.

The emergence of "new" social movements signals, for Melucci (*contra* Tamanaha), a decline in instrumentalism in collective action. New social movements are as concerned with symbols and meaning as they are with material outcomes, and the "reversal of cultural codes" can be a particularly resonant objective in complex societies, where "power lies increasingly in codes that regulate the flow of information."[62] Moreover, while political process models emphasize the state as a target of collective action, Melucci contends that new social movements "operate increasingly outside the established parameters of the political systems" creating "new spaces" within which the objective of collective action is not to aggregate the interests of the movement's constituencies, but to create and define them.[63] New social movements are not political, nor are they anti-political; rather, he says, they are "metapolitical," operating as their own subsystems,[64] addressing emergent social conflicts and crises of meaning.[65]

At the heart of Melucci's critique of political process models of collective action is an attack on the stable subject signaled by the term "identity" in "identity politics." Modernist conceptions of political life reflexively rely upon such a stable subject; without it, representational constitutional democracy is rendered incoherent.[66] But Melucci's critique points to a different conception

62. *Ibid*: 55.

63. *Ibid*: 56.

64. The reference to subsystems connects Melucci's theory to systems theory—further evidence, I think, of the difficulty theorists and researchers have had in locating constitutive processes within dynamic and permeable structural and institutional contexts.

65. *Ibid*: 222.

66. It should be noted that Melucci's critique is directed toward the *collective actor* as subject. Representational democracy relies upon an individualized, stable subject as well as collective subjects. The important point is that both mainstream accounts of

of subjectivity that is perhaps most evident in collective action undertaken by "new" social movements but which need not be limited to it. Melucci contends that identity, while characterized by temporal continuity, is always dynamic, fragile, and the outcome of an interactive process.[67] Recognition is crucial to the construction of identity, but it need not be conferred by the state. Rather, democratic institutions are important to the extent that they lead to "the creation of conditions which allow social actors to recognize themselves and be recognized for what they are or want to be; conditions, that is, which lend themselves to the creation of recognition and autonomy."[68]

Thus, Melucci posits a poststructural conception of social and political identity formation within the context of social movement activism. Collective action produces a collective identity that, in turn, informs social movement organization formation (and re-formation), as well as the selection (and evolution) of tactics, strategies, and targets (the state, culture, specific social institutions, etc.). In short, structural features of the political field are never entirely hardened in Melucci's account, rendering an instrumental view of cause lawyering at best an incomplete account of how law operates in the context of "identity-based" activism.

Melucci thus suggests a more permeable and dynamic set of boundaries between state-based institutions and those social structural formations that are deemed to exist "outside" or "beyond" the state. Moreover, his account of collective identity formation suggests that the process of institutional "recognition" is fundamentally constitutive. That is, the state does not

political life and social movements research rely upon stable, pre-legal, subjects that are said to give rise to particular social needs, desires, and demands.

67. Melucci 1996: 67.

68. *Ibid*: 219.

merely codify social categories but helps to constitute them in the first instance. How might we apply this insight to law as a particular incarnation of the state?

## IV. The Interpretive Turn

Melucci's critique of social movement theory coheres with *constitutive* theories of law—those that view law as fundamentally concerned with the production of social meaning. While social scientists working within this framework often focus on legal practices (e.g., mediation, participation in small claims court, appearing as a lay or expert witness at trial)[69] and the operation of law in everyday or organizational life,[70] legal scholars often adopt an implicitly or explicitly constitutive perspective in examining the complex substance of legal doctrine. Janet Halley's 1993 essay, "The Construction of Heterosexuality," is a particularly compelling example of the latter. In it, Halley describes the constitutive effects of legal doctrine in establishing heterosexuality as "stable, natural, and transparent" and as empowered to define homosexuality as well as itself as a class.[71] For Halley, legal doctrine produces diacritical classifications of sexuality; heterosexuality and homosexuality "acquire definition and meaning in relation to one another."[72] Specific constructions of hetero- and homosexual identity and essence are devised precisely as a result of law's reliance upon, and endless reproduction of, categories,

69. *See, for example*, Conley and O'Barr 2005.

70. Merry 1990; Silbey and Ewick 1998; Edelman 2002; Marshall 2005.

71. Halley 1993: 91.

72. *Ibid*: 83.

particularly within the context of Fourteeenth Amendment case law.

Halley's essay suggests the utility of examining legal doctrine within the context of its institutional location. In the balance of this chapter and in those that follow it, I expand upon Halley's insight, illustrating the institutional dimensions of the discursive production of sexuality by and around law. To do so, I draw from three contemporary social theorists, Michel Foucault, Pierre Bourdieu, and Jurgen Habermas,[73] seeking to bring certain of their contributions into conversation with new institutionalist paradigms in order to map out a route toward a more robust constitutive theory of law.

First, Foucault's work on disciplinary medico-juridical discourses offers a set of guiding concepts about law's operation in producing specific regimes of truth. For Foucault, law—like other discursive mechanisms implicated in the dispersion of knowledge/power—may be conceived as articulating both prohibitory and productive normative mandates. In short, law tells us in very precise ways what we may not do and what we must do. Moreover, embodied within these legal and disciplinary mechanisms are elaborate cultural codes and justificatory discourses. Much of the content of *States of Passion* constitutes an effort to disinter just such codes and discourses from within the law of homosex.

Second, Pierre Bourdieu offers the important notion of law as a "field" primarily concerned with the articulation, consolidation, and deployment of "symbolic power." If, per Weber, the state may profitably be defined as that actor or set of institutions that holds the monopoly on legitimate coercion, then law (per Bourdieu) is best defined as that set of institutions which

---

73. It is worth noting that Alan Hunt has previously suggested that Habermas and Foucault might be fruitfully engaged with one another in constructing a constitutive theory of law. Hunt 1993: 13–14, chapter 12.

monopolizes *symbolic* power. In addition, Bourdieu identifies a number of law's features that contribute to its force over social life, including the institutional conditions that give rise to juridical utterances (law's ritual and *habitus*) and the polysemic quality of legal discourse.

Finally, Habermas's communicative theory outlines the institutional conditions within which legal outcomes may achieve the status of normative validity via a kind of structured consent. For Habermas, law has the potential[74] to serve as an "ideal speech situation" within which social actors raise and redeem validity claims that arise as a result of the state's increased intervention into cultural lifeworlds. Habermas thus suggests that (1) new social conflicts and sources of disorder may result from the increased penetration of state institutions into the social, and (2) the state remains a particularly powerful site of resolution of such conflicts and disorder.

## A. Foucault: The Discursive Production of Truth Regimes

As Austin Sarat and Jonathon Simon have noted, law may be conceived not only as a set of social institutions that predictably and continuously produces material outputs such as distributive or redistributive orders, and rules coordinating economic and social activity, etc., but also as a producer of systems of meaning.[75] A focus on law as a producer of meaning can take many different forms. If one conceives of law as an arena or forum, then its power may lie in its ability to *adjudicate* between existing discursive claims as they contend for social ascendancy. Legal institutions may grant particular empirical or normative claims the

---

74. It has the potential, perhaps, but as noted below, this potential remains elusive—if not foreclosed.

75. Sarat and Simon 2001: 20–21.

status of truth and may codify these claims in specific institutional practices, giving them a place of privilege in a competitive discursive arena.[76] As suggested above, much research on the role of social movements in shaping legal practice and doctrine adopts this perspective. Alternatively, one might say that law produces its own discursive truth.[77] Instead of codifying pre-legal notions of empirical fact, law may serve to constitute the real via knowledge-making processes that derive their force from the formal procedures that mark law as neutral and authoritative.[78]

If one adheres to the former account, one is likely to focus on a particular sort of outcome resulting from activism targeting legal institutions: the creation or development of "legal consciousness" among ordinary social actors.[79] That is, one is likely to be interested in how social notions of identity, freedom, and conflict, for example, are linked to legally significant notions of classification/status, rights/obligations, and harm/redress, such that individuals and groups may identify how, when, and why they may make future claims upon legal institutions.

If one subscribes to the latter account, as I do, a different set of interests frames the analysis. What sort of truth does law produce? How does law take up claims made by individuals and collective actors and transform them in ways that may be both empowering and limiting? How does law, in producing a specific

76. Tamanaha 2006.

77. This idea derives generally from the work of Michel Foucault. *See, for example,* Foucault and Gordon 1980; Foucault 1990. *See also* Foucault, et al 1991.

78. *See* Bourdieu 1987. This idea is not far from Weber's notion that law derives its legitimacy (in Western democratic constitutional states) not from external will formation via democratic processes, but from the institutional features of law itself—its rationality, reliance upon abstract rules and procedures, judicial autonomy, and the like. *See* Habermas 1996: 73.

79. *See, for example,* Merry 1990; Ewick and Silbey 1998; Barclay and Marshall 2003; Marshall 2005.

regime of truth (here, a regime concerning sexuality and gender) select from specific corpora of knowledge, reconfigure them, and inscribe them upon social and material bodies? What sorts of justificatory narratives and claims about sexuality, the body, passion, desire, and the like are "put into discourse"[80] through and by law?

In his College de France lectures, Michel Foucault offers what I think is a useful distinction in thinking about how juridical discourses serve, in part, to constitute the social.[81] Foucault describes this distinction as that between "legality" and "discipline." Legality, he argues, is always essentially about prohibition—about telling us what we cannot do and be. As a result, he says,

> the movement of specification and definition in a system of legality always focuses with greatest precision on what is to be prevented, what is to be prohibited . . . order is to be established by taking the point of view of disorder . . . order is what remains [from law's intervention]."[82]

Discipline, on the other hand, focuses on what *must* be done. It is, in this sense, legality's complement: "In the system of the law, what is undetermined is what is permitted; in the system of disciplinary regulation, what is determined is what one must do, and consequently, everything else, being undetermined, is prohibited."[83]

One should not read Foucault's distinction between legality and discipline as referring to separate social spaces, however;

80. Foucault 1990.

81. Foucault, et al 2007: 46.

82. *Ibid.*

83. *Ibid.*

Foucault is not describing legality or discipline as disconnected institutions but rather as separate logics of state[84] intervention. As such, they often appear together as coterminous modalities of what he more expansively describes as the techniques of bio-power.[85] Indeed, legality and discipline are essentially intertwined—more closely analogous to positive/negative space formations than separate courses of influence. One may be foregrounded over the other, but discourses of prohibition and mandate are essentially inseparable.

This model may be contrasted to traditional social control models of the adjudicative and administrative state, which are predicated on a notion of specific loci of power from which emerge selective strategies of punishment and enticement.[86] Both Foucault's poststructural account and neoinstitutional accounts (such as the one offered by John Sutton)[87] suggest there may be little to distinguish "carrots" from "sticks." While the regulatory/redistributive distinction is one of long standing in political sociology, neoinstitutionalists and poststructuralists alike contend that this may be a conceptual distinction without a material difference, as both dimensions of state action operate to

84. The word "state" is always problematic when used in connection with Foucault's work, as he contests the term as unduly limiting (i.e., as tethered to a particular conception of state *vs.* society, and of sovereignty conventionally understood). *See generally* Foucault, et al 2007; Foucault, et al 1991. However, I think it important to mark my discussion here as being about the state (broadly conceived)—as that set of institutions (*a la* Weber) that holds itself out, specially ready to perform certain kinds of "legal" and "disciplinary" interventions. This is not inconsistent with Foucault's approach, I think. *See* Foucault, et al 2007: 277 ("The state is a practice.").

85. *Ibid*: 7. And *see generally*, *Ibid*, chapter one. Alan Hunt has argued that, taken together, Foucault's notion of "law and discipline" constitute modern "regulation." Hunt 1993: 268.

86. *See, for example*, Pound 1942; Black 1976; Parsons 1937, 1977; Piven and Cloward 1993. *See generally* the review in Sutton 1996: 943–45.

87. Sutton 1996.

discipline social behavior. Thus, John Sutton prefers the phrase "sanctioning regimes" to "social control mechanism(s),"[88] including within the former processes of stigmatization as well as instruments of punishment, and noting that normative and cognitive processes of legitimation are at least as important as coercive mechanisms in structuring such regimes. Sutton's focus on institutions leads him away from the structural roots of legitimation and control and toward intra- and inter-organizational processes in understanding the power of law to shape social norms and conduct.

Equally important, legality and discipline are fundamentally implicated in processes of normalization. Foucault notes that there cannot "fail to be a fundamental relationship between the law and the norm . . . every system of law is related to a system of norms."[89] Indeed, he continues, "there is something that we could call a normativity intrinsic to any legal imperative."[90] Discipline, too, is unambiguously normalizing. It normalizes by deconstructing individuals, movements, actions, places, time, and operations into their constituent components, classifying them according to certain objectives and establishing "optimal sequences or co-ordinations" designed to achieve those objectives.[91] Ultimately, "[discipline] divides the normal from the abnormal."[92]

In the chapters that follow, I argue that both legality and discipline operate through law upon sexuality in the ways described by Foucault as techniques of prohibition and mandate,

88. *Ibid*: 945.

89. Foucault, et al 2007: 56.

90. *Ibid*.

91. This account echoes, in many ways, Erving Goffman's description of the reconstruction of the individual which takes place in a "total institution." *See* Goffman 1961/2007.

92. Foucault, et al 2007: 57.

and therefore performs significant normalizing functions. For example, the jurisprudence that governs anti-gay hate crime and same-sex harassment creates prohibitory discourses of desire. It marks off "good" and "bad" desires; divides sexuality from animus, fear, and something called "horseplay"; and it generates categories of forbidden objects (and subjects) of desire. Same-sex marriage law, on the other hand, first deconstructs and then reconstructs social classifications that nominate "love" (marital or parental) over sexuality. In short, it *creates* families (of a particular sort).

Just as clearly, however, legality and discipline do not operate freely or without constraint. They do not impose social order upon groups or individuals external to the law so much as they take up extant discourses of desire, love, animus, fear, and identity, circulate them through the institutional processes that are the *sine qua non* of legalism, reduce them to certain predictable constituent parts, and reinscribe them upon the social body. Here, it is worth remembering, as neoinstitutionalists do, that the American state is frequently said to adhere to the "rule of law." This is no accident. The discursive objects that the law of homosex creates are rule-like in both origin (in that they are derived from a set of rational procedural rules that dissect, winnow, bracket, and disarticulate complex social inquiries and render them the solutions of discrete "questions presented") and effect, (in that they establish rules and grammars of prohibition and mandate).

But why should law be able to accomplish this? What features of legal discourse and legal institutions give law such social power? First, as Pierre Bourdieu has argued, law is organized in such a way as to produce a specific sort of linguistic object: a performative utterance, similar to that conceived by Austin, that results in social "magic." Put simply, law creates the reality it desires by virtue of the words it deploys. But this is not because words exist in specific linguistic relationships with each other or because they correspond to an underlying empirical reality that validates them as real or true. For Bourdieu, the authorizing power of legal speech acts is derived from the social power conferred upon legal institutions by a broad spectrum of social actors. Law is powerful because it is recognized as such.

Second, and relatedly, as both Bourdieu and Habermas note, certain features of legal institutions enhance law's ability to command the allegiance of the dominated as well as the dominant, and thus extend and deepen law's symbolic power. Legal institutions are characterized by a high degree of formalism and a predictability borne of countless explicit rules, yet they nonetheless appear permeable and responsive to social and cultural demands. Law is thus doubly seductive: it simultaneously assures us of its authority and its accessibility.

It is worth examining each of these points in greater detail.

## B. Bourdieu: Symbolic Power, Performative Utterances, and the "Force of Law"

According to Pierre Bourdieu, law serves as a site of the production and deployment of "symbolic capital"—that is, the power to define social reality.[93] Like economic capital, social capital, and cultural capital,[94] symbolic capital may be described as a resource—something to be deployed by dominant class[95] members

---

93. Bourdieu 1987.

94. *See* Bourdieu 1984.

95. To a significant extent, Bourdieu uses "class" to index socioeconomic class. However, he has expressly stated that the sort of classification process he describes as being produced by the deployment of symbolic power includes the creation of "classes" defined by other metrics, including age, sex, tribe, nation, and the like. Bourdieu and Thompson 1991: 105.

to further their class dominance. However, its value as a resource derives from its location within a social field that has secured participation from the *full* array of classes. As Bourdieu puts it, "[t]he specific property of symbolic power is that it can be exercised only through the complicity of those who are dominated by it."[96] The question that arises, then, is why we ought to expect the dominated to comply. The answer, for Bourdieu, lies at the intersection of language and social institutions.

By definition, symbolic power inheres in the construction of meaning, and thus language is the starting point of Bourdieu's analysis. He finds something of use in Chomsky's notion of linguistic competence, and in Saussure's semiotics, but finds both approaches insufficiently grounded in social and political relations.[97] Consequently, Austin's notion of speech acts—words that "do" things—is more appealing to Bourdieu because it is an expressly social conception of language. For Austin, language derives its ability to perform certain acts by virtue of its embeddedness in social convention—or "conditions of felicity."[98] If a minister pronounces to a group congregated in a church that two people are "married," the congregation understands those words to have a transformative quality—to, in essence, *create* the married couple. The power to "do things with words" is derived from the shared expectations of the group; if the appropriate conventions are followed, Austin contends, the words that are uttered are effective in transforming social reality.

Yet Austin, too, is insufficiently sociological for Bourdieu. He contends that the notion of "convention" is too vague and thin because it fails to specify the origin or source of social agreement.

96. Bourdieu 1987: 844.

97. *See* Bourdieu and Thompson 1991: chapter 1.

98. *Ibid*: 3.

Why does the group recognize the power of a given performative utterance? What underlies the ritualistic invocation of "magic" words? Bourdieu's answer is that the social power of language is located in the specific dimensions and qualities of social "fields," sometimes called "markets". Fields are structured configurations of social positions and the relations between them, which establish specific distributions of different kinds of resources, including symbolic capital.[99] Fields are similar to social institutions in that they are constituted by people and patterned social practices, but they are somewhat broader in jurisdiction. Religion may be a field, for example, or culture. Law, as well. Fields confer meaning and power upon speech acts: the import and force of language is derived from the "social position of the speaker"[100] within the field, and an effective performative utterance may be viewed as "a kind of photographic negative—of the set of institutional conditions which must be fulfilled in order for ritual discourse to be recognized."[101]

Although Bourdieu writes at length about the importance of structural correspondences existing across different social fields in empowering speech,[102] I believe his more theoretically puissant observations concern those within-field dynamics, features, and processes that confer linguistic competency and authority

---

99. *Ibid*: 76. "[A]ll speech is produced in and for the market within/for which it owes its existence and its properties."

100. *Ibid*:109.

101. *Ibid*: 115.

102. Bourdieu refers to these as "homologies." *See, for example, Ibid*: 41. In brief, the distribution of resources (forms of capital) within a field—for example, law—will correspond structurally to the distribution of resources in another field and in the social structure writ large. I find this claim of Bourdieu's to be among his least persuasive, not least because it is at odds with his assertions about the importance of field-specific dynamics, processes, and features.

on recognized speakers. At bottom, these are institutional in nature. The

> magical efficacy of . . . acts of institution is inseparable from the existence of an institution defining the conditions, *regarding the agent, the time, or place, etc.*, which have to be fulfilled for the magic of words to operate . . . these 'conditions of felicity' are social conditions, and the person who wishes to proceed *felicitously* . . . must be *entitled* to do so.[103]

Thus, for example, a priest who baptizes a child is able to secure the salvation of that child's soul because the priest has been properly credentialed, has uttered the proper words at the proper time, in the proper setting, and under the gaze of the proper witnesses. The religious field delimits the conditions within which baptism may be performed effectively, infusing the words uttered by the priest with the status and force of (socially meaningful) facticity.

It is not difficult to see how this conception of institutionally grounded linguistic power will operate in the juridical field. While Max Weber distinguished between modern rational legal systems (which, he claimed, derive their legitimacy from the neutral, technical, and bureaucratic processes that attend the formation and announcement of legal judgments) and pre-modern "charismatic" legal systems (which, he claimed, derive their legitimacy from the power of charismatic judges to utter "magic words"), Bourdieu contends that there is little to distinguish such systems from one another. For Bourdieu, rational law is no less the product of magic wrought by utterances.[104] Like the religious field, the

103. *Ibid*: 73 (emphasis in original).

104. *Ibid*: 42.

juridical field is structured by criteria of membership and competency, by rules of engagement (here, specifically, rules governing forms of contestation), and by the rituals of linguistic performance. The central dynamic animating law as a field is structured contestation over "the right to determine the law"; actors are effective speakers if they possess the technical competence that "consists essentially in the socially recognized capacity to *interpret* a corpus of texts."[105]

Substantively and stylistically, legal discourse is powerful because it partakes of a rhetoric characterized by impersonality and neutrality. Yet this is not merely a façade; it is the manifestation of a set of juridical dispositions–the *habitus* of legal practice—that serves to constitute the central mechanism defining law's performative power:

> This attitude constitutes the entry ticket into the juridical field—accompanied, to be sure, by a minimal mastery of the legal resources amassed by successive generations . . . This fundamental attitude claims to produce a specific form of judgment, completely distinct from the often wavering intuitions of the ordinary sense of fairness because it is based upon rigorous deduction from a body of internally coherent rules.[106]

Law takes "ordinary" conceptions of fairness and transforms them into real acts of justice. Lawyers are empowered to participate in this transformative process by institutional gatekeeping devices that ensure a relative uniformity of language, knowledge, and disposition.

105. Bourdieu 1987: 817.
106. *Ibid*: 820.

Yet it is not only lawyers who must satisfy certain admission criteria in order to enter the juridical field. Individual and collective actors who make claims upon the judiciary also must embrace the formalities of juridical practice as a condition of entry. Thus, the making of a legal claim signals the claimant's tacit acceptance of the rules of the game: he or she renounces extralegal means of resolving social and cultural disputes in favor of a juridical resolution.[107] This, in turn, requires more specific sorts of concessions. The litigant agrees to translate his or her broadly conceived grievances into the discrete language of a legal claim (he or she must "put the case" to the law); formulate the claim in conformity with certain procedural and substantive categories established by law; accept a discrete, binary resolution of the dispute (win/lose; guilty/not guilty); and sacrifice the nuance of ordinary experience in favor of a formalized, truncated account of the facts, the normative principles guiding the determination of a just outcome, and the judgment itself.[108]

These concessions seem minor in the face of all that law promises to confer in return. Judicial power is a special kind of power because it draws upon the state's unique capacity to impose a transcendent social vision. The "State alone holds the monopoly of legitimized symbolic violence"[109] and therefore law operates as "the quintessential form of the symbolic power of naming that creates the things named."[110] Indeed, it "creates social groups in particular."[111] Through its utterances, law produces social reality.

107. *Ibid*: 831.

108. *Ibid*: 832.

109. *Ibid*: 838.

110. *Ibid*.

111. *Ibid*.

It engages in the magical act of creating categories of experience and identity.

Finally, law is socially powerful because it plays upon the mutual dependencies established between "ordinary" language and the specialized language of lawyers.[112] While law traffics in a specialized discourse,[113] juridical utterances never remain contained within the juridical field. Like other field-specific discourses, juridical discourses "are diffused outside the restricted field and undergo a kind of automatic universalization,"[114] which elides the distinction between esoteric and commonsense linguistic meanings. Legal discourse is polysemic, resonant in ways that extend beyond the boundaries of law's institutional constraints. This is a crucial feature of law's power to define social reality because it serves to hide the traces of juridical origins. The law no longer announces merely a *legal* reality; it names a *social* reality that has the force of existential truth.

## C. Habermas: Law as a Mediating Category Between Facts and Norms

For Jurgen Habermas, too, the force of law is revealed at the intersection of legal institutions and social and cultural practices (or "lifeworlds"). According to Habermas, law is not an instrument but, rather, an achievement produced intersubjectively through communicative action. Yet only those communicative practices that link up in persuasive ways with the lifeworlds (normative and cultural structures—values and institutions—of a society) that exist "outside" of law will be effective in stabilizing

---

112. Bourdieu and Thompson 1991: 40–41.

113. It is a language that is enamored of Latin and of esoteric definitions of what are facially ordinary words (such as "proximate" or "damage" or "discriminate").

114. *Ibid*: 41.

dynamic societies.[115] As Habermas puts it, the "rationality" problem that law faces amounts to the question of how "the application of a contingently emergent law [can] be carried out with both internal consistency and rational external justification, so as to guarantee simultaneously the certainty of law and its rightness."[116] Law exists, according to Habermas, "between facts and norms"; it is a "category of social mediation" that helps to integrate societies no longer characterized by metasocial (sectarian) grounds of right, authority, and inequality.[117] In this "post-metaphysical" world—characterized by pluralism, Weberian disenchantment, and functional complexity—law works to the extent that it permits "the addressees of legal norms [to] understand themselves . . . as the rational authors of those norms."[118]

Thus, legal discourse has independent significance in advancing the aim of social integration by creating norms as social facts[119] but only if it is produced under conditions that inspire public confidence in the communicative processes from which it issues.[120] This makes sense because, for Habermas, legitimation crises arise precisely at the intersection of state rationality and the values of the lifeworld.[121] The increased administration of society by the state gives rise to "new validity claims" that are

115. Habermas 1996: 198.

116. *Ibid*.

117. *Ibid*., chapter 1.

118. *Ibid*: 33.

119. *Ibid*: 147.

120. *Ibid*: 297 ("practical reason no longer resides in universal human rights, or in the ethical substance of a scientific community, but in the rules of discourse and forms of argumentation that borrow their normative content from the validity basis of action oriented to reaching understanding . . . normative content arises from the structure of linguistic communication and the communicative mode of sociation.")

121. Habermas 1973: 72–80.

pressed by collective actors and which must increasingly be redeemed discursively.[122]

This is an important insight and one worth noting specially: Habermas's emphasis on the disjuncture between state and lifeworld, and the resulting production of new validity claims within legal institutions, suggests that law is arguably most powerful when it is taking up the sorts of cultural conflicts that are produced within the social space that is opened up by state action[123]:

> At every level, administrative planning produces unintended unsettling and publicizing effects. These effects weaken the justification potential of traditions that have been flushed out of their nature-like course of development. Once their unquestionable character has been destroyed, the stabilization of validity claims can succeed only through discourse. The stirring up of cultural affairs that are taken for granted thus furthers the politicization of areas of life previously assigned to the private sphere.

As we shall see, recent developments within the law of homosex offer particularly illustrative examples of how this process works. For now, it is important only to note two things: first, the way in which Habermas elevates the importance of discourse, arguing that *only* discursive processes can produce the level of normative agreement needed to legitimize an always contentious state-society relationship;[124] and second, Habermas's assertion that the administrative state creates, by its interventions

122. *Ibid*: 72.

123. *Ibid*: 72.

124. Of course, Habermas is skeptical of the idea of any easy distinctions drawn between "state" and "society." I use these terms provisionally—as placeholders

into lifeworlds, new sources of social conflict, new validity claims, and new uncertainties about social and juridical norms.

In this sense, Habermas's approach resonates in significant ways with the approach taken by queer theorist Cindy Patton. Patton contends that the contemporary Western state is a postmodern state. As such, she argues, it is centrally occupied with the task of "administering an incoherent, incommensurable plurality of interests."[125] This distinguishes it from the modern liberal state, which was characterized by "an overt concern with coordinating and integrating different claims on resources and power."[126] The postmodern state is concerned with creating and instating "governable subjectivities"; social and political identities serve less to organize claims upon the state for resources than they do to orient the disciplinary and constitutive power of a decentralized, self-effacing state. Consequently, "the crucial battle . . . for 'minorities' and resistant subalterns is not achieving democratic representation but wresting control over the discourses concerning identity construction."[127] While Habermas largely fails to specify *how* validity claims are redeemed by/within the state, Patton contends that it is the very assertion of identity that transforms the field of discursive power: "All identities effect . . . deontic closures . . . achievement of identities is precisely the staking out of duties and alliances in a field of power."[128]

designed to draw our attention to a zone of contentiousness, rather than to a specific divide separating two discrete spheres of activity.

125. Patton 1993: 172.

126. *Ibid*.

127. *Ibid*: 173.

128. *Ibid*: 174.

Yet Patton's account seems oddly optimistic about the cunning with which contemporary social movement organizations and actors might deploy identity constructs in the service of deeply ironic and performative postmodern politics.[129] What is missing from Patton's account—which (it must be said) is *not* intended to be a fully developed theory of postidentitarian politics and the state—is the institutional context within which discursive validity claims are adjudicated. In short, once new validity claims are raised, what sorts of conditions permit their discursive redemption? Habermas agrees with Weber that the institutional characteristics of modern legal systems are crucially important. Law must be rule bound, governed by abstract principles and procedures, and autonomous from political parties and interests.[130] Like Bourdieu, Habermas emphasizes the institutional basis of discourse production, noting the—to his mind—positive effects of legal procedural devices that reduce complex issues to "questions presented," narrow the scope of investigation and argument, and discipline evidentiary boundaries.[131] In a world in which no case truly stands on all fours with any prior case, these devices "define the bounds within which parties can deal with the law strategically" and enable the court to "decide each case in a way that preserves the coherence of the legal order as a whole."[132]

129. Patton is not entirely optimistic on this score. In fact, the main thrust of the essay in which she sets out this notion of postmodern identity performance is an effort to point out the ways in which queer/homo discursive identities are tethered to new right discursive identities. Still, she seems to wish for an ironic postmodern activism that, I would argue, has not yet crystallized. At the very least, it has not crystallized around juridical institutions.

130. Habermas 1996: chapter 6.

131. *Ibid*: 237.

132. *Ibid*.

Habermas describes the ideal speech situation—one that produces genuine discourse—in these terms:

> Discourse can be understood as that form of communication that is removed from contexts of experience and action and *whose structure assures us*: that the bracketed validity claims of assertions, recommendations, or warnings are the exclusive object of discussion; that participants, themes and contributions are not restricted except with reference to the goal of testing the validity claims in question; that no force except that of the better argument is exercised; and that, as a result, all motives except that of the cooperative search for truth are excluded.[133]

I have highlighted the phrase "whose structure assures us" because the important point here is not that these conditions actually exist in some real, material, empirically verifiable sense. Rather, what is important is that law's institutional structure assures us that they do. Tamanaha's critique of law as a field open to political opportunism notwithstanding, legal institutions retain a stunning array of procedural features and dispositions that serve to precisely structure the production of legal discourses and which, as a result, inspire the sort of confidence that Habermas associates with the redemption of validity claims.

## V. The Framework (In a Nutshell)

The juridical field is possessed of many legitimizing and authorizing features and dispositions of the sort identified by Foucault,

---

133. *Ibid*: 107 (emphasis added).

Bourdieu and Habermas, and each no doubt performs a good deal of work upon the extant social discourses, claims, and objects that present themselves to the law. Going forward, however, I think there are four such features that are particularly important and therefore require our sustained attention.

First, the language of law is principally a language that invokes and creates _justificatory narratives_. Here, we can draw from all three theorists in noting the importance of juridical discourse in contemporary governance projects, as well as the location of that discourse within specific institutional practices. As these theorists suggest, such practices both raise and resolve legitimation problems. To be cognizable as something that law can legitimately address—to be _justiciable_—a problem, conflict, or dispute must be described and justified in normative terms that law itself can understand.[134]

At a general level, justificatory narratives take a familiar form. As sociologists of law have understood for some time, people and groups engage the law through a process of "naming, blaming, and claiming"[135] where "claiming" is dependent upon a particular "naming" and "blaming" convention. Political theorist Wendy Brown has described this process as evincing a politics of _ressentiment_, of marking the claimant as injured and supplicating.[136] Because they articulate an account of why the state ought to intervene in a particular issue or dispute, justificatory narratives embody the substance of legality (in the Foucaultian sense of the word): conceptions of what is prohibited and what is mandated

---

134. I make no comparative claims in this book, focusing exclusively on American law and society. But it does not seem unlikely that this justificatory requirement is enhanced in this case, given American commitments to a laissez-faire state and a negative liberties conception of constitutional law. _See generally_ Barber 2005.

135. Felstiner, et al 1980.

136. Brown 1995.

in the law of homosex. But they do so within terms set by prior, legitimacy-conferring normative frameworks that prevail in American law. For example, claims for relief from anti-gay hate crimes draw upon retributive, utilitarian, and expressivist frameworks in establishing a narrative that justifies heightened punishment for crimes committed out of anti-gay hatred or bias. Same-sex harassment law partakes of an anti-discrimination/equity framework that has similar narrative force. And the same-sex marriage campaign invokes themes of equality and liberty in constructing a justificatory narrative designed to establish a basis for striking down state marriage bans and overriding majoritarian preferences.

Establishing these justificatory narratives requires certain first-order transformations of social problems, conflicts, and identities, rendering them intelligible within contemporary legal discourse. But this is hardly the only transformation that takes place. Law also reduces the complexity of social claims by _bracketing_ the most expansive, multifaceted, and uncertain dimensions of those claims, and delimiting compound questions and demands as discrete, singular, disconnected issues. For example, let us say that a woman is fired from her job and believes she has been discriminated against because she is a lesbian. She lives in California (which is a good place to live if you believe you have been discriminated against because you are a lesbian)[137] and visits her local gay-friendly employment litigator. Her claim—as she understands it—is a simple, yet profound, one: she has been treated unfairly by her employer because she is gay, and she understands that (in California at least) such conduct is considered unjust. Her attorney, however, sees her claim in terms of its constituent

137. Cal. Govt. Code § 12940.

parts. Was there an "adverse employment action"?[138] (She was fired—check!) Is she covered by the state and/or federal statute prohibiting employment discrimination—is she, that is, a member of a "protected class"? (Yes, under state law[139]; no, under federal law[140]—one cause of action down, one still alive.) What evidence is there that, but for his client's lesbianism, the adverse employment action would not have occurred? (Cf., e.g., prior case law and code provisions defining (a) causation requirements; (b) burdens of production and persuasion; (c) *bona fide* occupational qualifications; (d) pretextual defenses, etc. This is where the real fun (and work) begins.)

The operation here is quite clear: a claim about injustice and identity is reduced to a series of discrete elemental issues and questions.[141] Indeed, one can readily discern the bracketing function here by pursuing the following sorts of queries: What difficult, complex social realities are *not* interrogated in the movement from the term "lesbian" to "protected classification"? What complex questions of social knowledge, experience, identification, self- and other-definition, and the like drop out of the analysis before it has even really begun?

Second, law *disciplines evidentiary boundaries*—it establishes what counts as relevant evidence bearing upon the questions thus reduced—not only by deploying well-known gateway procedures such as rules of evidence and pleading but also through the structuring influence of prior doctrine. The principle of *stare decisis*, the rules establishing "binding" and "persuasive" authority, and the essential nature of legal reasoning—the process of

138. Yanowitz v. L'Oreal USA, Inc., 36 Cal. 41028, 1054-55 (Cal. Sup. Ct.).

139. Cal. Govt. Code § 12940(a).

140. 42 U.S. Code 2000e-2(a-d).

141. *See* Heimer 2001.

distinguishing cases (or pronouncing them on point)—all serve to constitute a drastically reduced field within which legal discourses are strategically invoked, circulate, and then validated, dismissed, or modified in judgment.[142]

Particularly important here is the way in which the analytical and doctrinal environment within which legal discourses are produced encourages law to engage in a bad sort of social science. In collecting, examining, and analyzing the "material facts" of a particular issue or dispute, legal decision makers frequently and consistently rely upon proxy measures in lieu of more complex, varied, and ontologically unruly empirical data.[143] So, for example, in deciding "what happened" in a same-sex harassment case, the trier of fact may deduce the presence (or absence) of sexual desire from the constructed "facts" of the litigants' sexual identities.[144] Law eschews complex social reality for categorical elegance; this makes sense for lawyers, but it does violence to lived social experience.

Finally, law relies upon the _polysemic quality of legal discourse_ to produce the appearance that it has not, in fact, addressed only a fractional component of the original claim but has, instead,

142. I conceive of this mechanism as largely analogous to what I have described elsewhere as the structuring influence of "policy environments" on legislative policymaking. Zylan 2000. As I conceive of them, policy environments are comprised of policy legacies (preexisting policy commitments), institutional mandates (the specific imperatives and objectives with which institutional actors are charged), and institutional/parainstututional resources (arguments, frames, and other discursive material with which state actors and those operating at the margins of state institutions have to work). In the legislative context, a given policy discourse will emerge as the interplay of each of these elements. Law is organized somewhat differently in that "policies" and "mandates" are more often implicit than explicit, but a similar sort of interplay may be observed. In short, legal discourses do not emerge out of whole cloth but are, rather, profoundly shaped by the institutional and discursive environment within which they are produced.

143. Heimer 2001.

144. See _infra_, chapter 5.

pronounced judgment on a larger social issue or conflict. So, for example, when a legal opinion announces that "X happened because of Y," lawyers will understand "because" to be a term of art indicating "but for" causation, application of the substantial factor test, a finding of proximate or legal causation, etc., but non-lawyers will hear "because" in its commonplace sense, which invokes a much broader, deeper, and consequential notion of causation.[145]

Each of these four mechanisms serves to constitute legal categories as social categories (and vice versa), to instantiate and authorize rules of prohibition and mandate, and—perhaps most importantly—to erase the traces of law's limiting and rendering processes, so that what remains is the appearance of a comprehensive resolution of those complex social questions and conflicts that law claims to have addressed. And it is this naturalizing quality of law's intervention[146] that makes it so powerful, and so problematic, as a source of social construction. Indeed, as invoked by the law of homosex, juridical utterances are doubly naturalizing. First, in setting out the rules of desire, identity, and the body, law authorizes particular expressions and experiences of sexuality that are profoundly limiting and narrowly constructed, yet which enjoy the status of unreconstructed social fact.[147] Second, the institutional processes by which law has selected, transformed, and announced a particular set of sexual categories and narratives are themselves masked and made to appear natural— an outcome then described as discovery, not construction.[148] In short, law performs magic, but it does so with the smooth,

145. I explore this particular example in great detail in Chapters 4 and 5.

146. Douglas 1986.

147. Durkheim 1982.

148. *See generally* Douglas 1986.

reassuring appearance of a fact-seeking technocracy. Ultimately, then, law's power to define sexuality for us derives from its commanding facade of neutrality, dispassion, and rationality not only because such features signal legitimacy and authority but because they are seductive. Law defines our desires because we desire the discipline of law.

To see how this is so and why we ought to be concerned about it,[149] it is first necessary to theorize a conception of desire, sexuality, passion, identity, and the body that explains how law—as a producer of representations—helps to construct sexed, gendered, desiring subjects. It is to this task that I turn in the next chapter.

---

149. One way of thinking about this project is as an effort to produce a *counterhegemonic* discourse of law and sexuality. *See generally* Hunt 1993: 232–235.

# 3

## Beyond the Binary Matrix: Theorizing the Social Construction of Sexuality

I have suggested that the law of homosex, examined closely, produces a discursive account of sexuality that is deeply problematic for sexual progressives—many of whom turn to the law precisely because they believe it is possible and desirable to create a liberatory sociolegal environment for the expression of multiple, diverse sexualities. In the chapters that follow, I will focus on the specific ways in which law both relies upon, and reproduces, a truncated notion of how sexuality operates in social life. To permit this sort of analysis, however, I must first articulate a fuller conception of how sexuality is socially constructed, a question that has long occupied theorists from a number of different disciplines, including psychoanalytic theory, sociology, philosophy, feminist theory, and queer theory. Doing so accomplishes two things. First, it renders visible the gaps, flaws, and omissions that pervade jurisprudential discourses of sexuality. Second, it offers an account of why and how jurisprudential discourses are themselves implicated in constructing—not merely describing—sexuality.

In what follows, I outline a theory of desire that explains the power, ambivalence, and social significance of the sexed boundaries of the body. I work with some foundational stories— psychoanalytic (especially those derived from Freud and Lacan), postmodern/poststructural, and feminist accounts of sexuality— but I reconfigure them in ways that make sense to me. Because some (many?) adherents of these accounts of sexuality value a more faithful rendering of their theories, my retelling of these stories is unlikely to be pleasing to them. So much the better. In the reproduction of social theory, fidelity is an unexamined (and unproven) virtue.[1] Indeed, all retellings such as this—all "reviews" of appropriate literatures—rewrite foundations in important ways, shifting frames of reference, emphasizing new elements of synthetic production, and creating a new intellectual terrain upon which to proceed.[2] If, as Janet Halley has written, "theory produces reality not only by making it visible . . . but by shifting the available terms for consciousness, desire, and thus interest"[3] (and I think that it does), then the rewriting and rereading of texts against, next to, and in conversation with one another is one way of achieving a different social reality of sexuality. And that, ultimately, is my goal.

1. I am not entirely unsympathetic to the criticism that one ought not to engage in cafeteria style theorizing. See, for example, Grosz 1997: 307 ("It seems to me that one must be aware of a certain 'ethics' of reading . . . One cannot simply buy into a theoretical system  without at the same time accepting its basic implications and founding assumptions . . . Problematic implications cannot be contained and prevented from infiltrating those considered unproblematic.") At the same time, I do not agree that efforts to reread and reconfigure texts in conversation with one another necessarily amount to a recuperative project. The key to avoiding the latter while engaging in the former is, I think, maintaining an explicitly critical posture that announces where it does (and does not) "buy into" the most salient and important tenets of those frameworks subject to reexamination and reconfiguration.

2. One might describe my approach as genealogical in a Foucaultian sense. That is, what I seek to do is trace a certain intellectual course of theorizing of sexuality without privileging any transcendent position of subjectivity (or objectivity). I do not claim, for example, that any one theory has the story "right." Rather, I seek to place certain conceptions and frameworks in relation to one another in an effort to see them anew, and productively. See generally Foucault 1972; Focault and Gordon 1980; Foucault and Hoy 1986.

3. Halley 2006: 4.

## I. How to Theorize Sex Without Really Trying

An important starting point of most popular conceptions of sexuality, including those deployed in law, is the notion that bodies are objectively real and material, made of the sort of stuff—bones, flesh, and blood—that manifests *substance*. Nobody who has ever woken up with the flu—with the sensation that she can suddenly and precisely identify the location and temperature of every single skin cell on her body—could be persuaded otherwise. And, more to the point of our inquiry, few gay men or lesbians would resist the notion that sexual desire is, perhaps above all else, a *physical* experience. Accordingly, what we might term "substantialist"[4] accounts of sexuality begin with observable material differences in genitalia, secondary sex characteristics, endocrinology, and chromosomal structure. These are posited as the wellspring of binary sex,[5] the division of males and females into two discrete classes[6] and, in turn, the material ground for both gender and sexuality. In the substantialist narrative, gender flows from sex—if not naturally,[7]

4. Mustafa Emirbayer has used the word "substantialism" to refer to the tendency of social science to objectify social phenomena, treating them as discrete entities or "variables," even as they would more profitably be conceived in relational terms. See generally Emirbayer 1997. My discussion of sexuality theory tracks that critique.

5. To avoid a potential problem that could easily lead to an infinite regress, let us simply agree that the word "sex" is deeply problematic. It is a multivalent homonym freighted with political baggage that no feminist theorist can hope to unload once and for all. For example, perhaps it references a *category* of reproductive anatomy. Or a particular set of genitalia, such as the "sex which is not one" that Luce Irigaray plays with and upon. Or, maybe it is a set of desire driven practices—the sex one "has." Janet Halley has a useful glossary of such definitions in *Split Decisions* (2006), and I see no reason to reinvent this particular wheel. When I use the word "sex," I take it to mean Halley's "sex1." For Halley's sex2, I use the word "sexuality."

6. See the discussion in Fausto-Sterling 2000.

7. *See, for example*, Wilson 1978.

then as a matter of socialization.[8] Similarly, sexual "identity" is derivative of sex categories; the terms "homosexual" and "heterosexual" are intelligible only within a grammar of dichotomous sex. Moreover, as elaborated by popular culture, the substantialist account describes the sexes as not only categorically different from one another but as "opposites"[9]—a relational claim that propounds oppositional mechanisms of gender and sexual identity.

The binarized, substantialist account of sex is so deeply anchored in American culture as to be axiomatic and virtually invisible.[10] And yet researchers and scholars in a wide variety of disciplines have all but debunked it,[11] demonstrating that the stuff of sex differences simply cannot bear the social and cultural work it is asked to do. Instead, anatomical, endocrinological, neurological, and chromosomal sex differences must be wildly exaggerated in order to materially ground the binarization of gender and sexuality. As the late Eve Kosofsky Sedgwick put it, with characteristic elegance and pith:

> Under no matter what cultural construction, women and men are more like each other than chalk is like cheese, than ratiocination is like raisins, than up is like down, or than 1 is like 0. The biological, psychological, and cognitive attributes of men

8. Chodorow 1978; West and Zimmerman 1987; Thorne and Yalom 1992, 1993; Messner 2002.

9. See for example Gray 1992.

10. The taken-for-granted quality of substantialism is the *sine qua non* of its power to construct reality. Berger and Luckmann 1990: 16 ("All typifications of common-sense thinking are themselves integral elements of the concrete historical socioeconomic Lebenswelt within which they prevail as taken for granted and socially approved.").

11. See generally Fausto-Sterling 2000.

overlap with those of women by vastly more than they differ from them.[12]

Sedgewick's list makes plain that the differences we observe between men and women—and consequently between masculine and feminine subjects, and gay and straight people—are relatively minor in a biological sense. The amplification of such differences at the social level is thus evidence of a process of *social construction*: the constitution of an objective world through the repetition and reinscription of social practices and norms that come to evince a quality of taken-for-grantedness.[13]

The fact that sex, gender, and sexuality are socially constructed does not render them any less real, however. While substantialist and constructionist accounts of sexuality are often discussed as though they are ontologically irreconcilable, sociologists have long understood materiality and signification to be two sides of the same coin. As John Berger and Peter Luckmann put the matter some 40 years ago:

> Society does indeed possess objective facticity. And society is indeed built up by activity that expresses subjective meaning... It is precisely the dual character of society in terms of objective facticity and subjective meaning that makes its 'reality sui generis'... The central question for sociological theory can then be put as follows: How is it possible that subjective meanings become objective facticities? Or, in terms appropriate to the afore-mentioned theoretical positions: How is it possible that human activity... should produce a world of things?[14]

12. Sedgwick 1993: 7, n.6.

13. Berger and Luckmann 1990.

14. Berger and Luckmann 1990: 18.

Berger and Luckmann begin to answer their own question by describing social reality as a lifeworld constituted by processes of "typification" and "reification." Human beings engage in a variety of face-to-face encounters that become the basis for expectations about how the world is likely to present itself ("typification"). Indeed, such interactions are doubly "typifying": "I apprehend the other as a type and I interact with him in a situation that is itself typical."[15] Such typifications multiply and interlace to form what sociologists call "social structure," a term of art that bears the marks of both signification and materiality. Social structure exists in a conceptual space (the phrase partakes of metaphor), but it is nonetheless real in that it shapes, constrains, channels and directs human behavior.

Similarly, Berger and Luckmann argue, we view the products of human interaction as thing-like: as possessing objective, material, and natural qualities (reification).[16] In so doing, we come to experience them as having a life of their own, perhaps connected to us in important or intimate ways, but in a crucial sense standing apart from us. Importantly, Berger and Luckmann note that identity can function in precisely this way: "a small part of the self is objectivated and held out as something other than the self."[17] Identity—such as sexual identity—becomes thing-like[18] and, at the same time, is the product of an ongoing relational process: *identification*.

Typification, reification, and identification are constitutive of social reality: they produce and emerge from interpersonal and

15. *Ibid*: 31.

16. "[R]eification is the apprehension of the products of human activity as if they were something else than human products—such as facts of nature, results of cosmic laws, or manifestations of divine will." Berger & Luckmann 1990: 89.

17. *Ibid*: 91.

18. See, for example, Bernstein 1997.

social dynamics that create—and subsequently turn upon—conceptions of self and others. Berger and Luckmann say little about what the content of "self" and "others" might be, but they do suggest that language plays a particularly important role in mediating material, social, and cognitive worlds.[19] The production and use of signs allows the products of human consciousness and interaction to appear tangible because language has a transcendent quality: it is "detachable" from present experience.[20] Words, grammars, and "symbolic universes" help actors bring confusing, weird, and unruly experiences into conformity with their understanding of themselves and their worlds. Signification thus facilitates the construction of a coherent lifeworld: "[b]ecause of its capacity to transcend the 'here and now,' language bridges different zones within the reality of everyday life and integrates them into a meaningful whole."[21]

Though Berger and Luckmann are rarely (if ever) described as postmodern or poststructural theorists, their account of the constitutive properties of language has much in common with antifoundationalist theories. Such theories, including certain variants of feminist and queer theory, echo Berger and Luckmann's social constructionism by asserting that reality is both material *and* the product of social discourses, including medical, cultural, and juridical discourses (among others). In short, poststructural and postmodern theories of sexuality contend that bodies are not merely described or constrained by discourse but respond and feel and are experienced in certain

19. Berger and Luckmann 1990: 19–35; 42, 98.

20. *Ibid*: 36–39.

21. *Ibid*: 39.

ways because discourse has written meaning into and upon corporeal forms.[22]

## II. Inside, Out

As Elizabeth Grosz has argued, one useful way of thinking about the discursive and social construction of the body and sexuality is as a process that works from the inside out and from the outside in—as inscription upon a kind of Mobius strip.[23] The body and the self are "written" on both sides of the strip by intrapsychic, interpersonal, social, and cultural processes, producing a self that is simultaneously and mutually cognitive and corporeal. Grosz offers the image of the Mobius strip to convey that neither dimension is reducible or superordinate/subordinate to the other. Experiences of the body are imprinted upon the mind, and the mind maps the body as an array of signifying planes, surfaces, openings, and limits.

First, the inside. Drawing upon psychoanalytic and phenomenological literatures, Grosz describes a psyche that is forged intrapsychically and interactively through individualized experiences that involve the social and material world and the body's dynamic, physical boundaries. The psyche reaches out to meet the world

22. Steven Seidman (2003) notes that one can conceive of "strong" and "weak" social constructionist accounts of sexuality. In the weak account, sexual impulses and desires preexist social order but are shaped, constrained and directed by a variety of normative, political, and economic forces. In the strong account, normative, political, and economic forces *constitute* sexuality, producing desires, identities, and behaviors. Just as I find constitutive theories of the law/society relationship more compelling than instrumental theories (and for similar reasons), I find constitutive theories of sexuality more persuasive than those that limit the role of sociality to its channeling functions.

23. Grosz 1994b: xii. The Mobius strip has also been invoked by Jacques Lacan and Ann Fausto-Sterling. In Grosz's account, the strip represents the boundaries, or surface, of the body.

and, in so doing, develops a sense of its own corporeal subjectivity. Grosz's description of this inside-out dynamic relies upon a feminist reading of Freud and Lacan that underscores the (largely unrealized) radical potential of the psychoanalytic model. While it has long been criticized for its phallocentrism, ethnocentrism, and occasional biologism, psychoanalytic theory offers promise as an approach that problematizes sexuality, gender, and the body as *outcomes*: the products of processes that involve the body, the mind, and the limitations of material and social environments. According to Freud, infants arrive in the world ungendered, unsexed, and polymorphously perverse, capable of eroticizing the entire body in connection to just about any sort of external stimulation. This moment of capacious and narcissistic lustiness is short lived, however. Thoroughly dependent on proximate others for their very survival, infants immediately begin a course of psychosexual development that painstakingly and predictably winnows the possibilities of gender, sex, and sexuality into a neatly functional binary array.[24]

There is a kind of chicken-and-egg quality to the Freudian account (how did those Oedipal mothers and castrating fathers become gendered and heterosexed in the first place?), and feminists, including Grosz, have rightly pointed out Freud's reflexive equation of the penis with all that is powerful and good in the

---

24. *See* Weeks 1985. The process by which this occurs—involving, as is well known, passage through Oedipal and Elektra conflicts, castration anxiety, penis envy, and the like—is a set of developmental dynamics that incorporate the mind, the body, and the (gendered and heterosexed) social environment. That is, the infant develops increased cognitive and physical capacities, and works through experiences of desire and satisfaction, in the context of particular social environments. The body produces sensations (hunger, satiety, tension, release), but those sensations are given meaning and significance by how they are recognized and responded to by others—especially (for the infant) by primary caregivers. Thus, while the infant may begin life as a narcissistic and polymorphously perverse sovereign (the world is "His Majesty The Baby's" oyster), his or her options are soon radically reduced and simplified through an iterative process starring already gendered and sexed others.

world. But the psychoanalytic story is a promising start—first, because it suggests how bodies and selves might begin to be formed in sex- and gender-specific ways and, second, because it describes a mechanism by which generalized desires and satisfactions may be specified and then mapped simultaneously to cognitive representations and corporeal sensations. The Freudian account describes a body that is not a thing, but a series of projections—a topography of the psyche's libidinal investments and cathexes. The ego, in turn, "is not a point-for-point projection of the body's surface but an outline or representation of the degrees of erotogenicity of the bodily zones and organs."[25]

In the Lacanian account, meaning and language occupy an even more central place in the binarization of sex, gender, and sexuality. For Lacan, sexuality is not partial because it is the enemy of the social (as it is in the Freudian account),[26] but because it is the price of entry *into* the social. Lacanian theory contends that the key process forming the self occurs at the acquisition of language. It is in seeking what s/he lacks (food, a toy, a clean diaper) that the infant is compelled to create certain symbolic and material linkages that crystallize in language—first, a single sound designed to signal to one's others (especially mothers) a generalized desire that may be directed toward a specific object and later, a variety of signifiers that take shape in relationship to the material and social world and to the elaborate architecture of the symbolic. The self is thus constituted as an "I"—the speaking subject whose identity is formed around the division between what is present and what is absent: a formative binary relation. So far, so good.

25. Grosz 1994b: 37.

26. Freud and Strachey 2005.

Lacan goes further, however, and renders binary subjectivity fundamentally gendered and sexed. The phallus is inextricably connected to "presence" while the Other is connected to what is lacking—to "absence." The self is thus phallic, defined in repeated contradistinction to a universe of Others, including caregivers, objects, and linguistic signifiers. Consciousness is sexed and gendered; language mirrors and instantiates this physical, social, and symbolic reality. It is this further step that—like Freud's reflexive privileging of the penis—takes Lacanian psychoanalytic theory down a troublingly deterministic path. Feminists and others have rightly asked why presence should be marked as phallic and absence marked as the feminine and female Other. It seems terribly convenient that the ungovernable id would be the source of the feminine,[27] while the ego (entering the world as the speaking subject) is materially and culturally male: assertive, forceful, imposing of its will, and *desiring*. In response, the Lacanian account either embraces the Freudian just-so story of reproductive essentialism[28] or elides the question of why and how ego and id are sexed and gendered and so assumes, rather

27. The transvaluation of the id and the feminine as the source of creativity and productive (as opposed to destructive) power is the central tenet of the French feminist intellectual project known as *Ecriture Feminine. See, for example*, Cixous and Segarra 2010.

28. Lacan's privileging of the phallus is, at times, even more hilariously circular and self-referential than Freud's. Thus, Lacan has written about the phallus: "One could say that this signifier is chosen as the most salient of what can be grasped in sexual intercourse [*copulation*] as real, as well as the most symbolic." Lacan and Fink 2006: 581. In other words, the phallus is significant because it looks significant (in sexual intercourse, as seen from the phallic/male/masculinist perspective) and/or because, well, it's *significant*. Like Freud, Lacan equates (a) what he imagines to be the centrality of the phallus in reproduction (i.e., its role as the active carrier of sperm) with (b) the active position of the phallus in sexual intercourse. But he adds an additional term to the equation: (c) the privileging of the phallus as linguistic/cultural signifier. *See, for example*, Tyler 1997: 244–45.

than explains, the binary expression of sexuality, gender, and the sexed body.

Thus, psychoanalytic theory seems to offer the promise of socially constructed sex, gender, and sexuality, only to snatch it back in the service of biological or cultural determinism. Feminist and queer[29] theorists of sexuality have noted that this may render psychoanalytic theory not only a theoretical *cul de sac* but also a political one. A failure to think beyond sex, gender, and sexual binaries would seem to require capitulation to their endless reproduction. Indeed, even by their own terms, Lacanian and Freudian theories understand this binary framework to be fundamentally limiting and constraining of human desire and experience.[30] For Grosz, however, the nascent determinism of Freudian and Lacanian accounts is counterbalanced (if not outweighed) by their radical potential, but only if one leverages the indeterminacy built into the inscriptive mechanisms themselves. Recall that the embodied ego, imagined from a psychoanalytic perspective, is a series of projections—a "psychical topography" that maps "not .. the real or anatomical body but . . . the degree of libidinal cathexis the subject has invested in its own body."[31] To the extent that cathexis is an ongoing process, the possibility is opened for reconstitution of the self in ways not faithful to sexed, gendered, and sexual binaries.

And, indeed, in both the Freudian and Lacanian accounts, the mapping of the embodied ego continues throughout a human being's life. While Freud and Lacan famously focused on infancy

29. I find the category "queer" as it has been deployed in contemporary theory and activism to be incoherent, and so I don't replicate such usage here. However, I do mark it as needed to identify it as a named intellectual and political project.

30. See generally Weeks 1985.

31. Grosz 1994b: 27, 34.

and early childhood,[32] Grosz notes that both theorists describe body/ego construction as perpetual—and as perpetually unfinished. For Lacan, the ego is a "constant achievement" that "must be constantly renewed, not through the subject's conscious efforts but through its ability to conceive of itself as a subject and to separate itself from its objects and others." The subject, in short, is what s/he does, in constant negotiation and conversation with significant (and signifying) others.[33] Similarly, for Freud, the body/ego is subject to reconfiguration as, according to Grosz "any corporeal process, event, or experience is capable of sexualization."[34] The biological is always insufficient, always poses an element of lack, which—in the Freudian account—is what we know and experience as *desire*. Thus, "[d]esire is based on a veritable cartography of the body (one's own as well as that of the other)" and, through sexuality (broadly conceived), the "body is quite literally rewritten, traced over, by desire."[35]

For Grosz, phenomenology extends this notion of subjectivity's reinscription through its emphasis on consciousness as both embodied and intersubjective.[36] In the phenomenological account,

32. For Lacan, the key moment in ego development is the "mirror stage," (at about six months of age) during which the child establishes what Grosz calls a "provisional identity" that is distinct from that of the mother. Grosz 1994b: 42.

33. *Ibid.*

34. As described by Freud, the mapping of the embodied ego is a dialectical process that involves physical movement through the material and social world, experienced as cognitive, linguistic, and emotional moments that are written upon the psyche as "memory traces." These memory traces, in turn, inform future experiences of the body, causing them to resonate in particular ways for the self, which then incorporates the new experiences as new memory traces. As Freud described it, each new set of inscriptions builds upon, while qualitatively changing, prior inscriptions, creating new architectures of the mind (and body). *See* Freud and Strachey 2005: chapter 1.

35. Grosz 1994b: 56.

36. *See Ibid*: chapter 4.

echoes of which can be discerned in the sociology of ethnomethodologists such as Erving Goffman and Harold Garfinkel,[37] experience is the anchor of the self, and it occupies the space between mind and body.[38] Subjects move through the world as apprehending, corporeal, purposeful actors—their consciousness of themselves and others the product of perceptual, embodied and intentional[39] experience. On this view, sexuality becomes explicable as a modality of desire, rather than the satisfaction of an instinct or drive:

> It is only the sensory, perceiving subject, the corporeal subject, who is capable of initiating (sexual) desire, responding to and proliferating desire. The libido is not an effect of instincts . . . It emanates from the structure of sensibility, a function and effect of intentionality, of the integrated notion of affectivity, motility, and perception. Sexuality is not a reflex arc but an 'intentional arc' that moves and is moved by the body as acting perceiver.[40]

Thus, sexuality is embodied and intersubjective—rendered possible by what the subject can perceive and understand. In short, it is enabled by social *knowledge*, which shapes perceptions of the material and social world. Here, we begin to see

37. The relationship between phenomenology and ethnomethodology is complex and disputed, but sociologists generally understand there to be at least a phenomenological cast to ethnomethodology and symbolic interactionism.

38. Grosz 1994b: 95.

39. "Intentionality" is a term of art in phenomenology. It refers to the sense of purpose and direction that characterizes experience; that is, experience is always directed *toward* some aim or object. Jacob 2010.

40. Grosz 1994b: 109.

how Berger and Luckmann's concepts of reification and typification may take gendered and sexed form. In the phenomenological account, it is socially produced knowledge of the world and of the people around us (our Others) that structure sexuality as a modality of desire. Our bodies–inside, outside, and surfaces— are intersubjectively understood and experienced. We are our selves only in relation to certain Others, whom we experience as specific *kinds* of bodies and actors. They are men and women, gay and straight: typified by gendered and sexed performances and interactions, and reified into categorically defined bodies and identities. We become who *and what* we are in relation to them.

This rather abstract and general description can perhaps be made more accessible and concrete if we consider a few applications. In "Master and Slave: The Fantasy of Erotic Domination,"[41] feminist psychoanalytic theorist Jessica Benjamin develops an intrapsychic and intersubjective theory of erotic domination (a set of practices that includes, but is not limited to, sadomasochism) that conceives of it as a dialectical relationship between subjects. Highlighting the relational and fundamentally social character of psychosexual development, Benjamin contends that, beginning in infancy, each of us moves through the world engaged in embodied interactions with others. These interactions are animated by two primary, conflicting desires: the desire to be recognized and the desire to exert individual will. We engage in this dialectical struggle on a nearly continuous basis because it is what defines the contours of our sense of self:

> What I am describing here is a dialectic of control: if
> I completely control the other, then the other ceases to exist,

---

41. Many of these themes are explored in greater depth in Benjamin's book, *The Bonds of Love* (1988).

and if the other completely controls me, then I cease to exist. True differentiation means maintaining the essential tension of the contradictory impulses to assert the self and respect the other.[42]

The intrapsychic dimension of this account is clear, but when Benjamin writes of "true differentiation," she means the differentiation of bodies as much as of egos. As an articulation of the self/other divide, the dialectic of control creates and recreates corporeal borders. As infants and young children, these lines are crudely drawn: we learn that we do not control the universe and develop an increased awareness of where we end and others (especially nurturing others) begin.[43] Later, we replicate these border-making and border-crossing experiences with sexual partners. We experience sexual intimacy as a transgression of bodily boundaries—a transgression that is invited or pursued willingly, but always symbolically promises the ultimate collapse of the distinction between self and other. Echoing the work of Georges Bataille, Benjamin contends that the loss of the self in communion with another (romantic bromides notwithstanding) is an experience that can threaten a kind of death.[44]

42. Benjamin 1983: 284.

43. As in the classical Freudian account, Benjamin describes the earliest period of childhood as a concatenation of experiences and changing capacities, leading to increasing awareness of the limits of the physical and thinking self. It is a dance between need and will, frustration and pleasure, all experienced within the gaze and embrace of significant others—themselves gendered, sexed, and sexual beings. *See* Benjamin 1983, 1988.

44. Benjamin, citing Bataille, contends that consciousness of the body's limits is essential to the very existence of the self. Dissolution of those limits—making the physical self continuous with its environment—calls to mind the "oceanic feeling" of the womb and the commingling of matter that is the defining feature of the graveyard. *See* Benjamin 1983. The morbidity of such an image notwithstanding, this account does indicate why death metaphors abound in cultural depictions of intense sexual attraction and orgasm (e.g., the notion of orgasm as "la petite mort").

Moreover, because this dialectic is embedded in a culture shot through with social inequality, systematic expressions of domination and submission are inevitable. This is especially visible in relations between men and women, which provide a blueprint for erotic domination. The gendered nature of erotic domination is "co-created" by male and female (and masculine and feminine) subjects and replicated through the process of "splitting": the division of gendered, sexed, and sexual attributes, practices, and qualities into polarized oppositions (e.g., relational vs. rational, female vs. male, active vs. passive, etc.). Benjamin shifts the traditional Freudian framework, which sees such replicative processes as determined and/or inevitable, by demanding that we examine psychosexual development as a meeting of selves, rather than self and other (or self and object). The primary caregiver is not simply the negation or alter of the child. Instead, embodied, gendered, and sexed caregivers intersubjectively create (with the children they care for) specific, recurring dynamics of recognition/assertion. In this account, the relative strength of the caregiver's sense of herself as an erotic agent is crucially important in structuring the kind and level of polarization that will characterize the child's dynamic of control and subsequent erotic subjectivity.[45] Of course, to the extent that adult women embody sex, gender, and sexual norms of receptivity and passivity, the intersubjective account echoes other psychonalytic approaches in expecting the process of splitting to replicate itself, producing new generations of sexually assertive men and sexually passive women. Yet if one can intervene[46] to

*See generally* Oxford English Dictionary 7th ed. (citing Shakespeare, John Donne, and—wait for it—American songwriter John Denver).

45. *See* Benjamin 1988; *see also* Benjamin 2006.

46. Benjamin contends that such intervention is possible and has posited the notion of "thirdness" (a triangular configuration of subjects) as one path toward resolving the phenomenon of "splitting." *See* Benjamin 2006.

enhance women's erotic power such that sexuality (and sexual subjectivity) might be more balanced and "mutual," the intersubjective approach suggests that the entire binary framework might be destabilized, to liberating effect.

Leo Bersani's work on gay male sexuality is similarly evocative of the psychoanalytic and phenomenological accounts but with a darker cast. For Bersani, male homosexual desire is what appears at the intersection of hegemonic masculinity and a specifically gay or "homo"[47] set of bodily acts and postures. Examining the phenomenon of "gay macho," Bersani notes that its hypermasculine styles and gestures—the attention to musculature, the cultivation of traditionally and normatively male positions and aesthetics—is not (as it is often described) offered as a kind of parody or subversion. Parody and subversion are, in Bersani's words, a "turn off,"[48] and none of these men are trying to turn each other *off*. What makes hypermasculinity sexy is, rather, its deconstruction of the distance between identification and desire: gay men can experience an almost "mad identification" with hegemonic masculinity while, at the same time, "they never cease to feel the appeal of its being violated."[49] Plainly, this is a dangerous proposition in a culture that evinces an often murderous commitment to asserting the incommensurability of gay and straight:

> The logic of homosexual desire includes the potential for a
> loving identification with the gay man's enemies . . . a sexual
> desire for men can't be merely a culturally neutral attraction
> to a Platonic idea of the male body; the object of that desire

47. *See* Bersani 1995.

48. Bersani 1987: 208.

49. *Ibid*: 209.

necessarily includes a socially determined and socially pervasive definition of what it means to be a man.[50]

Thus, gay sexuality takes its cultural and physical specificity from what might be described as difference-within-sameness: gay men threaten hegemonic masculinity because of their (real or imagined) willingness to simultaneously embrace it and experience its violation—that is, to invite penetration. Homophobia circulates around the "infinitely more seductive and intolerable image of a grown man, legs high in the air, unable to refuse the suicidal ecstasy of being a woman."[51] This image's ability to unsettle (and excite) is a product of both cultural and corporeal phenomena that are intrapsychic and intersubjective:

> To be penetrated is to abdicate power . . . Human bodies are constructed in such a way that it is, or at least has been, almost impossible not to associate mastery and subordination with the experience of our most intense pleasures . . . [T]hose effects of power which, as Foucault has argued, are inherent in the relational itself (they are immediately produced by "the divisions, inequalities, and disequilibriums" inescapably present "in every relation from one point to another") can perhaps most easily be exacerbated and polarized into relations of mastery and subordination, in sex, and [this] potential may be grounded in the shifting experience that every human being has of his or her body's capacity, or failure, to control and to manipulate the world beyond the self.[52]

50. *Ibid*: 208–09.

51. *Ibid*: 212.

52. *Ibid*: 212–16.

If exerting power, especially phallic power, is definitional of hegemonic masculinity, then the abdication of power through receptivity—especially receptivity to the phallus—is deeply hreatening of same.

Note that Bersani's account is intersubjective in a sense quite different from that suggested by Benjamin, who longs for mutuality and communion between two internally balanced selves. In Bersani's world, gay man partake of sex, gender, and sexuality as a set of social, cultural, and physical possibilities and limits that come together in relations between gay subjects. In receiving the phallus, the real and iconographic gay man is not the reverse image of hegemonic masculinity. Rather, he embodies the promise of a seductive reconfiguration of subjectivity in the presence of another masculine male subject, one which is predicated on his active submission. Here, phallic powerlessness is alluring not because it signals the abdication of selfhood, but because it has the potential to disorganize, disturb, and even destroy it. As Bersani describes it, the self is shattered in the moment of penetration, which amounts not to an offering of one man's body to the subject-completion project of another, nor to a joining of two selves in (degendered) sexual communion, but to a dissolution of subjectivity itself into a kind of bodily excess and confusion. On this view, sexuality—and perhaps homosexuality in particular—reveals itself to be thrillingly anticommunitarian.[53]

Whether promising communion (as in Benjamin's work) or the pure physicality of egolessness (as in Bersani's), sexuality in

---

53. *Ibid*: 216. Bersani's ambivalence on this point is palpable. On the one hand, he seems to embrace a non-redemptive sexual project and argues that the assertion of the self is the central mechanism implicated in the use of sexuality as a form of power. On the other hand, his invocation of the "grave" (the title of the article is "Is the Rectum a Grave?") is not merely an allusion to the death of the subject in a Freudian sense. It is also a recognition (in 1987) of the literal death of gay men during the AIDS pandemic.

these inside/out accounts is a complex phenomenon that is equal parts materiality and meaning. Eros is far from mechanical in these stories, and bodies do not simply express and seek to satisfy the preconstituted desires of the self. Bodies and egos are produced, reproduced, and deconstructed simultaneously and in interaction with other bodies and egos and always with an eye toward social and cultural *representations* of sex, gender, and sexuality. Recall Berger and Luckmann's notion of reification. The reified qualities of socially constructed sex and gender categories give sex and gender the appearance of stability and materiality that, in turn, permits the self to have particular experiences of corporeal sexuality (to experience penetration, for example, or domination, or the specifically homo[54] quality of sexual contacts between women or between men). They make sexuality what it is—what it feels like—but they do so in ways that suggest the potential for subversion and reconfiguration. This is because sex, gender, and sexuality are performative: they take shape and meaning in action. As Judith Butler has written (about gender):

> In this sense, gender is not a noun, but neither is it a set of free-floating attributes, for we have seen that the substantive effect of gender is performatively produced and compelled by the regulatory practices of gender coherence. . . . In this sense, gender is always a doing, though not a doing by a subject who might be said to preexist the deed.[55]

Thus, gender is both real (reified, in the term favored by Berger and Luckmann) but also always an approximation—movement

---

54. Bersani 1995.

55. Butler 1990: 33.

toward a point on the horizon—that constitutes the subject as a gendered being as s/he engages in repetitive, iterative gender performances.[56] Similarly, sexuality, as a function of identity and as a marker of specific sorts of bodies, is enacted with an eye toward social and cultural constructs. As Bersani's work suggests, "homo"sexual desire requires a notion of sameness (juxtaposed to gender and sex difference) in order to be intelligible on a visceral, as well as a cognitive, level.[57]

Moreover, sex, gender, and sexual categories are revealed to be provisional: they are placeholders establishing the rubric within which the interior self may make sense of "bodies and pleasures"[58] as indicators of identity,[59] but they are not the direct manifestation of biological or otherwise "hard wired" attributes or behaviors.[60] Performativity is a "citational" practice[61]; as with all such practices, it is prone to incremental deviations from its normative center. Like a photocopy of a photocopy—or, in some cases, an edited or annotated photocopy of a photocopy—gender, sex, and sexual performances shift gender, sex, and sexual norms,

56. Note that such performances need not be normative; they may be subversive or parodic performances. But the very possibility of subversion or parody requires a normative point of reference.

57. Bersani 1995.

58. *See* Foucault 1990: 157.

59. Here we can see the importance of Berger and Luckmann's notions of typification and reification. Intersubjective encounters rely on both processes in defining the sex, gender, and sexual rubrics that inform and enable specific kinds of practices and identities.

60. Because the body is constantly engaged in the process of (psychosexual and phenomenological) reinscription, it is subject to change. This is one reason Grosz describes the body as "volatile."

61. Butler 1997.

meanings, and practices over time.[62] The notion of performativity invites the possibility of subversion, play, parody, and creativity in expressions of sex, gender, and sexuality.

Of course, a playful and changeable conception of sexuality is not without its critics. Butler's work is often attacked for what some view as its implied voluntarism—the idea that performances of sex, gender, and sexuality may be undertaken freely, individually, and without material constraint.[63] Some lesbian and gay theorists, for example, mock poststructuralism for its refusal to recognize the "real" world in which gay and lesbian people live, contending that such theories instead posit a universe of "free floating signifiers" that may be played with at will.[64] Considered next to the hydraulics of biologically or structurally determinist accounts, performativity would seem to be rather ethereal. But this critique makes sense only if one assumes a radical disjuncture between the material and the symbolic world. As Berger and Luckmann demonstrate, language, representations, and social discourses constrain human action as deeply and as profoundly as do structures of material and physical possibility and limitation. Indeed, in shaping how we understand and experience the material and physical world, representations and discourses are indistinguishable from it. They constitute the "outside" from, and within which, we may manifest and be seen to manifest specific kinds of subjectivity.

62. "Thus, gay is to straight not as copy is to original, but, rather, as copy is to copy. The original [is revealed] to be nothing other than a parody of the idea of the natural and the original." Butler 1990: 31.

63. *See, for example,* Stein and Plummer 1996; Braidotti and Butler 1997; Adam 1998.

64. Stein and Plummer 1996:137–38; *see also* Adam 1998: 395.

## III. Outside, In

> If the psychical writing of bodies retraces the paths of biological processes using libido as its marker pen, then the inscription of the social surface of the body is the tracing of pedagogical, juridical, medical, and economic texts, laws, and practices onto the flesh to carve out a social subject as such, a subject capable of labor, of production and manipulation, a subject capable of acting as a subject and, at the same time, capable of being deciphered, interpreted, and understood.[65]

As this quote from Grosz suggests, subjectivity may be conceived as a process of placement, discipline, and positioning by social, political, cultural, juridical, and other institutional dynamics and practices. These processes address the body as a set of surfaces, or texts, and render it a "sociohistorical artifact" or "social object."[66] They enable and delimit corporeal experiences, produce the possibility of certain kinds of identifications and practices (while foreclosing others), and constitute subjects of various sorts (citizens, workers, mothers, fathers, lovers, women, and men, etc.). If the self that inhabits the body may be described as the expression of a psychical topography, then the corporeal subject produced from the "outside/in" may be described as part of a social typography.

This conception of the outside/in includes a phenomenon familiar to sociologists: socialization. That is, one can conceive of the "outside" as a set of prescriptions that enforce normative behaviors and movements through the repeated imposition of positive and negative sanctions—individuals are socialized into

---

65. Grosz 1994b: 117.

66. *Ibid*: 116.

conformity with social norms. Examples of this process spring readily to mind: little boys being given detailed instruction in heteromasculinity via participation in Little League or Pop Warner,[67] young women internalizing a belief that "math is hard" as a by-product of heterosexualization during adolescence,[68] and newly out gay men and lesbians being subjected to gay makeovers and other LGB membership rituals.[69]

But the concept of socialization is limited by its tendency to describe a unidirectional and largely bilateral process of norm enforcement. Consistent with the prior discussion of the inter-subjective creation of corporeal subjectivity, it makes more sense to think about the "outside/in" dimension of this process in more dynamic terms, incorporating relations that work in multiple directions. Film theorist Teresa de Lauretis offers a particularly compelling description, one that envisions subjectivity emerging within a network of ongoing sociality and signification.

> . . . sexuality is one form of (self)representation, and fantasy is one specific instance of the more general process of semiosis, which enjoins subjectivity to the social signification and to reality itself . . . there is always something real in psychic fantasy, real for the subject's internal world and real for the external world, from which the fantasy is mediated and to which it returns, again mediated and to a greater or lesser extent resignified through the subject's agency in the social. For in the infinite universe of signs that is social reality,

67. Messner 2002; Anderson 2005.

68. Brown and Gilligan 1992.

69. See, for example, Will & Grace "Fagmalion, Parts 1–3" (Season 5, Episodes 13–15; orig. aired 1/16/03, 1/30/03, 2/6/03); Queer as Folk (U.K.) "Meeting People is Easy" (Episode 1.1, orig. aired 2/23/99); Ellen."The Puppy Episode, Part 2" (Season 4, Episode 22, orig. aired April 30, 1997).

each subject is in turn object and sign ... individual sexual structuring is both an effect and a condition of the social construction of sexuality.[70]

Sexuality is a form of semiotics, but it is also a social *practice* involving culturally and historically specific forms of desire. Sexual identity "is neither innate nor simply acquired, but dynamically (re)structured by forms of fantasy private and public, conscious and unconscious, which are culturally available and historically specific."[71]

What does it mean to be "culturally available and historically specific"? De Lauretis has in mind the products of the macro level discursive processes described by Michel Foucault in his canonical work, *The History of Sexuality*. Foucault's history attacks conventional chronologies of sexuality, which tell a story of increasing social, political, and cultural "repression" of sexuality over the course of the seventeenth and eighteenth centuries, culminating in a particularly austere Victorian Era. In the course of this project, he rejects the idea that power is primarily or exclusively expressed as a negation—a denial or a prohibition— of universal, transhistorical sexual desire. Rather, he argues that sexual practices and identities are constituted by discourse as a set of possibilities:

Sexuality must not be thought of as a kind of natural given which power tries to hold in check, or as an obscure domain which knowledge tries gradually to uncover. It is the name that can be given to a historical construct: not a furtive reality that is difficult to grasp, but a great surface network in which

70. De Lauretis 1994: 303–09.

71. De Lauretis 1994: xix.

the stimulation of bodies, the intensification of pleasures, the incitement to discourse, the formation of special knowledge, the strengthening of controls and resistances, are linked to one another, in accordance with a few major strategies of knowledge and power.[72]

Discourse joins power and knowledge together and produces sexuality, primarily through various historically specific mechanisms of self-disclosure:

Rather than the uniform concern to hide sex, rather than a general prudishness of language, what distinguishes these last three centuries is the variety, the wide dispersion of devices that were invented for speaking about it, for having it be spoken about, for inducing it to speak of itself, for listening, recording, transcribing, and redistributing what is said about it: around sex, a whole network of varying, specific, and coercive transpositions into discourse. Rather than a massive censorship, beginning with the verbal proprieties imposed by the Age of Reason, what was involved was a regulated and polymorphous incitement to discourse.[73]

Discourse is a term of art for Foucault (and Foucaultian scholars). It is not merely what is said by someone—that is, it is not reducible to language. Rather, it is a set of statements (or "*enoncements*") that serve to coordinate certain ideas, objects, and relations.[74] Discourses both emanate from and serve to constitute social institutions (such as psychiatry, the family, or law). Taken

72. Foucault 1990: 105–06.

73. *Ibid*: 34.

74. Foucault 1972.

together (often collected from disparate institutional loci), *enoncements* may produce a discursive formation: a unified system of discursive statements possessed of durability and relative coherence.[75] As such, discourse becomes part of the fabric of signification within which actors understand and move through the worlds around them. It becomes the language with which people describe themselves and what they do, but it is hardly open to unbounded selection or sampling. No free-floating signifiers here; discursive formations constitute a powerful set of ordering principles that channel and delimit social action and identifications from multiple directions. Power is capillary; the disciplining of the sexual self is "eminently social"[76] in that it need not rely on hierarchical authority for its regulatory force. To a significant extent, we engage in self-regulation through a process that looks like revelation: we confess, describe, recapitulate, and report in narrative form a sexual truth that is rendered coherent by the terms of the ascendant discourses of the day.[77]

Thus, for Foucault, what matters in the history of sexuality is not how and when sexuality has been allowed to appear or express itself in its "natural" or prediscursive state. What matters are the specific forms that have served to shape and induce particular kinds of statements about one's sex as indicia of personal truth. So, for example, the confession is a regulatory mechanism that is

75. Hunt and Wickham 1994: chapter 1.

76. De Lauretis 1994: xx.

77. Thus, Foucault compares the practices associated with the confession to those of psychoanalysis. In each case, the self is "revealed" in utterances that are shaped and enticed by specific discursive practices. In the confession, the truth emerges in the language of sin and redemption, while in psychoanalysis it takes the form of dysfunction or pathology and health. One could readily extend Foucault's analysis to contemporary discourses of revelation: YouTube, Facebook, and the ubiquitous "confessional" of reality TV each share similar tropes and rituals designed to designate and deliver revelatory truth (especially about sexuality).

embedded in, and evoked from within, Catholic institutional discourse. It elicits accounts of the self that describe the body and its desires in terms of sin and morality, good and evil. Psychoanalysis deploys similar techniques to elicit narratives of the self, but these stories sound in health and dysfunction. The "incitement to discourse" takes form in historically specific sexual truth regimes comprised of taxonomies; rules of prohibition, taboo, and normalcy; and conceptions of causality. These regimes do not describe or emanate from sexuality but, rather, constitute it in the first instance as a fully social experience.

De Lauretis wishes to tether this "eminently social Foucault" to the "fully private Freud" in order to understand how the inner and outer worlds of the self are joined together. Training her eye on lesbian sexual desire and practice (a woefully undertheorized topic), De Lauretis marshals Foucault's suggestion that discourse produces sexuality in support of an argument for the importance of public representations. Her solution to the "problem" of lesbian desire—namely, its failure to achieve specificity as something other than the negation or repudiation of heterosexual desire or a political elaboration of mother-love[78]—is as simple (and as profound) as advocacy for "the production of a discourse . . . in which sexual activities between women are given representation and signified as desire."[79] For De Lauretis, contemporary discourses of lesbian desire are "all inadequate to the task" because they are discourses of sexual *indifference*—a pun she deploys to signify both the elision of gender differences between lesbians and a kind of limpness and passivity such discourses ascribe

78. ". . . the sweeping of lesbian sexuality and desire under the rug of sisterhood, female friendship, and the now popular theme of the mother-daughter bond, has become canonical in feminist criticism to the point where it vitiates the analytical efforts even of those critics . . . who are wise to it." De Lauretis 1994: 116.

79. *Ibid*: 75.

to women's sexuality.[80] In a culture that marks agency and subjectivity—especially and including sexual subjectivity—with difference, sexual indifference amounts to invisibility.[81]

How, then, can lesbian desire manifest itself as a specific, real, and resonant form of sexual subjectivity? De Lauretis contends that representational practices have the potential to "restructure" subjectivity via the creation of specific intrapsychic, intersubjective, and cultural paths between subject and fantasy. So, for example, she contends that the film *She Must Be Seeing Things* produces lesbian desire by "constructing particular paths of spectatorial access to the fantasy it re-presents, inscribing a particular subject-position in its very mode of enunciation and address."[82] Representation here is not realistic imitation, and the spectator is not a passive recipient of imagery; she is an active participant in creating an experience of desire through fantasy that may, in turn, become incorporated into her sexuality. Like Bersani, De Lauretis argues forcefully for a specifically homosexed form of desire and identification. Homosex is not, in their accounts, a variation on heterosexuality—its inversion or approximation. It is qualitatively different. For De Lauretis, lesbian desire is gender-specific and predicated on an experience of gendered sexual difference. She writes:

> What the lesbian desires in a woman ('the penis somewhere else') is indeed not a penis but a part or perhaps the whole of

80. Here, De Lauretis echoes Benjamin's suggestion that the problem of erotic domination is, in part, traceable to women's weak sexual agency. *Ibid*: 185.

81. "In all the culturally dominant forms of representation that surround us, from television to museum art, from the most banal . . . to the most sublime . . . desire is predicated on sexual difference as gender, the difference of woman from man or femininity from masculinity, with all that those terms entail . . . whatever women may feel toward other women cannot be sexual desire, unless it be a 'masculinization,' a usurpation or an imitation of man's desire." *Ibid*: 110–111.

82. *Ibid*: 142.

the female body, or something metonymically related to it, such as physical, intellectual, or emotional attributes, stance, attitude, appearance, self-presentation—and hence the importance of clothing, costume, performance, etc., in lesbian subcultures.[83]

In creating the stuff of gender and sexual difference, lesbian subcultural practices produce sexual subjects and sexual objects. (As De Lauretis notes wryly, it takes two women to make a lesbian.[84]) What a lesbian desires is a woman socially constituted *as a woman who desires women*. This is a discursive construct with material origins and material consequences: "individual sexual structuring is both an effect and a condition of the social construction of sexuality."[85]

Similarly, recent sociological research on transsexualism indicates the importance of discourses of sex, gender, and sexuality in shaping the ways in which we experience our interior and corporeal selves. Drawing upon the work of phenomenologist Maurice Merleau-Ponty, sociologist Henry Rubin contends that many female-to-male transsexuals (FTMs) experience a kind of "reverse phantom limb" phenomenon with respect to their genitalia. Born with anatomically sexed bodies that failed to match their evolving identifications as (often heterosexual) men, many of the FTMs that Rubin interviewed did not recognize the genitalia they were born with, understanding their female reproductive anatomy as a kind of "error of expression." That is, they understood themselves to be fundamentally male—male underneath

83. *Ibid*: 228.

84. *Ibid*: 235, n. 17 (it is the gendered difference between two women that "makes desire"). See also Nestle 1992: 139.("Butches were known by their appearance, femmes by their choices.").

85. De Lauretis 1994: 309.

it all, and prior to the ill-fitting bodily encasement that they wore, uncomfortably, as adult subjects. As a consequence, they pursued body modification efforts not as constructive but as *reconstructive* projects—intended to restore the (missing) penis.[86]

Rubin's research poignantly and starkly demonstrates the materiality of discourse. The prior (interior) male self that drives a female-to-male transsexual to pursue difficult, costly, and often painful bodily modifications is a culturally and historically specific discursive outcome. It takes a particular physical attribute to be its centrally defining feature—a functioning and aesthetically faithful penis—because the penis is defined culturally and socially as the essence of maleness. But the very notion that a penis might be constructed at all, and that it might be done in service of reconciling internal and external dimensions of gender, sex, and sexuality, owes its existence to specific late-modern developments in the social production of knowledge. As Rubin notes, the development of medical discourses and practices that have rendered phalloplasty feasible have also created the possibility of imagining a "reconstruction" of the penis. Without this development, it is hard to see how FTMs would be able to conceive of their bodies as open to being made "right."

The evident constructedness of this moment of social and technological capacity—which has created the ability to change the *boundaries* of the body—does not make it any less authentic

86. This is somewhat more complicated than the word "restore" might imply. In fact, many of the FTMs interviewed by Rubin experienced their bodies as both male and not-male. Internally, they felt like men. And their gender performances faithfully expressed this core sense of anatomical sex. But they recognized that, intersubjectively, their external corporeal selves were (too) frequently misrecognized by others and that they were not always capable of performing their anatomical sex as they wished to be (particularly in sexual encounters). Sex reassignment procedures thus offered the hope of correcting what Rubin terms "expressive errors": failures of the body to express itself in conformity with the subject's understanding of its form and function. Rubin 2003: chapter 4.

or visceral to transsexual men seeking surgical *reconstruction*.[87] It is simply part of the material world that they may draw upon as they seek to harmonize their inner and outer selves, to resolve the pain produced by "category conflicts."[88] Moreover, the materialization of "category conflicts" is itself the product of the social production of knowledge. The late twentieth-century emergence of feminist discourses and practices has revealed sex, gender, and sexuality to be conceptually and materially distinguishable from one another, such that it is now possible to think of sex and gender as separate dimensions of experience.[89]

Rubin's research also demonstrates the importance of discursive struggles within feminist and lesbian communities in producing ever more refined identity categories: butch, femme, lesbian feminist, lipstick lesbian, dyke, etc.[90] Today, transmen

87. A study of male-to-female transsexuals ("MTFs") by Schrock et al. illustrates the same point in a slightly different way. In that study, the authors followed MTFs as they actively worked to transform their physical selves (voice, breasts, dress, gesture, genitalia) from male to female. Though many felt their early efforts to be awkward and intentional, eventually they described themselves as feeling more "natural" than they had as men. Schrock et al 2005. This makes sense because they had simply accomplished (in a remarkably short time) what most girls achieve through the longer stretch of childhood and adolescence: they had been socialized to be women. Reiteration and repetition of the physical self—of gestures, movements, actions upon the world and with other bodies—requires less and less intention and thought over time to accomplish its aims. Hence, it increasingly feels "natural." The difference here is that our gender/sex dimorphic culture asserts that women who were born female are in fact expressing their gender as a manifestation of their "nature," while women who were born anatomically male are not.

88. Rubin 2003: chapter 2.

89. The work of feminist anthropologist Gayle Rubin, for example, has been profoundly influential in spreading the idea that it is productive to think of sex and gender as separate conceptual dimensions, which combine variously in "sex/gender systems" to (among other things) structure social and sexual life. Rubin 1975.

90. The multiplication and subdivision of sex and gender categories may be viewed as an instance of the larger phenomenon of internal struggle within social movements—a process well documented by social movement scholars. *See, generally,* McAdam 1995.

and bois may be added to the list.[91] Each new categorical divide is the product of contested, troubled individual engagement with discourses that are embedded in material, lived practices. Community institutions structure resource distribution along categorical lines, sexual and romantic encounters and relationships are enabled or foreclosed by specific identifications, and aesthetic and occupational possibilities are delimited by the gendered and sexed opportunity structure that characterizes a given moment in LGB history.[92]

While Rubin's research focuses on the specific case of female to male transsexuals, there is no reason to think that any of us experiences our bodies or selves any differently—though not all of us will be as cognizant of category conflicts as those who identify as transsexual. We each draw upon the material, discursive, and technological worlds in which we exist as we seek to make sense of who or what we are and who or what we might become. We each struggle with categories, which rarely, if ever, fit snugly around our complex, volatile, fluid, and multidimensional experiences of sex, gender, and sexuality.[93] What De Lauretis, Bersani, Grosz and

91. The addition of these latter categories is potentially destabilizing in a way that the appearance of prior categories may not have been. Are transmen more like lesbians or more like men? The FTMs in Rubin's study plainly conceived of themselves as men, though many had experienced a (more or less difficult) prior "lesbian career" and thus remained connected in important ways to lesbian communities. Rubin 2003. Indeed, transmen are an increasingly visible presence in lesbian social, erotic, and political communities. Some embrace a more "gender queer" understanding of identity, but those who understand themselves to be male (especially heterosexually male) would seem to have little to bind them with women who understand themselves to be lesbian. The particular mixture of essentializing and de-gaying discourses that are in ascendance (at least within the law of homosex) does not, I believe, auger well for lesbians seeking community with heteronormative men (whether they are bio-men or transmen).

92. *See, for example*, Kennedy and Davis 1994; D'Emilio 1983; Armstrong 2002; Nestle 2003.

93. Or, for that matter, race, belief, ability and the endless array of socially inflected dimensions of existence that one might think of or name.

others offer in their revisiting of Foucaultian and Freudian theories is a conception of gender, sex, and sexuality that is equally attentive to the social and the intrapsychic and in which the mind and the body are equally fluid and labile.[94] Both are also equally the result of inscriptive processes. We have corporeal experiences of the world that we feel, understand, and take in; and these, in turn, cathect the body in specific ways that shape future corporeal experiences. These readings of contemporary theorists of sexuality allow us to simultaneously appreciate the importance of sexed bodies in constituting selfhood, and the possibility of transcending those sexed bodies and gendered selves. Bodies are "volatile," even as they are never ungendered and unsexed. They are material, but they are not under the sway of the mind. Quite the contrary: the mind and the body are engaged in an always active exchange of inputs and outputs, themselves made consequential and powerful by the social meanings ascribed to, and through them.

## IV. The Erotics of the Possible

Contemporary theories of sexuality range far beyond the mechanical binarisms that characterize "common sense" (and, as we shall see, jurisprudential) accounts of sex, gender, and the body. These theories describe a body and a self that are yoked together in an ongoing project of becoming—one that is auto-referential, but which takes place within specific cultural, social, and historical contexts. Bodies and minds are not blank slates, but active, changing, material agents, reaching out to meet the social and physical worlds in which they are embedded, and feeding into one another to create an experience of selfhood that is indistinguishably

94. Grosz 1994b.

corporeal and cognitive. The mind/body dualism collapses in these accounts, except as an analytical device intended to illuminate the mutually constitutive nature of the cognitive, the physical, and the social. Feminist, psychoanalytic, phenomenological, and queer theories reject a simple, unidirectional relationship between bodies, desires, and behaviors. They unsettle the idea that the body is the prior ground of identity (sexed, gendered)[95] and identity-based conduct (sexuality), and draw our attention to the ways in which the embodied self is always and necessarily constituted within social and cultural systems of meaning. Inside/out theories, such as psychoanalytic theory and phenomenology, conceive of the body as a boundary that negotiates the introjection and internalization of meaning in the creation of subjectivity: a coherent body *image*. Such images must not only be internally coherent; they must also cohere across the body's boundaries. Outside/in theories tell us about the cultural, historical, and discursive processes that inscribe the surface of bodily boundaries and offer the substance from and within which sex, gender, and sexuality are performed.

Contemporary theories also offer an account of how sex, gender, and sexuality (and the relations between them) might change. The intentional and unintentional deviations that are part and parcel of sex, gender, and sexual performances provide the space within which subversive practices and identifications might emerge. They open the space within which those who seek to resist the stultifying and oppressive practices of sex, gender, and sexual normativization might live and love. Put simply, they suggest the possibility of sexual freedom. But while identity politics often promise a kind of comfortable inclusion, the freedom I describe may feel unsettling and unfamiliar—even threatening.

95. Namaste 1996.

The inside/out and outside/in stories recounted above suggest that desire often takes surprising and troubling forms.[96] Disparate and discordant ideas, feelings, sensations, and emotions may freely coexist and commingle in a world understood as intersubjective, intrapsychic and corporeal. Indeed, the distance between desire and disdain is radically reduced in these accounts; both are constitutive of identity and experience. Perhaps then, our inclination toward dualisms may be understood as a recuperative project: in seeking to neutralize the discomfort posed by such configurations, we sift through the cultural and social traces of longing and revulsion and array them in binary form. Such practices produce a rational and actionable set of master narratives—a way of understanding not merely what has happened in the past but how to engage the world on an ongoing basis. They contrive to form a recipe knowledge[97] of desire.

As I detail in the chapters that follow, courts are particularly likely to embrace this rationalizing project. Indeed, they may be institutionally compelled to do so. Law embraces and relies upon a substantialist account in which sex, gender, and sexuality are reified and, in turn, serve as the foundation for legal subjectivity.[98] In disposing of cases that implicate the body or sexuality, courts and lawyers repair to a mechanistic notion of desire in which

---

96. One can readily see the appeal of the unexpected here. In fact, I suspect that it is precisely the unexpected quality of certain forms of desire and satisfaction that maintains and reproduces the tension that eros requires—without it, we live in a pretty unsexy world. At the individual level, Benjamin's discussion of the transgression of bodily boundaries via a recounting of *The Story of O* suggests why sexual interaction is often described as a series of progressive steps—each one breaking down an ever more intimate boundary between one's body and that of another. (Think of the baseball metaphor here: first base, second base . . .) The progression works to maintain erotic tension because it keeps our focus on our own corporeal limits—the physical map of where I end and you begin. *See* Benjamin 1983, 1988.

97. Berger and Luckmann 1990: 83.

98. *See, for example,* Meier 2008.

sexed, gendered, and sexual beings act and are acted upon. As Alan Hyde describes it, law addresses itself to "[the] nice body with a self at home in it."[99] The self—understood as the psyche, identity, thought, and/or intention—is conceived as distinct and separate from the body. The body may serve as the self's instrument, or as a machine, or as the corporeal representative or manifestation of the inner person, but there is little doubt that it is the mind or self that is in charge and that the body is its (mostly) obedient servant.[100] The body pursues satisfaction of the Cartesian self's desires— its wants and needs—which emerge from preconstituted, fully formed, gendered, sexed, and sexual beings. On this view, law merely *processes*—takes in, examines, disposes of—men and women who "are" gay or straight, masculine or feminine. It deduces a structure of desire, animus, love, passion, disgust, and the like from the positions and manifest actions of such subjects vis-à-vis similarly preconstituted sexual, sexed, and gendered *objects*.

In other words, activists, lawyers, and judges work with what appears to be a commonsensical,[101] largely biological, and mechanical conception of how sexuality is experienced and embodied. I call this conceptual framework a *predictive binary matrix*: sexuality, gender, and the body are conceived as categorical status

99. Hyde 1997.

100. One exception, noted by Hyde, is the potentially unruly penis. *See* Hyde 1997: ch. 10.

101. The word "commonsensical" is used advisedly here. What I mean is that the account deployed by specific institutional actors by and large matches a lay or popular account. At the same time, as Foucault has demonstrated, a popular account of sexuality is invariably an effect—a distillation—of a specific set of institutional discourses: psychiatric, medical, juridical, and (I would add) cultural-political (i.e., located within and around social movement organizations). The discursive construction of sexuality is, accordingly, a self-reflexive process: juridical discourses of the body, gender, and sexual expression become part of popular discourses of the same, which then feed back into the process by which new juridical definitions of the body, gender, and sexuality are produced.

descriptors that exist in determinate, predictive relationship to one another. The framework is constituted according to the following terms: (1) the body is deemed divisible into two sexes, male and female; (2) legal actors and institutions recognize as real only two polar genders, masculine and feminine; and (3) they further understand there to be only two categorical sexual orientations, heterosexual and homosexual.[102] Those binaries thus established, courts then engage in a kind of probabilistic reasoning: by first locating a relevant subject or object at the intersection of two of the categories, they may then establish the subject or object's location in the third category. For example, if a court "knows" that a plaintiff in a sexual harassment case (let's call her T[103]) is a woman and, further, that she is masculine, it is likely to predict her sexual orientation to be homosexual. Knowing this, the court would also "know" that T did not and, indeed, *could* not have harbored any desire to be pursued sexually by a male defendant. Once established, the configuration of genders, sexes, and bodies "reveals" the "truth" of what happened in a way that can then be made visible and real. The categories are discrete, dichotomous, and rigidly relational.

This is a simple, straightforward, and—above all—practical conception of sexuality, gender, and the body. It is serviceable in

102. The ready objection to this characterization is that these binaries are *not* categorical but are, rather, the poles establishing the limiting points of three continua. Let me be clear that I am not describing these categorical assignments as empirically accurate or verifiable—quite the contrary. As should be apparent, I believe the predictive binary matrix is fundamentally wrong, misleading, and the source of endless grief for those who would live freely and creatively. But as feminist and queer theory have suggested—and as my analyses of same-sex harassment law, hate crimes legislation, and marriage demonstrate—the tendency to *recognize* two and only two categories of sex, gender, and sexual orientation is a deeply ingrained social, political, and institutional habit.

103. Objects of harassment are often referred to as the "target" of an alleged harasser.

many respects relevant to the institutional functioning of the judiciary. However, when viewed through the lens of the rich, deep, and nuanced literatures on gender, the body, and sexual desire, the predictive binary matrix reveals itself to be, at best, a heuristic device and, at worst, a reinscription of a regressive sexual narrative. More troubling, the process by which the matrix is deployed masks its institutionally specific quality. Instead, as a result of the processes outlined in Chapter 2, court pronouncements about causation, harm, responsibility, and obligation serve to authorize the predictive binary matrix as social fact.[104] As institutional bodies engaged in a kind of amateur social science, courts are compelled to deploy predictive devices because they are incapable of working with complex social and psychological accounts of human existence and behavior. One can readily admit and understand this limitation of judicial practice; courts, after all, may be very good at very many things, even if they are not particularly good at understanding and acting upon the complexity of human desire. For sexual progressives, however, this should be cause for alarm.

This is because there can be little doubt that law participates in the construction of an increasingly important, salient, and disciplinary sexual truth regime. Foucault's observation that "Western man has become a confessing animal"[105] is as evocative of law as it was of psychoanalysis or the rituals of Catholicism. Like these other institutionally specific practices, juridical practices produce, shape, and entice specific sorts of statements about gender, sex, and sexuality. With increasing frequency and fervor, LGB organizations invite legal actors and institutions to define narratives of the self and desire—in adjudicative proceedings but also in the

104. On social facts, see Durkheim 1982.

105. Foucault 1990: 58–59.

"shadow of the law" through a process law and society scholars refer to as "legality" or "legalism."[106] Within adjudications themselves, the articulation of sexed, gendered, and sexual subjects and objects according to the terms of the predictive binary matrix is routine, as subsequent chapters will demonstrate. But juridical narratives are also constitutive of broader social and cultural discourses of sexuality. They establish relations of knowledge that join sexual subjects and objects, and elaborate notions of motivation and desire. To the extent that sexuality is rendered real and specific by what the embodied and intersubjective subject can perceive and understand—by the social production of knowledge—the importance of the law of homosex in creating a field of representational (im)possibility must be acknowledged and interrogated. It is time we come to terms with the consequences of indulging our "desire [for] the state's desire."[107]

106. *See, generally* Ewick and Silbey 1999. *See for example,* Hull 2006; Marshall 2005.
107. Butler 2004: 111.

# 4

## I Hate the Way You Make Me Feel: Anti-Gay Hate Crime Laws and the Analytics of Emotion[1]

I have suggested that law helps to constitute social reality and—in particular—that it helps to constitute the predictive matrix of sex, gender, and sexuality that limits and constrains social expressions of sexual desire and experience. I have further suggested that law does this by producing certain discursive objects (doctrine and argument) within a specific set of institutional practices that legitimate these limiting narratives, in part by establishing us as (in Habermas's term) their "authors." We desire the law's discipline, and the law does not disappoint us.

But how, precisely, do we signal our desire for law's discipline? Certainly there are cases of individual actors who, through bad luck or happenstance, find themselves in the position of making a claim upon the juridical state and thus invoking its power to define and create narratives of sexuality and identity. More frequently, however, such claims are pressed via the strategic interventions of lesbian, gay, and bisexual (LGB) social movement organizations. The most recent generation of LGB activism has been characterized by a distinct turn toward legalism, as activists working through social movement organizations (SMOs) seek to intentionally, tactically, and strategically deploy legal doctrine

1. A different version of this material appeared previously as "Passions We Like . . . And Those We Don't: Anti-Gay Hate Crime Laws and the Discursive Construction of Sex, Gender, and the Body," *Michigan Journal of Gender & Law* 16: 1–48.

and argument.[2] Legal "wings" of SMOs are organized for precisely such purposes: to change formal legal institutions and doctrine to advance the aims of their foundational organizations and, more importantly, the aims of those organizations' social and political constituencies. Such entities use the tools at their disposal in skillful and thoughtful ways, frequently achieving their stated objectives in spite of great resistance and limited resources. At the same time, however, such legalistic strategies produce particular discursive effects—effects that are unintended and often unmarked, but which flow inevitably from law as a set of specific institutional practices. Consequently, I think it important to examine which legal interventions have been pursued by LGB activists and what, precisely, constitutes the discursive terrain that has been produced as a function of this pursuit. Returning to the core questions framing my analysis, I want to ask: How does law take up claims made by these collective actors and transform them in ways that may be both empowering and limiting? What sorts of justificatory narratives and claims about sexuality, the body, and desire are "put into discourse" as a result of the claims advanced by LGB activists? How do the claims and arguments offered in response by opponents and adversaries divert, contextualize, and/or transform these discursive objects? In short, how does this set of processes produce a specific regime of sexual truth?

This task is made a bit less challenging by virtue of the relative conformity observed between the agendas of national and state LGB gaylegal advocacy organizations. According to the information published on their Web sites, for example, the Human Rights Campaign; the National Gay and Lesbian Task Force; the ACLU's Lesbian, Gay, Bisexual, and Transgender Project; the National Center for Lesbian Rights; and Lambda Legal are all working on

2. Brown and Halley 2002.

the same relatively small group of issues: same-sex marriage, hate crime legislation, workplace discrimination, health care and/or HIV treatment and prevention, transgender rights, parenting, protection of LGB youth and elders, immigration, and the status of LGB people serving in the military.[3] The high degree of overlap may be the product of organizational or institutional isomorphism[4] or a product of strategic coordination, or both. In any case, most of these organizations' efforts focus on the civil law, a fact of some significance since, not so long ago, homosex was considered *per se* criminal conduct in the United States.[5]

The once criminal status of same-sex sexuality was deeply influential in shaping the experience of the modern gay and lesbian movement and, with it, the trajectory and quality of gay-legal advocacy. From the earliest days of the modern LGB movement, activists knew they had to attack the criminalization of homosex before they would be able to advance any other aims of the movement.[6] For one thing, the fact that same-sex conduct was considered a crime made the lives of those who engaged in same-sex sexuality difficult, dangerous, and fraught with peril,

3. *See* http://www.hrc.org/Content/NavigationMenu/HRC/Get_Informed/Issues/Index.htm; http://www.thetaskforce.org/issues; http://www.aclu.org/lgbt/index.html, http://nclrights.org/projects/index.htm; http://www.lambdalegal.org/. There are, of course, differences across these organizations in terms of emphasis, and some tackle issues that are not listed here. However, certain issues—particularly marriage, workplace discrimination, and hate crimes—clearly predominate across a wide range of LGB organizations.

4. Soule and Earl 2001.

5. Criminal sodomy statutes varied across jurisdictions, and many prohibited both opposite- and same-sex "sodomy." Moreover, "sodomy" was itself variously defined, sometimes referring to oral-genital contact, sometimes referring to anal contact, sometimes referring to anything that didn't qualify as missionary position heterosexual sex. *See* Eskridge 2008: Appendix. However, even those statutes that prohibited both heterosexual and homosexual "sodomy" were frequently enforced only against persons engaged in (or suspected of) same-sex sexual behaviors. *Ibid*: chapter 8; *see also Bowers v. Hardwick* 1986; Bernstein 2003.

6. D'Emilio 1983.

as the law authorized draconian penalties for even single acts of fellatio, cunnilingus, or anal intercourse.[7] And even where violations of state sodomy statutes were not prosecuted, they could provide grounds for police harassment or a path to civil commitment.[8] Equally as important, the criminal status of homosex underwrote many, if not all, other forms of anti-gay discrimination, including workplace bans on gay men and lesbians, immigration policies that disqualified applicants based on sexual identity, and discrimination in housing.[9]

Thus, as they emerged from around and within the organizations that formed the nucleus of the modern LGB movement, gaylegal advocates focused much of their work and resources on efforts to repeal or invalidate state sodomy statutes.[10] It was not an easy task. True, a number of states effectively repealed their sodomy laws when they adopted the American Law Institute's Model Penal Code, a uniform statutory scheme that omitted sodomy from its list of crimes, beginning in 1955.[11] And other jurisdictions showed declining interest in enforcing their laws, perhaps as a result of changing social and sexual norms.[12] But full decriminalization proved elusive to gaylegal advocates, as 24 states and the District of Columbia retained criminal sodomy statutes on the books well into the 1980s.[13] In 1986, advocates suffered a crushing blow when the Supreme Court reaffirmed the right of state governments to criminalize same-sex sexual activity

7. Eskridge 2008: chapters 5–6.

8. Eskridge 1999; Bernstein 2003.

9. Eskridge 2008: 235. *See also* D'Emilio 1983; Bernstein 2003.

10. Eskridge 2008: chapter 7; Bernstein 2003.

11. Bernstein 2003: 360.

12. Eskridge 2008.

13. Harvard Law Review 1990: 9, n.2.

in *Bowers v. Hardwick*, a case that tested the constitutionality of Georgia's sodomy statute.[14] In an opinion that was simultaneously sweeping in its effect and narrow in its framing of the issue, the *Bowers* Court held that state sodomy statutes did not violate the United States Constitution because there is no "fundamental right to engage in homosexual sodomy."[15]

As bleak as it looked at the time—and as decisive and unsettling as the language of the opinion was[16]—*Bowers* turned out to be a decision of limited force and duration. The case was decided 5-4, and Justice Powell, who had sided with the majority, later admitted that he had "probably made a mistake" in voting to uphold the Georgia statute.[17] By 1996, the Court's approach to homosex had plainly shifted. While the *Bowers* Court had rejected Hardwick's claim that a belief in the immorality of homosexuality could not be a legitimate basis for a law criminalizing gay sex,[18] in *Romer v. Evans*, the Court reversed course. It held that

14. The facts of the *Bowers* case are now the stuff of legend and include an arrest in respondent's own bedroom courtesy of a careless or overly trusting houseguest, a warrant issuing as the result of a half-finished can of beer, and a suspiciously diligent police officer. William Eskridge offers a vivid account of the case in *Dishonorable Passions* (2008).

15. *Bowers v. Hardwick*, 478 U.S. 186, 191 (1986). ("Precedent aside, however, respondent would have us announce, as the Court of Appeals did, a fundamental right to engage in homosexual sodomy. This we are unwilling to do.")

16. The majority's tone was both stentorian and a bit snide in its dismissal of Hardwick's claim. The Court's framing of the issue as being about a "right to engage in sodomy" had a belittling effect, making the case sound easier to decide than it surely was (as the 5-4 result and multiple opinions reveal). And while the majority claimed that it took no position on the wisdom of sodomy statutes, it also pointed out that prohibitions on sodomy "had ancient roots." *Ibid*: 192. A concurring opinion by Justice Burger was even more emphatic in its condemnation of homosex, citing everything from Judeo-Christian law to Blackstone in support of his conclusion that "[t]o hold that the act of homosexual sodomy is somehow protected as a fundamental right would be to cast aside millennia of moral teaching." *Ibid*: 215.

17. Marcus 1990.

18. 478 U.S. 196.

anti-gay sentiment was *not* a legitimate state interest and therefore could not properly underwrite a law that discriminated broadly against gay men and lesbians.[19] And in 2003, the Court expressly disavowed *Bowers*, ruling in *Lawrence v. Texas* that states could no longer punish same-sex sexual conduct as a violation of their criminal codes because doing so infringed a fundamental right to privacy, autonomy, and personal liberty.[20]

So ended the long period of homosex's criminalization in the United States and, with it, most of what remained of gaylegal advocates' interest in the criminal law. Indeed, many gay men and lesbians were more than happy to turn their attention away from the criminal justice system. Having long suffered the harassment and punishment that attended criminal sodomy statutes, they remained skeptical of law enforcement's commitment to equal treatment—even if all that meant was "the [equal] right to be let alone."[21] Thereafter, most gaylegal activism centered on matters implicating civil law, especially laws touching upon marriage and anti-gay discrimination.[22] There was one exception, however. In the years following the *Romer* decision, many

19. *Romer v. Evans*, 517 U.S. 620, 632 (The "sheer breadth [of Colorado's law] is so discontinuous with the reasons offered for it that the amendment seems inexplicable by anything but animus toward the class it affects; it lacks a rational relationship to legitimate state interests."). It should be noted that *Bowers* was decided on due process grounds, while *Romer* was an equal protection case—and one frequently held up as exceptional in its application of the "rational basis" test (see *infra*, pp. 14–17 for a discussion of equal protection analysis and the standard of review). Whether or not *Romer* represented a doctrinal shift, however, it clearly produced a discursive one.

20. *Lawrence v. Texas*, 539 U.S. 558 (2003).

21. 478 U.S. 199 (Blackmun, dissenting) (quoting *Olmstead v. United States*, 277 U.S. 438, 478 (1928) (Brandeis, J., dissenting).

22. This includes, most saliently, attempts to amend state and federal anti-discrimination laws regulating housing, education, and employment, as well as those governing the status of gay men and lesbians serving in the armed forces. *See* 10 USC. § 564.

gaylegal advocates began to pursue an expansion of police powers by calling for the enactment of anti-gay "hate crime" laws.

## I. A History of Anti-Gay Hate Crime Legislation

Hate crime legislation is quite new. The drive to criminalize bias motivated crime began in the 1960s but only took on real momentum during the 1980s, as the result of some peculiar political dynamics. According to Valerie Jenness and Ryken Grattet, the emergence of the anti-hate crime movement in the United States was the product of a "strange bedfellows" arrangement between the civil rights and feminist movements (on one hand) and a nascent "victims' rights" movement (on the other). The latter had begun to take shape in the late 1960s, as a loosely coalesced set of political and social actors demanded greater attention to the needs of crime victims for "assistance, support, and rights."[23] As Jenness and Grattet note, the alliance of these movements was more than a little odd: the victims' rights movement had emerged within conservative political domains and discourses, while the civil rights and feminist movements operated within and from the politics of the Left.[24] But the movements cohered around the notion that violence was a social problem of great, and perhaps increasing, magnitude. For those in the civil rights and feminist movements, it had long been identified as a brutal tool of racial or gendered oppression. For those in the victims' rights movement, violence seemed to be on the rise in American society, and the needs of victims were being

23. Jenness and Grattet 2004: 28.

24. *Ibid*: 27.

overlooked by legislative and judicial reforms that expanded the rights of defendants.[25]

Awkward alliances notwithstanding, the evolving anti-hate crime movement has had significant legislative success, with states passing dozens of anti-hate crime laws during the 1980s and 1990s. The laws took several different forms, the result of strategic choices and institutional processes of diffusion.[26] Some modified preexisting criminal statutes or enhanced penalties for existing crimes when the motivation for the crime or selection of the victim is bias related. Others created new laws that referred to existing statutes or created new crimes of "intimidation" or "interference with civil rights."[27] The laws emerged in waves, with earlier versions addressing only ethnic, racial, or religious bias and intimidation. Later, the categories of gender, sexual

25. *Ibid.* (citing Weed 1995 and Maroney 1998).

26. *See* Jenness and Grattet 2004, chapter 4. *See also* Soule and Earle 2001. Jenness and Grattet argue that the spread of anti-hate-crime legislation resulted from social movement activism responding to the increased (or perceived) increase in incidents of anti-gay hate crime. They also contend that the legislation diffused mimetically— that is, that the enactment of hate crime laws follows a pattern of isomorphic diffusion across contiguous spaces. Jenness and Grattet 2004: chapter 4. Diffusion does appear to have been at work in accelerating the passage of anti-gay hate crime laws during the 1990s. However, in their analysis of the enactment of criminal hate crime laws, Soule and Earl find evidence of a more complex, heteromorphic process of diffusion, and identify several intrastate factors of importance as well (including partisanship, per capita income, and a jurisdiction's overall innovativeness). Soule and Earl contend that criminal hate crime laws—while diffusing rapidly—nonetheless evince a complex pattern of adoption, where states in the same region may actually have been less likely to adopt criminal hate crime laws where a region-mate had already done so. Indeed, there is evidence that the relative publicity associated with passage of hate crime laws may have led some jurisdictions to resist adopting criminal hate crime laws—particularly where they had already adopted civil hate crime laws or tracking laws. Soule and Earl 2001: 297–300.

27. Jenness and Grattet 2004: 80–86.

orientation, and gender identity were sometimes, but not always, added.[28]

Once they began to be considered as part of anti-hate crime statutes, however, laws prohibiting anti-gay hate crime spread quickly. Currently, 31 states and the District of Columbia have some sort of anti-gay hate crime statute on the books.[29] There are also civil hate crime laws in place, but most of the focus of the anti-violence[30] movement's activities has been on amending the criminal code. These laws do one or more of the following things: (a) create tracking mechanisms to collect data on incidents of anti-gay hate crime;[31] (b) create special enforcement mechanisms, such as vesting jurisdiction over anti-gay hate crimes in federal law enforcement authorities; and/or (c) mandate enhanced criminal sanctions by elevating or changing the underlying charge that attends a hate crime prosecution.[32] Different approaches imply different kinds and levels of state intervention. Tracking mechanisms, for example, require little institutional change, as most local, state, and federal law enforcement agencies already collect a great deal of data on crime and crime victims.[33] The vesting of prosecutorial authority and jurisdiction over hate crimes in federal law enforcement occupies a middle ground. Because it

28. *See* Jenness and Broad 1997: 44.

29. National Gay and Lesbian Task Force 2009 http://www.thetaskforce.org/downloads/reports/issue_maps/hate_crimes_7_09_color.pdf.

30. *See* Jenness and Broad 1997: chapter 3.

31. *See, for example,* Hate Crime Statistics Act, P.L. 101–275 (1990).

32. *See, for example,* Cal. Penal Code §§ 422.6–422.76.

33. *See, for example,* the F.B.I.'s Uniform Crime Reports. The FBI provides some guidance to local law enforcement in how to determine whether crimes ought to be characterized as hate motivated or not, but its guidelines are broad, nonspecific, and necessarily delegate discretion to the officers on the street. *See generally* McVeigh, et al., 2003; U.S. Dept. of Justice 2006.

might lead to prosecution of some alleged anti-gay hate crimes that would otherwise be ignored by local authorities, it is more interventionist than tracking mechanisms but less so than sentence enhancements. The legislation allows the Justice Department to take the lead in investigating and/or prosecuting an alleged hate crime but does not require it. It also promises some amount of resource distribution to local law enforcement for training and investigation, but probably not enough to significantly alter the existing practices of local authorities.[34] Sentence enhancements intervene more deeply. Particularly where charging or sentencing elevations are mandatory and of general application, the enactment of laws that enhance penalties upon a finding of hate or bias motivation can dramatically alter the practices of police officers, prosecutors, defense attorneys, and courts.[35] The introduction of such laws is also likely to have a palpable impact on victims and defendants.

Because they invoke the coercive power of the state, each of these mechanisms for combating anti-gay hate crime raises significant political, jurisprudential, and normative questions. But as the mechanism that extends the power of the state most deeply into the lifeworld, sentence enhancements raise particularly troublesome questions of legitimacy.[36] Consequently, they have been the focus of much of the scholarly work undertaken

34. Still, efforts to establish this federal authority were met with a great deal of resistance. After numerous unsuccessful attempts to move a stand-alone bill through Congress, the Matthew Shepard and James Byrd, Jr. Hate Crimes Prevention Act was only enacted when it was attached as a rider to a Defense Authorization Bill in 2009. *See* Public Law No. 111–84.

35. Herek and Berrill 1992a. As Jenness and Grattet demonstrate, there is wide variation among hate crime statutes with respect to how sentence enhancements are determined and applied, as well as to which crimes they may attach. Jenness & Grattet 2004: chapter 4.

36. *See generally* Habermas 1973, 1996.

on behalf of hate crimes legislation.[37] This work—much of it rich, careful, and thoughtful in its analysis of the implications of criminalizing hatred or bias as it is expressed in particular acts of violence—constitutes the heart of the discursive field produced in and around the legal definition of anti-gay hatred. Political, social, and legal advocates (and adversaries) draw upon and contribute to these scholarly debates. If we examine this discursive field closely, however, we see that it socially constructs sex, gender, and sexuality by reifying categorical distinctions in ways inimical to a project of sexual freedom. That is, the intersection of hate crime discourse and LGB identity discourse produces a sexual truth regime that defines hatred as a categorical emotion and as a particular intrapsychic and corporeal experience that is produced at a boundary, marking off fixed sexual categories. This fictive construction of animus, in turn, defines an equally fictive construction of desire (as its antithesis), thus positioning desire as the disciplinary outcome of a legal mechanism of prohibition. Put simply, in the truth regime produced by anti-gay hate crime jurisprudence, we understand sexual desire primarily by what it may not be: the transgression of binary sexual status categories.

The perilous contours of anti-gay hate crime discourse are shaped in large measure by the institutional processes of knowledge production outlined in Chapter 2. They are fashioned by the production of a set of *justificatory narratives* that are constructed out of the discursive interplay of advocates and opponents, undertaken within specific policy environments. These environments—especially doctrinal environments—inform the kinds of questions that may be posed around the question of anti-gay hate crime laws while *bracketing* others. Here, Fourteenth

37. *See, for example*, Jenness and Grattet 2004; Lawrence 1999 (justifying hate crime laws, in general); Herek and Berrill 1992a; Igansky 2001; McDevitt, et al., 2001.

Amendment jurisprudence is particularly influential, as it works to reduce the complex and messy facts of social inequality to categories of heuristic elegance and utility. Once identified in these terms, the victims and perpetrators of violence can be described as having acted in a radically reduced potential array of scenarios. This *disciplines the evidentiary boundaries* within which courts and litigants operate, ruling out certain kinds of questions and inquiries, especially those that might confirm or disconfirm hypotheses that would call into question the predictive binary matrix of sex, gender, and sexuality. Finally, the legal articulation of "anti-gay hate crime" in scholarship and in adjudicative practices is given social force by the *polysemic* quality of legal discourse. The word "hatred" is particularly important here. While law increasingly finds evidence of actual hatred to be unnecessary to satisfy a hate crime charge, social discourse continues to rely upon the statutory language of "anti-gay hate crime" to reify and act upon an image of unmitigated animus as a defining feature of crimes committed against LGB people.

## II. Justificatory Narratives and the Policy Environment of Anti-Gay Hate Crime Law

How does one justify treating a "hate crime" more harshly than other kinds of crime? Anti-gay hate crimes *seem* worse, but why? And are they? More to the point, can anti-gay hate crime law advocates make the case that they are without rendering incoherent the premises upon which the project for sexual freedom is based? What is anti-gay hate crime, exactly? What legal mechanisms are implicated in an effort to define and establish the terms of proof for this new category of crime?

Answers to these questions present and suggest themselves in a now-expansive literature seeking to justify and define the operation of hate crime legislation.[38] As noted earlier, for reasons both moral and political, criminal punishments must be justified in some way. Simply put, if the state is going to deprive someone of his or her liberty and, in the case of capital crimes, his or her very life, it must demonstrate a compelling reason to do so.[39] Moral philosophy has tended to divide justifications for criminal punishment into three broad categories: retributivist accounts (which assert that punishment is just to the extent that it is deserved by the defendant), utilitarian accounts (which assert that punishment is just if the benefits it provides to a society outweigh the costs incurred by imposing it), and expressivist accounts (which assert that punishment is just if it serves an important symbolic purpose). Legal scholars, particularly philosophers of law, have spirited debates over which of these three frameworks ought to prevail, and defend clear and decisive boundaries between them. Political and gaylegal advocates of anti-gay hate crime laws, however, tend to combine elements of each, creating a justificatory narrative that is more bricolage than precise architectonics.[40] Within this narrative, retributivist and expressivist arguments are most prominent. For example, the Human Rights Campaign contends that hate crimes should be

38. Because much of the normative heavy lifting on behalf of hate crime legislation is not specifically addressed to anti-*gay* hate crime laws, what I will be doing in the following discussion is beginning with existing claims about hate crime laws generally and then applying them to anti-gay hate crime sentence enhancements specifically.

39. *See* Katz et al. 1999.

40. Elsewhere, I have critiqued this framework for, *inter alia*, its internal inconsistencies. *See* Zylan 2009. Here, I seek only to identify the narrative themes at work and to demonstrate the ways in which they draw legal and social practice into a project that reinscribes the predictive binary matrix of sex, gender, and sexuality.

punished specially because they are more harmful than other crimes:

> All violent crimes are reprehensible. But the damage done by hate crimes cannot be measured solely in terms of physical injury or dollars and cents. Hate crimes rend the fabric of our society and fragment communities because they target a whole group and not just the individual victim. Hate crimes are committed to cause fear to a whole community. A violent hate crime is intended to "send a message" that an individual and "their kind" will not be tolerated, many times leaving the victim and others in their group feeling isolated, vulnerable and unprotected.[41]

The National Gay and Lesbian Task Force echoes this theme of terroristic harm generated by anti-gay hate crime and adds the expressivist claim that hate crime laws "*send a message* that certain crimes that strike at this country's core values, such as the freedom to live free of persecution, will be punished and deterred by both enhanced penalties and federal involvement in the investigation and prosecution of the crime."[42]

Whether they sound in utilitarianism, retributivism, or expressivism (or some combination of the three), justificatory claims concerning hate crime laws are primarily normative claims. That is, they establish arguments explaining why hate crime laws ought (or ought not) to exist as distinct instruments of punishment. However, in establishing these normative claims, advocates and opponents of hate crime legislation also deploy and instantiate certain empirical and ontological arguments

41. http://www.hrc.org/Template.cfm?Section=Hate_Crimes1.

42. http://www.thetaskforce.org/issues/hate_crimes_main_page (emphasis added).

about sexuality, animus, desire, identity, and the purpose of the criminal law. In what follows, I seek to unpack these empirical and ontological assertions because it is here that law produces an account of sexuality that is both institutionally specific and poly-semic. Legal scholarship and practice draw from cultural and political discourses of desire, animus, fear, and identity in pro-ducing a lay behavioral science of hatred: a set of predictive and reconstructive maxims about categorical sexual status. In so doing, however, the complexity of desire and animus must be sacrificed in service of evidentiary practices that make sense within law as it is constituted, but which, when exceeding the bounds of this institution, inscribe an unduly limiting concep-tion of sexuality upon the social body.

### 1. The Hate Crime Statistics Act: Conduct, Status, and the "Principal Categories of Hate"

In 1990, the efforts of anti-gay hate crime law advocates to extend hate crime protections to LGB victims produced a key vic-tory: inclusion of persons identified in terms of "homosexuality or heterosexuality" as a protected group under the newly enacted Hate Crime Statistics Act (HCSA).[43] The inclusion of the new category had been vigorously resisted, however, by conservatives in both houses of Congress. Some advanced now standard arguments about increasing the cost of the measure or making enforcement more burdensome to local authorities. Many others, however, made jurisprudential arguments. According to Jenness and Grattet, "the primary objection to the inclusion of sexual orientation in the HCSA was that the federal government should not provide gays and lesbians with 'special rights' and that to do

---

43. 28 U.S.C. § 534.

so would render violence against gays and lesbians equivalent to violence against racial, ethnic, and religious minorities."

The invocation of the phrase "special rights" is important here, as are two key amendments of the bill: one which replaced the phrase "sexual orientation" with the phrase "homosexuality or heterosexuality"; and a second which created a new section of the bill designed to preclude an interpretation of the HCSA that would extend anti-discrimination protection to LGB people. A third amendment added Congress's belief that "the [sic] American family life is the foundation of American society" and affirmed that "Nothing in this Act shall be construed . . . to promote or encourage homosexuality." These extraneous affirmations signaled other discursive themes that were just beginning to surface in national politics: an emergent narrative linking a perceived decline in family integrity to gay sex (on one hand) and the welfare state (on the other), and a preoccupation with the possibility of same-sex marriage. The former is a topic for another day.[44] The latter is a matter I take up in Chapter 6, but it is worth noting here the early tethering of all things gay to the specter of same-sex marriage.

On the surface, one might view these amendments and rhetorics as the tried-and-true methods of social conservatives seeking to resist legislation designed to advance the status of LGB people, or as incidental measures of little material consequence. For example, one congressman complained that the phrase "sexual orientation" was an "ambiguous" protected classification that might require the FBI to track hate crimes perpetrated against "child molesters."[45] But there is more to the story than

44. Zylan (in progress), "The Salacious State: Postmodern Patriarchy and the Enforcement of the Marriage Contract."

45. Congressional Record 1988: 11405, cited in Jenness and Grattet 2004: 60.

this, and focusing on the outcome alone, or chalking the rhetoric up to reflexive homophobia misses the specific discursive effects produced by the legislative debate. Even as it included LGB people in the catalog of those against whom hate crimes would be recognized and tracked via the HCSA, this debate signaled the emergence of several discursive inconsistencies and difficulties for anti-gay hate crime law advocates.

To understand why this is so, we must first spend a little time getting to know the Fourteenth Amendment's Equal Protection Clause and the Civil Rights Act of 1964, two provisions that were frequently invoked, confused, switched, and conflated by both opponents and proponents of the HCSA bill. Both measures have played critical roles in shaping the discursive and institutional environment within which LGB legal activism was operating in the 1990s and in which it continues to operate today. The Fourteenth Amendment is one of three constitutional amendments that was passed in the immediate aftermath of the Civil War. Along with the Thirteenth Amendment, which abolished slavery, and the Fifteenth Amendment, which guaranteed voting rights to all Americans, regardless of race, the Fourteenth Amendment was enacted to rectify the most expressly racist dimensions of the Constitution, provisions that authorized slavery, identified black Americans as not fully human, and restricted the right to vote to white Americans.[46] It guarantees several things. It safeguards the "privileges and immunities" of citizenship, mandates the "equal protection of the laws," and ensures "due process of law" to all persons residing in the United States.

Yet, because the language of the Fourteenth Amendment is rather broad and general, it is subject to varying interpretations,

46. *See generally* Maltz 1992; Foner 2002.

including the notion that it might apply to forms of social inequality beyond those marked by race. For example, courts have long had to consider whether, given its provenance, the Fourteenth Amendment's Equal Protection Clause ought to be interpreted to apply only to state practices that implicate racial classifications or whether it should be given a broader application. Equal protection analysis has evolved over time, but it is now well established that race occupies a special place in the jurisprudence. Racial classifications provoke the strictest scrutiny by the courts as they determine whether a given state action comports with the equal protection guarantee of the Constitution. No other social classification—not gender, not wealth, and certainly not sexual identity—automatically provokes the same level of scrutiny. Still, feminists and gaylegal advocates have managed to obtain some limited traction in their efforts to ground legal challenges to sexist and anti-gay state practices in the Fourteenth Amendment's equal protection guarantee.

Arguably, one reason federal courts have struggled to formulate a coherent approach to equal protection analysis implicating questions of gender-, and sexuality-based inequality, among others, is that running alongside the constitutional questions posed by social inequality are a series of statutory questions that echo similar themes. In 1964, Congress passed, and President Lyndon Johnson signed, the 1964 Civil Rights Act: a landmark piece of legislation that became the cornerstone of American anti-discrimination law. The legislation was designed, in part, to respond to the Supreme Court's crabbed interpretation of the Reconstruction Amendments and so, at its inception, was clearly focused on racial discrimination. It took some time for other forms of social inequality to adopt the language and praxis of "civil rights." Still, even as early as 1964, some well-placed feminist state actors were canny and skillful enough to insert the word "sex" into Title VII of the bill as an additional protected classification.[47]

Despite its early inclusion, however, "sex" as a protected Title VII classification has long occupied an unsettled status. Courts that have readily dismissed race-based classifications as grounded in wrongheaded notions of race as a social, psychological, or biological category remain hesitant to dismiss similar sorts of generalizations about sex or gender. Much of this reluctance can be attributed to the contested character of the notion of "equality" when applied to gender. First, even among feminists, there is no consensus over whether "equal" means "same" or, alternatively, "different, but equitable" when applied to gender. This question lies at the heart of anti-discrimination discourse, yet it eludes a definitive answer. Instead, it generates only more questions: What is the status of the body in shaping women's political, social, and legal status? Do biological differences between men and women "matter" in a sociolegal sense? Should they? What does the law mean when it speaks of "gender" and "sex"? Are these the same meanings that operate politically or socially? Is gender an innate characteristic, or is it something that is achieved or enacted? Is "woman" an intelligible concept of political subjectivity? Case law not only doesn't answer these questions, it doesn't even attempt to. While appearing to define "equality," anti-discrimination law brackets the most difficult and essential

47. Stories vary about the provenance of this amendment. Some believe it was the result of clever strategy and vigorous lobbying by feminists within Congress. Others assert that it was the consequence of a political miscalculation by a white Southern Congressman who had inserted it as a kind of "poison pill" (or joke) in an effort to kill the entire bill. Either way, "sex" was included as a protected classification in Title VII (the employment nondiscrimination provision of the bill) when it emerged in its final version. *See* Freeman 2008: chapter 13.

questions one ought to answer—or at least pose—in order to produce an intelligible definition of the term.

Where homosex is concerned, another layer of confusion appears, muddying the essential ontology at issue. Is sexuality a status like race, like gender, or is it a quality of conduct? That is to say, is it what you are or what you do? If it is conduct, then it begins to look a lot less like the legal conceptions of race and sex embedded in equal protection and Title VII doctrines and more like something else . . . perhaps expression? But even if it is a character of the self, or of the body, sexuality faces the additional difficulty that it must be disclosed in order to become the basis of discrimination and litigation. In that case, it indeed appears to be something closer to conduct. But is it expressive conduct? Or is it private conduct, like watching dirty 8 millimeter movies at home or using contraception while having sex with your spouse?[48]

Certainly activists and scholars have considered these questions in great depth, but the answers they formulate enter the legislative and judicial discourse over anti-gay hate crime laws in, at best, partial and fractured form. The parameters of the justificatory narratives that ground such laws are delimited by the equal protection/Title VII institutional and discursive framework that brackets these first-order questions of being and doing. The big questions of conduct and status are reduced and particularized, and (as a consequence) specific answers begin to suggest themselves. In the debate on the HCSA, for example, advocates and opponents fought over the inclusion of the phrase "sexual orientation" because it would codify a *status*—not in the ontological sense but in the jurisprudential sense. The debate boiled down to two subinquiries: First, is LGB identity the sort of social

---

48. *Stanley v. Georgia,* 394 U.S. 557 (1969); *Connecticut v. Griswold,* 381 U.S. 479 (1965).

phenomenon that, like race and gender, ought to serve as the basis of a legal definition that sorts out invidious discrimination? That is, is discriminating on the basis of sexual orientation "bad" in a way which justifies state efforts at redress? If so, then LGB activists were merely seeking "equal" rights under the law. But if there was some difference between sexual orientation and race/gender that made LGB identity something other than, or more than, a status category, then discrimination might not always be invidious. In that case, LGB activists were seeking not equal but "special" rights.

The second subinquiry concerned the implications for Title VII of codifying LGB identity as a protected status category in the HCSA. As noted above, Title VII did not then, and does not now, include protection for LGB people at the federal level. Time and again, federal courts have looked to the absence of such protection as evidence that Congress affirmatively refuses to extend nondiscrimination protection to LGB people. Consequently, there were clear strategic reasons for congressional conservatives to vigorously resist the inclusion of "sexual orientation" in the list of HCSA-protected categories. Still, even as they contested the inclusion of "sexual orientation" primarily for strategic and instrumental reasons, conservatives did so in terms that—like the inquiry into status—served to underwrite a categorical discourse of sexuality, sexual identity, and animus.

In the earliest manifestation of their opposition to the inclusion of LGB people in the HCSA, dissenters to the House report to the Committee of the Whole House, which recommended passage of the bill, claimed there was no "federal nexus" justifying inclusion of sexual orientation as a protected category because "[t]here is no mention of homosexual rights in the Constitution." Including LGB people would, they argued, raise their status vis-à-vis other would-be claimants, including "women, the elderly, members of the police or passengers on urban mass transit."[49] In short, it would give them "special rights." Congressman William Dannemeyer put the point bluntly: the gay community, he argued, was trying to create a "rational basis on which to suggest we should change the laws of the culture of our society so that we will accept and equate homosexuality with heterosexuality."[50] He objected "in a very firm way to an effort . . . to elevate sexual preference, whether you call it heterosexuality or homosexuality, on the same basis as race, color, religion, or natural [sic] origin."[51]

Although Dannemeyer and others invoked the language of constitutional status, much of the stated opposition to the bill seemed to confuse constitutional status with statutory status under the Civil Rights Act. Dannemeyer claimed that including sexual orientation in the HCSA would "change the basic definition of the 1964 Civil Rights Act to include a new status that would have the dignity of being within the proscription of that act."[52] These arguments, as well as claims like that of Congressman Gerry Studds that the categories included in the bill made sense

49. H.R. Rep. No. 100-575 at 12 (1988) (Reps. Gekas et al. dissenting from the report).

50. 135 Cong. Rec. 13,545 (1989) (statement of Rep. Dannemeyer) (emphasis added). "Rational basis" resonates in a very specific way in antidiscrimination law. As noted above, a key threshold question in Fourteenth Amendment equal protection cases is which standard of review applies to the facts at issue. Most legal classifications are examined under the lowest level of scrutiny: rational basis review. Dannemeyer's concern here was the possibility that LGB advocates would find support in the HCSA for future claims alleging the irrationality of laws distinguishing between heterosexuality and homosexuality.

51. *Ibid.*

52. 135 Cong. Rec. 13,545 (1989).

because "these are the principal categories of such acts of hate,"[53] demonstrate the movement between legal and social categories and the polysemic quality of legislative language. For Studds, it was not members of Congress, but perpetrators of hate crime, who were analogizing between race, gender, and sexual orientation.

Anti-gay hate crime law advocates also sought to justify the inclusion of sexual orientation in HCSA's catalog of protected categories by invoking the discourse of sexuality as an innate human characteristic. In this account, sexual orientation was like race or gender, not a choice or form of conduct that might be changed or variable but an essential feature of personhood. Was this purely a strategic choice on the part of advocates? Probably not; the false opposition between "biology" and "choice" resonates throughout LGB politics and activism. But even as it was strategically useful in the short term (the bill passed, after all) and even as it is intuitively appealing to many LGB people, this approach represents a discursive *cul de sac* with respect to larger projects of sexual freedom. This is because status-based arguments on behalf of LGB equality are necessarily tied to a binary construction of sexuality. That is, to determine one's "status" within this framework, courts and litigants must repair to static definitions of sexual identity. One either is or is not gay or lesbian and—by operation of the binary—if one is heterosexual, then one is not gay and cannot experience or express same-sex desire. This seems an unremarkable, unobjectionable, and pretty functional approach to take in one's daily life. But the radical division between gay and straight is a key feature of heterosexism. Anti-gay hate crime discourse may, therefore, invite a set of justificatory and evidentiary practices that serve to reify a

53. *Ibid*: 13, 547.

division that underwrites social practices of sexual exclusion and limitation.

## 2. Elaborating the Narratives: Reason, Emotion, and the "Normal" Anti-Gay Hate Crime

The legislative debate over the Hate Crime Statistics Act was, as Valerie Jenness and Ryken Grattet have noted,[54] a crucially important discursive and political moment in the life of the anti-gay hate crime law movement. But it also ushered in a more vigorous debate between advocates and opponents of such laws, undertaken by activists and scholars from a wide array of perspectives, and so resulted in a more elaborate and carefully considered set of justificatory discourses. In this phase, utilitarian, expressivist, and retributivist rationales have been more explicitly engaged.

Utilitarianism is a consequentialist theory of justice. It understands punishment to be just if the consequences that it produces are, on balance, favorable for society as a whole. Because utilitarians find punishment itself to be a social evil, the burden is on the advocate of punishment to demonstrate that the good it will produce will outweigh the harm wrought by imposing it. Utilitarianism is also collectivist in the sense that it aggregates costs and benefits over a group. An individual may experience a great deal of harm, but if the society as a whole receives a benefit greater than that harm, all is well.[55] Thus, a pure utilitarian approach to the criminal law may be indifferent to whether an individual defendant is actually deserving of a specific kind or

54. Jenness and Grattet 2004: 45; Jenness 1999.

55. Bentham 1996: 158–59.

degree of punishment—a notion that can be disquieting, to say the least.[56]

Perhaps because it is unsettling, this sort of pure utilitarianism does not drive debates about proposed changes to the American criminal justice system, and it is infrequently invoked in anti-gay hate crime discourse. Where they do invoke utilitarian justifications, advocates emphasize theories of deterrence.[57] When the House of Representatives added "sexual orientation" to the list of protected classifications in federal hate crime legislation in late 2009, Senator Carl Lewin stated that he hoped that the new law would "deter people from being targeted for violent attacks because of the color of their skin or their religion, their disability, their gender or their sexual orientation."[58]

Levin's confusing construction, "deter people *from being targeted*," might be attributable to the fact that deterrence is a peculiar rationale when applied to hate crimes. After all, deterrence is predicated on a model of human action that evokes cold, calculating rationality.[59] Deterrence works (if it does) when the marginal utility gained by committing a crime is outweighed by the severity of the criminal sanction imposed if caught committing it,

56. Moore 1987.

57. Hart 1968:8. ("Even those who look upon human law as a mere instrument for enforcing 'morality as such' . . . would not deny that the aim of criminal legislation is to set up types of behaviour . . . as legal standards of behaviour and to secure conformity with them."); *see also* Andenaes 1974. LGB organizations have not elaborated much of a deterrence justification, but they do sometimes adopt the language of deterrence. *See* National Gay and Lesbian Task Force Action Fund 2009 ("[Laws that enhance penalties for crimes against certain targets] do not value some lives more than others. Instead, they send a message that certain crimes fundamentally at odds with this country's core values, such as the freedom to live without persecution, will be punished and deterred by both enhanced penalties and federal involvement in the investigation and prosecution of the crime.").

58. Hulse 2009.

59. See Andenaes 1974; Gibbs 1975; Zimring and Hawkins 1973.

multiplied by the risk of being caught and prosecuted.[60] The econometric dimensions of this account underscore the cognitive rationality required by the aspiring criminal whom the state seeks to deter. Deterrence requires several cognitive transactions: first, the would-be offender must make an educated guess about the likely costs and benefits of a given criminal act. Next, s/he must calculate the benefits of crime minus its costs, conditioning the latter on the likelihood of being caught and prosecuted. Finally, s/he must choose and carry out the course of action that efficiently implements the result of this calculation.

I will leave it to others to decide whether this is a plausible account of human action. But, in any case, it fundamentally conflicts with the discursively constructed archetypical hate crime—what criminologists call the "normal" hate crime.[61] In a formal legal sense, a finding of hatred may be more or less important in establishing liability for a hate crime. Some jurisdictions require a finding of "but for" causation in a hate crime prosecution. That is, they require the state to demonstrate that but for the hate or bias motivation (or the victim's sexual orientation), the crime would not have occurred.[62] Others, such as California, only require hatred or bias to have been a "substantial factor" in

---

60. *See, for example,* Posner 1985.

61. Sudnow 1965; Jenness and Grattet 2004: 92 ("The documentation and publicizing of hate crimes provided by social movements and social movement organizations has produced an image of the ordinary circumstances under which hate crime—or, to use a more technical sociological term, a 'normal' hate crime—occurs . . . A sample of such images might include an assault outside a gay bar, arson directed at a black family's home . . . Scenarios like these have emerged as the "normal" victimization pattern in social movement, and eventually legislative, discourse about hate crime. Such examples draw on and contribute to a portrait of hate crime as involving a specific range of stereotypical victims and conduct.")

62. Jenness and Grattet 2004: 117–118. On causation generally, see *infra,* chapter 5.

causing the crime.[63] As a discursive matter, however, hatred is essential.[64] As articulated by advocates of anti-gay hate crime legislation, the normal hate crime—the basis of social and legal processes of typification[65]—is a sudden, unprovoked manifestation of simmering animus[66]:

> The empirical studies available suggest that the normal hate crime construct is made up of key elements [police] officers consider to represent an ordinary occurrence of hate crime: namely, the facts of the crime reveal no provocation by the victim, no prior encounters between the victim and the perpetrator, a specific target, accompanying derogatory insults, observable graffiti or other hateful words or epithets, the victim's fears about the perpetrator or beliefs about the crime, and recognizable indications of association with known, organized hate groups.[67]

63. Jenness and Grattet 2004: 117–118.

64. *See generally* Jenness and Grattet 2004.

65. *See supra*, chapter 3.

66. *See, for example*, National Center for Lesbian Rights 2003 (describing beating of three men leaving a gay pride event as "a blatant display of hatred and violence") (on file with author).

67. Jenness and Grattet 2004: 134. *See generally*, Herek and Berrill 1992. Gregory Herek and Kevin Berrill open their book *Hate Crimes* with a first person account of perhaps the most haunting and well-known act of violence against two lesbians—an incident that left one grievously injured and the other dead. In "A Survivor's Story: Eight Bullets," Claudia Brenner tells of being shot by a stranger while camping on the Appalachian trail. The shooter followed Brenner and her lover, making contact several times, then hid in the woods and watched them make love before "explod[ing their] world with his hate and his bullets." Herek and Berrill 1992:11–15. The story is deeply disturbing and (at least in part because of this) iconographic of the notion of an "anti-gay hate crime."

The normal anti-gay hate crime is characterized by *irrationality*—the irrationality of homophobia, bias, and prejudice.[68] Within the juridical and discursive field upon which anti-gay hate crime legislation is debated, it is precisely this irrationality that renders a hate crime more dangerous and malevolent than conventional crime. It is also what justifies the gaylegal turn toward a criminal justice system that has historically disdained and disparaged homosex and the people who engage in it. In other words, the polysemic quality of the phrase "anti-gay hatred" is what makes a demand for greater policing a politically progressive act.

The narrative theme of hatred as an irrational and dangerous motive for crime is powerful and resonant, at least in part because it finds evidentiary support in social practices. First, the fact that crimes perpetrated against gay victims have been under-reported, under-prosecuted, and under-punished can be attributed in some measure (and perhaps entirely) to the baseless disapprobation of homosex, which has been at least as pervasive in the criminal justice system as anywhere else.[69] Second, crimes committed

68. Herek 1992b; Adam 1998; National Coalition of Anti-Violence Programs 2007: 17 (" . . . anti-LGBT violence is revelatory of social pathologies more fundamental, and ultimately more dangerous, that other violent crime."). The National Center for Lesbian Rights offers a similar account of anti-gay hate crime as pathology. Describing attacks on transgendered woman Gwen Araujo and lesbian Sakia Gunn, the NCLR's Executive Direction Kate Kendall wrote: "These crimes are separated by seven months and 3,000 miles but they share the deep-seated misogyny and homophobia of every hate crime directed at a lesbian, gay, bisexual or transgendered person. These two women tell the same story from a different lens: transgressions of gender, whether based on who one loves or how one identifies, will be brutally repressed and savagely responded to." "The Story of Two Newarks: Kate Kendall's Op-Ed on the tragic deaths of Gwen Araujo and Sakia Gunn," http://www.nclrights. org/releases/newark060603.htm.

69. McVeigh et al; ACLU, "Letter to the House Urging Support for the Local Law Enforcement Hate Crimes Prevention Act (5/2/2007)" http://www.aclu.org/lgbt/ crimjustice/29600leg20070502.html (quoting one report of a victim who claimed her gang rape was ignored by her local police department: "They closed their book,

against gay people because they are gay seem to be irrational on their own terms. Consider homophobia, a psychosocial phenomenon that embodies a simultaneous disgust of gay sexuality and a fear that homosex is almost irresistibly seductive.[70] Indeed, the homophobic mind imagines gay men (within the normal hate crime narrative, the prototypical victims of anti-gay hate crime)[71] as effeminate and weak, yet also deeply threatening.[72] These irrational dynamics serve to construct the homophobic social and cultural fabric out of which, activists and scholars contend, hate

and said, 'Well, you were asking for it.'") The ACLU has also relied upon the failure of state and local police departments to adequately prosecute crimes against gay people to assert a jurisdictional basis for anti-gay hate crime laws in terms sounding in the language of equal protection: "Federal legislation addressing such criminal civil rights violations is necessary because state and local law enforcement officers are sometimes unwilling or unable to prosecute those crimes because of either inadequate resources or their own bias against the victim. The prospect of such failure to provide equal protection of the laws justifies federal jurisdiction." *Ibid.*

70. Drawing upon Georges Bataille and Sigmund Freud, Leo Bersani has written provocatively and convincingly about the nature and source of this simultaneous loathing and desire. *See* Bersani 1987: 209–12. *See also* Nussbaum 2004: 166.

71. The (widely recognized and admitted) limitations of data collection render generalizations about the gender composition of the population of anti-gay hate crime victims perilous at best. But recent figures offered by the Anti-Violence Project do not offer empirical support for the normal hate crime narrative's almost exclusive focus on male victims. According to the AVP, in 2006, 57 percent of anti-gay hate crime victims identified as male, while 41 percent identified as female. Interpreting these numbers invites extensive speculation, especially since 13 percent identified as transgendered, meaning that some victims identified themselves as male or female and as transgendered. But if one assumes that women and men are about equally represented in the population of gay people (as they are in the general population—an assumption that almost certainly overstates the number of self-identified lesbians)—the gender imbalance is minimal at best. National Coalition of Anti-Violence Programs 2007: 9.

72. The discursive construction of gay men as effeminate and weak is powerful and of long standing. *See, for example,* Messner 2002. At the same time, a subordinated discourse—perhaps most salient in the debate over whether gay people should be permitted to serve openly in the U.S. military—conceives of gay men as sexually threatening (especially in communal showers). *See* Lehring 2003: 127.

crimes emerge as the almost inevitable consequence.[73] Yet because homophobia is this objectively irrational, it is also manifestly ill-suited to respond to legal mechanisms of deterrence relying upon rational cost-benefit analyses.

Still, hatred (while irrational) is not conceived as thought*less* in the anti-gay hate crime narrative. There is a certain ideational content in the normal hate crime, whether it is in the selection of the victim or in the specific quality of the motivation to commit violence. Indeed, philosopher and legal scholar Martha Nussbaum contends that emotions (even powerful ones like hatred) always embrace a significant cognitive element.[74] In Nussbaum's account, while emotions are often mistakenly thought of as drives, reflexive actions, or "animal" instincts, they are always "about" something. Emotions require an "assent" to a "judgment" and embody beliefs about their objects. Beliefs, of course, can be wrong, mistaken, or unreasonable. Indeed, a central insight of Nussbaum's work on emotions and law is that some emotional states offer valid and reliable indicators of important social aims and goods and ought to inform legal doctrine and practice, while others, including disgust and shame, are generally unreliable.

However, Nussbaum's theory of the cognitive bases of emotion distinguishes them from the cognitive operations that inform the *mens rea* categories familiar to students and practitioners of

---

73. Herek 1992b. *See also* GLAAD 1998 ("Hateful rhetoric fosters a fearful and intolerant environment—all the ingredients necessary for putting people in harms (*sic*) way . . . That there are people who hate [Matt Shepard] for being open and honest about his life is unconscionable."); National Coalition of Anti-Violence Programs 2007: 19 ("As is evidenced in the data included in this report, the political and cultural environment may not have been as toxic for LGBT people in 2006 as it was in 2003, 2004, or much of 2005, but given the community's experience over the last few years, any optimism must be exhibited cautiously when looking at concerns of violence and safety. The dynamics that helped contribute to the astounding jump in reports of violence in the preceding years can and may again occur.")

74. Nussbaum 2001, 2004; *see also* Kahan and Nussbaum 1996.

criminal law. She explicitly distinguishes between the kind of thought that is coexistent with an emotional response and the kind of thought that the law thinks of as "motivation":

> Emotions, in short, are acknowledgements of our goals and of their status. It then remains to be seen what the world will let us do about them. Desires may all contain a perception of their object as a good; but not all perceptions of good give rise directly to action-guiding desires. This suggests that the tendency to explain actions in terms of two distinct sorts of items, beliefs or judgments and desires, needs to be made more complicated. Emotions are judgments, but not inert judgments; on account of their evaluative content, they have an intimate connection with motivation that other beliefs do not; on the other hand, because they may not hook into the situation at hand in a way productive of a concrete plan of action, they are different from desires as well.[75]

Emotions stand somewhere between desires and "motivation" because they indicate "a certain passivity before the world."[76] They are distinguishable from action-relative mental states (the traditional *mens rea* categories of intent, knowledge, recklessness, and negligence), which are about acting upon the world and which are the objects of efforts to deter crime.[77] This might lead

75. Nussbaum 2001: 135.

76. *Ibid*: 43.

77. The Model Penal Code identifies the key *mens rea* categories as intentionality, knowledge, recklessness, and negligence. The categories arise directly out of the relationship between thought and action; culpability increases in direct proportion to the level of cognitive deliberation that attends a given prohibited act. This framework conforms to a utilitarian conception of deterrence; the culpability scale roughly responds to various levels of resistance to social and criminal prohibitions. Knowledge and foresight form the backdrop within which the economic model of

one to expect that Nussbaum would be skeptical of the possibility of deterring anti-gay hate crime, but she is not:

> The criminals who prey on gays and lesbians are not, on the whole, a bunch of committed desperados who would go to their death for their principled opposition to the 'gay agenda.' As Gary David Comstock showed in his comprehensive study of antigay violence, they are for the most part young male troublemakers who don't have a particular political aim, but just want to beat up on someone whom the police probably won't protect . . . they probably would go do something else—many of them, at least—if they got the signal that this is something society was going to take really seriously.[78]

Still, Nussbaum's advocacy of anti-gay hate crime laws is predicated on a discursive move away from hatred and toward something else: something like discrimination. Instead of the hatred-fueled gay-basher, we are drawn toward the image of the opportunistic thug (and back to the rational actor of utilitarianism proper).

This is not accidental. There is, in fact, a discernible tension within political, practical, and scholarly accounts of anti-gay hate crime. In spite of the frequent use of the word "hate" in legal and political discussions of the object of the law, the language of hate crime statutes actually tracks the language of anti-discrimination law, emphasizing intentionality and selection of the victim (impliedly because of his or her perceived vulnerability) rather than the emotional component of hate motivation. Still, as Jenness and Grattet describe, the political will behind hate crime

deterrence operates; deterrence presupposes a distance between thought and action within which one may interpose informed free will.

78. Nussbaum 2004: 295.

legislation has been grounded in a notion of hate crime taking the form of deeply emotional, almost primal brutality.[79] Both themes are prominent in anti-gay hate crime discourse, and both find their way into adjudication, but hatred is the concept that exerts polysemic force over the social body.

Nussbaum's theory also suggests another way in which law might effect change via interventions that target emotional states. She notes that the evaluative content of emotions is profoundly socially constructed. If I feel grief over the loss of my mother, the content of that grief—and its "appropriateness"—is constituted by the social construct "mother" (or "mother love").[80] Emotions are "localized" and eudaimonistic (oriented toward the flourishing of the self), but their content varies with social norms. If this is true, changes in the content of an emotion must come from deep and extensive changes in social norms. Sentence enhancements might contribute in some small measure to such a normative shift and, if so, such an effect might provide sufficient justification for the imposition of additional criminal penalties.

Such an argument takes us away from utilitarianism, however, and into the realm of expressivist justifications. Expressivism makes a straightforward claim: whatever else it might do, law serves an expressive function in communicating what a society values and what it disdains.[81] Rooted in Durkheimian functionalism, expressivism highlights the symbolic import of laws and of their enforcement in changing, publicizing, and/or solidifying social norms.[82] The criminal law is particularly important in this

79. Jenness and Grattet 2004.(*see* especially chapter 3).

80. Nussbaum 2001: 157–165.

81. Kahan 1996 (on expressivism generally); Beale 2000: 1254–61 (on expressivism as applied to hate crime legislation). *See also* the critique of expressivist rationales for hate crime laws in Hurd and Moore 2004: 1100–17.

82. Durkheim and Halls 1984; McAdams 1997; Sunstein 1996; Balkin 1997.

respect because, expressivists contend, it is in the very business of denunciation. Not only do criminal laws permit of much harsher penalties than civil laws do, but the stigma associated with criminality lends their interventions added symbolic value.[83] Thus, apart from whether or not a given law "fits" a crime (which is of interest to the retributivist) or whether it is likely to deter future crimes (as the utilitarian hopes), laws may be justified on expressivist terms if they communicate a socially valuable message.[84]

With respect to hate crime laws, expressivists make two claims. First, they argue that hate crimes send particularly malevolent messages to victims and their communities and consequently demand equally strong denunciatory replies.[85] Second, expressivists claim that hate crime legislation is important not only for what it says about hate crime (that it is considered even more destructive than the same crime without the hate motivation), but for what it affirmatively says about the targets of hate crimes (that they are valued members of the civic community) or about equality more generally (that it is an important social objective).[86]

These seem to be fairly unassailable values (violence is bad, equality and dignity are good) but surely this is not all there is to the expressive content of hate crime laws. If hate crime sentence enhancements are important because they express important social values, what, precisely, are those values, and how are they specifically conveyed by sentence enhancements? Heidi Hurd and Michael Moore have argued that expressivist defenders of

83. Beale 2000: 1266–67.

84. Kahan 1998: 1641; Kahan 1996: 599. *See also* the summary in Hurd and Moore 2004: 1100–01.

85. Kahan 1996: 599; *see also* Beale 2000: 1265–66.

86. Hurd and Moore 2004: 1100–17.

hate crime sentence enhancements assume that the denunciatory effect of such laws begins and ends with passage of the legislation.[87] But actual defendants are charged with, and tried for, offenses characterized as "hate crimes." And sociologists of law have observed that crime victims often give voice to their experiences of suffering in the language of hate crime discourse.[88] As we saw in Chapters 2 and 3, naming, as a set of social, legal, and representational practices, matters a great deal. Indeed, empirical evidence suggests that the normal hate crime narrative informs charging and prosecution; one of the important factors officers and prosecutors consider in determining whether or not to pursue a hate crime charge is how the victim describes the offense and the offender.[89]

The legislative discourse of anti-gay hate crime has been deployed and refined by juridical practices–by advocates seeking to prod law enforcement into defining and prosecuting specific incidents as hate crimes, prosecutors seeking to fulfill their professional mandates of doing justice and protecting the public, defense attorneys seeking to fulfill their professional mandates of representing clients and forcing the state to prove its cases, and by judges seeking to make sense of the formal and practical dictates of the criminal code. There can be little doubt that this is highly expressive work. But noting the expressive quality of the discourse only tells part of the story here; what is most prominent

87. Hurd and Moore 2004: 1114–15 ("[t]he question remains as to why so many proponents of hate/bias crime legislation regard the need to 'send a message' to be a sufficient justification for such laws. We think it is because such proponents are focusing only on the passage of the bills enacting hate/bias crime legislation . . . Forgotten is the obvious fact that when one uses the criminal law as a medium for sending a message, one then has to punish those who do not get the message.").

88. McVeigh, et al, 2003.

89. Jenness and Grattet 2004: chapter 6.

in the polysemic *content* of anti-gay hate crime law is a set of themes that sound deeply and specifically in retibutivism.

Retributivists contend that punishment should always follow culpability. As Michael Moore puts it, "[a] retributivist punishes because, and only because, the offender deserves it."[90] Desert is defined in terms of the amount of *harm* that is wrought by the conduct at issue and by the level of *culpability* with which the harmful conduct is undertaken. Accordingly, hate crime laws may be justified on retributivist grounds in one of two ways.[91] First, such laws may be justified if it can be demonstrated that the enhanced penalties they impose correspond to the greater wrongdoing that results from hate crimes. Alternatively, enhanced penalties may be justified if hate motivated crimes imply greater culpability on the part of those who perpetrate them than do crimes that do not implicate concerns about social equality.

The first claim poses certain difficulties for advocates of LGB equality. Retributivism begins with the assumption that each life is equally dignified and valuable by virtue of being human. This is why some retributivists argue that the state has an obligation to impose the death penalty on those who commit murder; any lesser punishment would fail to accord the murderer respect as a dignified, sentient being.[92] The claim here is straightforward: because each human life is morally equal in weight, one cannot assign greater wrongdoing to the violation of one person's rights than is assigned to the violation of another's. The level of harm may only be traceable to characteristics of the victim if it can be said that those characteristics are indicative of greater protectable rights or interests. One might make such a claim about

90. Moore 1987: 179.

91. Dillof 1997 at 1032.

92. Lewis 1987.

children, for example. But the argument that LGB people enjoy greater rights or protectable interests than others runs orthogonally, at best, to the central thrust of LGB political and legal discourse: namely, the idea that gay and lesbian people are morally and socially equal to heterosexuals and therefore deserving of equal legal rights. In other words, it runs headfirst into the opposing discourse of "special rights."

To be fair, there is another and perhaps more common invocation of the greater wrongdoing claim: that each hate crime amounts to greater wrongdoing because of the secondary harms that are produced by a hate crime.[93] For example, advocates point to the harm inflicted on an entire community by a single hate or bias motivated attack. In the social construction of the normal hate crime, these secondary harms are not only common but are almost part of the definition of the concept "hate crime." Still, even as it speaks of harm, this claim doesn't really work as a retributivist argument; retributivism eschews punishment by proxy where there is no reason to believe that the targeted harm could not be directly addressed by the criminal law.[94] Consequently, retributivist opponents of hate crime laws have vigorously resisted this formulation, noting the ways in which it runs counter to general principles of criminal justice.

Indeed, something other than conventional retributivism seems to animate both the "terrorism" and the "greater harm"

93. *See* Berrill and Herek 1992: Levin and McDevitt 2002. The secondary harm claim has been particularly salient in legislative discourse. *See* Jenness and Broad 1997: 38-39. Recall, as well, the claim made by the Human Rights Campaign: "Hate crimes rend the fabric of our society and fragment communities because *they target a whole group* and not just the individual victim. Hate crimes are committed to cause fear to a whole community." *See supra*, note 42.

94. *See* Dillof 1997: 1050-1061. The use of proxies is problematic for retributivists because they tend toward both over- and under-inclusiveness. *See also* Hurd and Moore 2004.

elements of the quasi-retributivist narrative justifying anti-gay hate crime laws. The essence of the argument is not that LGB lives are worth more or simply that other LGB people ought to be counted as secondary victims, but that the very calculus of the law must be rebalanced because LGB people and the LGB community have historically been deemed by the state to be *less* valuable than other people and communities. That is, while pure retributivists assume an equal moral playing field, advocates of hate crime legislation assume a profoundly unbalanced terrain in articulating their retributivist justifications of hate crime laws. On this view, the retributive satisfaction that is experienced upon the enhanced punishment of a hate-motivated offender is derived in part from the sense that a larger social wrong (heterosexism) has been, to some extent, righted.

This claim is not one grounded in notions of distributive justice, however.[95] Rather, it distills group-based wrongs via the operation of the criminal law, which (like all law) requires a specific adjudication of the facts involving specific parties. That is, the moral and political calculation is directed to the individual victim and perpetrator: *this* victim deserves *this* additional measure of justice, and *this* perpetrator deserves *this* subtracted measure of privilege.[96] As a rule of general application, the calculus may assume too much (that the victim has experienced sexuality-based injustice and that the perpetrator

95. *See* Harel and Parchomovsky 1999.

96. For example, consider this observation attributed to Judy Shepard, whose son was killed in what has been widely characterized as an anti-gay hate crime: "Matt is no longer with us today because the men who killed him learned to hate. Somehow and somewhere they received the message that the lives of gay people are not as worthy of respect, dignity and honor as the lives of other people." Human Rights Campaign, *Issues and Legislation: Hate Crimes, available at* http://www.hrc.org/ issues/hate_crimes/index.asp. The enhanced penalty associated with hate motivated criminal conduct thus is a punishment for the *bias driven devaluation* of the victim, an act that is deemed an independent wrong.

has experienced heteronormative privilege). Failing evidence of such actual experiences, the attempt to measure wrongdoing in this way may amount, as Hurd and Moore have argued, to finding wrongdoing in the mere increased risk of harm.[97] Advocates of hate crime legislation counter that individual victims and perpetrators are the products of social forces of inequality: whether individuals experience in a conscious way their relative levels of oppression or privilege is irrelevant to whether it actually exists. Indeed, the very fact of the crime itself provides *prima facie* evidence of the victim's socially constituted vulnerability and the perpetrator's socially constituted sense of entitlement.[98]

Of course this is right. But if one recognizes that the perpetrator is socially constituted as such, then it becomes difficult to also say that s/he ought to be held personally and individually responsible for his or her actions. Put another way, solving the "harm" question in this way only begs the question of why people who commit offenses in a manner evincing homophobia are more deserving of blame and punishment than those who commit them without such motivations. We are thus directed to a second type of retributivist argument raised in favor of hate crime legislation: that based on the culpability of the offender. Here, advocates contend that punishment should be enhanced not because the harm of a hate crime is greater but because the offender is more blameworthy in some way.

The focus on culpability refocuses justificatory efforts on the core concepts of the normal hate crime narrative: hatred and bias. The discourse revolves around the notion that there just seems to be something particularly loathsome about someone who kills or maims others out of hatred or bias. And advocates of

97. Hurd and Moore 2004:1144.

98. Herek 1992b.

anti-gay hate crime law point out that the state has long recognized that equivalent wrongs may be attended by different levels of accountability and responsibility and ought to be punished differently in response. While intuitively sensible, this narrative of justification raises an important and difficult prior question: on what principle ought the state to distinguish between levels of culpability?

Here we are returned to the reason/emotion problematic that courses through utilitarian justifications of anti-gay hate crime laws. As noted above, law generally distinguishes between different levels of forethought in characterizing crimes as implicating greater or lesser culpability. That is, a person who commits a crime with intent to do so is considered more blameworthy than someone who is merely reckless in engaging in the same prohibited conduct. Emotional states may be relevant but usually only to demonstrate, as a defense, that one's cognitive abilities were impaired.[99] This may be part of the reason why anti-gay hate crime discourse invokes the notion of "bias" (a more clearly cognitive state) alongside the notion of "hatred" (which evokes emotion). In fact, advocates of anti-gay hate crime legislation have largely failed to settle on an account of what a hate crime really is.[100] Advocates frequently move back and forth between

99. Lee 2003. Nussbaum points out that defenses predicated on emotional states (such as the doctrine of "reasonable provocation") are themselves the product of social norms: "The doctrine of 'reasonable provocation' in the Anglo-American criminal law embodies social norms about the occasions on which a "reasonable man" will get violently angry . . . Although judges know well that people got [sic] angry at many other provocations, the assumption behind the doctrine is that social norms should guide norms of sentencing: the well-brought-up person responds with violence to some provocations only. Today the doctrine remains, but the objects have changed." Nussbaum 2001: 162–63.

100. Much of the scholarship on anti-gay hate crime law fails to address this question in any satisfying way. Levin and McDevitt (2002: ch. 1) suggest that some crimes are "obviously" hate crimes, or that one can identify hate crimes on the basis of certain common characteristics (i.e., they tend to be more violent, they often

references to "bias" and "hate" in describing the characteristics of the conduct that the legislation seeks to prohibit. This linguistic slippage has the effect of installing hatred as the touchstone of culpability, while retaining an emphasis on the cognitive processes that are familiar to law. The use of the phrase "hate crime" highlights the egregious and indefensible quality of such crimes, and is favored by political advocacy groups, such as the HRC and the National Gay and Lesbian Task Force, when speaking to their constituents.[101] Legislators, on the other hand, tend to use the term "bias," perhaps deeming it a more appropriate object of legislative disapproval or (alternatively) a more amenable object of the apparatus of deterrence.

But this probably does not reflect a strategic or instrumental discursive choice. Rather, the movement back and forth between discussions of "hatred" and "bias" signals a fundamental lack of clarity about how anti-gay hate crime actually works and why, consequently, a hate crime ought to be punished more severely than its predicate crime. That is, advocates have yet to develop a clear theory of how bias and hatred differ from each other and operate together to produce the necessary degree of culpability.

involve groups of offenders, etc.). But this approach begs the question, What makes a crime "obviously" a hate crime is that there has already been created a socially meaningful category—hate crime—that then defines its contents. And determining which crimes count as hate crimes by describing the characteristics of average hate crimes is plainly tautological. Jenness and colleagues rightly point out that there is no simple one-to-one "mirror" between the material reality of hate crime and what is legally, socially, and politically *recognized* as hate crime. Jenness and Grattet 2004; Jenness and Broad 1997. While some scholars, such as Jacobs and Potter (2000), find this observation to be fundamentally damning to the very notion of hate crimes, I think it signals only that it is crucial for us to determine *how* those legal, social, and political definitions are fleshed out via the justificatory discourses under examination here.

101. Human Rights Campaign, Issues and Legislation, LLEEA Background, available at http://www.hrc.org/issues/federal_leg/lleea/background; National Gay and Lesbian Task Force, Understanding Key Elements of Hate Crime Legislation, available at http://www.ngltf.org/statelocal/hatecrimes.htm.

Instead, they have tended to gloss the issue by asserting that where bias and hatred are found together in the commission of a crime, they create a synergistic effect that renders the resulting offense worse in some way than it otherwise would have been. Whether it is bias that feeds hatred, or hatred that finds particular expression in bias, or whether the two are unintelligible in isolation from one another, remains largely unexplored. Indeed, it is here that justifications based on wrongdoing and culpability tend to blend into one another. For example, one common argument on behalf of hate crime laws suggests that enhanced penalties are warranted because hate crimes tend to be more violent and/or tend to produce greater psychological harm in their victims.[102] Putting aside the empirical uncertainties associated with this claim,[103] what is striking about it is the way it uses harm, or perceived harm, to deductively establish the mental state of the perpetrator.[104]

There are several other ways in which one might conceive of the relationship between hatred and bias in the anatomy of an anti-gay crime, however. One possibility is that hatred and bias are coexisting mental states of significant duration.[105] Unlike action-relative mental states (such as intentionality and knowledge), hatred and bias function together as a kind of foundational cognitive or emotional terrain, upon which particular encounters are played out with more or less predictable consequences. But this account comes too close to suggesting that a person might be punished for beliefs rather than action-as-an-expression-of-belief and so invites the sort of First Amendment challenge that

102. Iganski 2001.

103. *See generally* Jacobs and Potter 2000; Ehrlich 1992.

104. Again, many retributivist theorists find this sort of proxy mechanism unnacceptable. *See supra*, note 91.

105. *See* Hurd 2001 at 219–24.

has nearly extinguished the very viability of hate crime legislation in the past.[106]

Instead, advocates have advanced a more nuanced claim that permits recognition of both bias and hatred as operative in the normal hate crime. In such a crime, bias operates as the dispositional state, while hatred appears as an emotion specific to the circumstances. The mechanism operates something like this: generalized bias against the group is condensed via the emotion of hatred, which is directed toward a particular group-identified victim.[107] Hatred, in this sense, is a vehicle through which bias operates as a kind of prior, foundational mental state. How accurate is this model of the workings of hate and bias? Let us start with what should be an easier question: how certain are we that bias motivated crime even requires the presence of hatred for its accomplishment?[108]

On one level, it seems clear that the ability to physically violate another person requires that the perpetrator suspend his or her belief in the victim's fundamental humanity. Hatred is one way of accomplishing this. But there are others. Rage, for example, or disdain. The key process seems to be *objectification*, whereby one person becomes an object for the enactment of another's passions. Yet objectification alone tells us little about its emotional or cognitive specificity or provenance.[109] As we saw in Chapter 3, feminist, queer, and many other theorists contend that sexual desire may be the most common form of objectification that we observe in contemporary societies. Certainly, advocates

106. *Wisconsin v. Mitchell*, 508 U.S. 476 (1993).

107. Lawrence 2003: 9.

108. Jenness and Grattet observe that hatred may be disappearing as a required element of the offense. Jenness and Grattet 2004: 112–119. *See also* Brick 2007.

109. Nussbaum 2001.

of hate crime legislation do not contend that *all* expressions of objectification are culpable, and one might expect LGB advocates of anti-gay hate crime laws to be particularly be sensitive to the risks of criminalizing them.

Instead, advocates content that only some kinds of objectification are reprehensible and that we can identify what they are and when they occur. It is not objectification *per se* but the quality of objectification that is culpable, which is another way of saying that advocates of hate crime laws are inviting courts to examine passion. But how confident can we be that courts will properly indentify the passions in play? Empirical evidence suggests this may be difficult not only because emotions leave unreliable evidentiary trails in their wake, but also because they may not be identifiable even to the person who experiences them.[110]

## III. Discipline and Punish

Instrumental efficacy aside, this construction of the nature of anti-gay hate crime gives rise to another concern, one centered on a discursive process that has been largely unmarked by LGB activists, theorists, and legal practitioners. This problem emerges as a result of the ways in which law disciplines the evidentiary boundaries within which hate crime cases may be adjudicated. Specifically, law uses a mechanical approach to identify the presence of hatred as a motivation through the deployment of proxy measures. Thus, the inquiry is constructed as a series of questions: Was the defendant heterosexual? How do we know? Was the victim gay? How do we know? How did the *defendant* know? What conduct occurred between the victim and the defendant such that we can infer the existence of animus on the part of the defendant?

110. Kahan and Nussbaum 1996: 284.

This discursive process is both legally and socially powerful. It disciplines unruly facts, rendering them intelligible within an overall story of hatred when, in fact, violent encounters are rarely so simple:

The H. family—mother, father, two young daughters and 17-year-old Joshua, lived on Guadalupe Street in San Jose. William Kiley, *a gay man*, lived across the street; he also owned a rental unit next door to the H.'s. In 1988, Kiley's tenant's dog bit Mrs. H . . . . [a]nimosity between the neighbors was ongoing from that date.

Around June 1990, Kiley bought a lawn mower, which did not have a grass catcher. When he mowed his tenant's lawn, grass clippings would blow onto the H.'s' driveway. This incensed the H.'s . . . In television interviews admitted as evidence at trial, Kiley said the H.'s constantly harassed him because of his sexual orientation. When he contacted an attorney about the harassment, he was told he would need to get proof. *He obtained that proof* on June 11, 1991.

On that date, Kiley again mowed the lawn at his rental. As he was finishing, Mr. H. came home, looked at Kiley, and said, "You cocksucker, I'm tired of your fucking games." . . . Later Joshua appeared at his door, asking if Kiley was "gonna clean up the grass on our driveway." . . . By 8:08 p.m., tensions were so high that Mr. H. called the police hotline to see what could be done. The police recorded the call, which lasted 12 minutes . . . At a certain point during this 12-minute conversation, a fight broke out between Joshua and Kiley.

The fight was captured on Kiley's videotape. It showed an agitated Joshua dancing around Kiley like a boxer, yelling at him to clean up the grass clippings, and pointing at his driveway for approximately one and one-half minutes. During this time Joshua repeatedly called Kiley a "faggot," "queer," and "punk." He taunted Kiley, "come on, let's get it on you faggot queer." After Kiley ordered Joshua to "[g]et off my property," Joshua hit him. Kiley did not respond at first, but then he squirted Joshua with the hose. Joshua became enraged. He took off his shirt, threw it on the car in his driveway, then came after Kiley, hitting and kicking him several times. Kiley never hit back.[111]

In affirming the hate crime conviction of Joshua H., the California Court of Appeals said surprisingly little about this complex set of facts. Instead, in upholding the constitutionality of the state's hate crime statute against vagueness and overbreadth challenges, the court obliquely affirmed the propriety of inferring bias from "speech, writing, or conduct"[112]—a reference perhaps to the epithets Joshua used, or the fact that he selected "a gay man" as an outlet for his brutality.[113] But did Joshua H. beat William Kiley "because" he was gay? Or was it because of a property dispute between neighbors? Perhaps it was both. What is important here is the way in which the inquiry is structured. The material facts bearing on the hate crime inquiry are surprisingly few: evidence of Kiley's homosexuality; Joshua's use of the words "faggot," "queer," and "punk," and the violence of the conduct itself.[114] Of these, references to the homosexuality of victims

111. *In re Joshua H.*, 13 Cal.App.4th 1734 (Cal. Ct. App. 1993) (emphasis added).

112. *Ibid*: 1743.

113. Appellate opinions rarely convey the true brutality of crime (no doubt as a consequence of the formality that attends the appellate process), but the beating suffered by Kiley was a savage one. Hoping to capture the harassment he believed he was suffering at the hands of his neighbors, Kiley set up a video camera in a house across the street from the contentious property line. The videotape of the beating and the battered condition of Kiley's face following the attack are graphically featured in a documentary film by Arthur Dong, *Licensed to Kill* (1997).

114. The court found the violence of Joshua H's conduct to preclude a finding that it was merely expression (and therefore protected under the First Amendment). 13 Cal. App. 4th at 1742–43.

(or the gayness of the neighborhood where an attack has taken place) are probably most common.[115]

The use of categorical assignments is prevalent in such cases, regardless of whether a "hatred" theory or a "discriminatory selection" theory of anti-gay hate crime is at issue.[116] Indeed, where the latter theory is in play, identification of the parties' actual or perceived sexual identities is required. For example, in *People v. Fox*, a New York court rejected a motion to dismiss a hate crime charge predicated on a discriminatory selection theory, on the grounds that the prosecutors did not have to establish actual animus as long as they demonstrated that defendants selected a victim whom they perceived to be gay.[117] With respect to the case at bar, the court noted that

> the grand jury evidence shows that the defendants devised a plan to lure a gay man to a particular location in order to rob him, as Fortunato told Fox and Timmins he had done in the past. The evidence further shows that the defendants followed through on this plan by (1) using the Internet to enter a gay chat room; (2) engaging in conversations in that gay chat room with Sandy, whom they believed to be a gay man; (3) luring Sandy to a remote location with false promises of sexual favors; and (4) attempting to rob Sandy upon his arrival.[118]

115. *See, for example, State v. Timothy K*, 27 P.3d 1263 (Ct. App. Wash. 2001); *People v. Diaz*, 188 Misc. 2d 341 (N.Y. Sup. Ct. 2001); *Cuevas v. State of Florida*, 770 So. 2d 703 (Dist. Ct. App. Fl. 2000); *Bennett v. Texas*, 831 S.W.2d 20 (Ct. App. Tex. 1992); *In re MS*, 10 Cal. 4698 (Cal. Sup. Ct. 1995); *Marcicky v. Renico*, 2003 WL 22272142 (E.D. Mich. 2003); *People v. Fox*, 17 Misc. 3d 281 (Sup. Ct. N.Y. 2007).

116. *See, for example,* In re MS, 10 Cal. 4698 (Cal. Sup. Ct. 1995); People v. Fox, 17 Misc. 3d 281 (Sup. Ct. N.Y. 2007).

117. Fox, 17 Misc. 3d at 281.

118. *Ibid*: 285.

Note that the implication of both cases is that the defendants were not—indeed *could* not—have been gay themselves, even though these "facts" are never explicitly established but only inferred.

These particular cases don't give rise to a suspicion that the defendants might have had more complicated dispositional or emotional states, but one can imagine additional questions that might complicate these stories. For example, what led Fortunato to start trolling gay chat rooms in the first place? What caused Joshua H. to ask William Kiley if Kiley was "going to suck some faggot dick" immediately after he had viciously attacked him—that is, why was this particular image in his mind so soon after such a brutal encounter?[119] These are purely hypothetical questions, of course, and there is no reason to think that the courts got these cases "wrong" by failing to ask them. I pose them only to draw attention to the ways in which evidence that might complicate the animus/desire opposition is bracketed out of a jurisprudence that cares only about categorical status.

The discursive effect of these evidentiary processes is the linking of specific sexual identity categories to a limited array of possible states of passionate engagement. A heterosexual man can only be feeling hatred for his gay male target when he feels this much emotion. The discourse therefore reaffirms the polarization of gay and straight, a process of reification that increases social investments in categorical identity. As a matter of instrumental advocacy, this leads to good outcomes and certain retributive satisfactions. But if we are interested in the social construction of sexuality, law's reconstitution of the predictive binary matrix ought to give us pause.

119. 13 Cal. App. 4at 1740.

One way of illustrating this is to look at a quite different class of cases involving sexuality and violence—cases that stand in uneasy tension with those that allege the commission of anti-gay hate crimes. In these cases, it is the defendant who raises the sexual orientation of the victim (as well as his own) in an effort to establish a particular account of sex and violence. A "homosexual panic" or "sexual advance" defense seeks to mitigate liability or to establish legal justification for an act of violence by asserting a claim that the victim aggressed sexually against the defendant.[120] The defendant may claim that he was fearful of an assault (specifically, of being penetrated) or enraged by the attempt to render him gay.[121] Both of these constructions depend on a notion of male heterosexuality that is gendered in ways predicted by the binary matrix of sex, gender, and sexuality.

What they also do is invite courts to construct particular kinds of stories about the nature of animus—stories that occlude the possibility that desire and hatred might sometimes coexist in the same person and in the same interaction. For example, in *Riddle v. Texas*, Granville Riddle was convicted of capital murder after a judge refused to offer an instruction on a sexual advance defense. Prosecutors alleged that the defendant had killed the victim by hitting him repeatedly with a tire iron, and the court plainly found the evidence of brutality in the crime (the victim was struck over a dozen times) dispositive. On these facts, the

---

120. *See* generally Suffredini 2001; Lee 2003; Howe 2000. So far as I have been able to determine, this is always a "him." I have yet to come across a case involving female defendants and victims that makes the same claim.

121. *See generally* Comstock 1992; Mison 1992; Smythe 2006. *See, for example, State v. Christian* 984 So.2d 132 (Ct. App. La. 2008); *Broome v. State*, 687 N.E.2d 590 (Ct. App. Ind. 1998); *Wiggins v. State*, 1997 WL 124253 (Tenn. Ct. Crim. App. 1997); *Commonwealth v. Pierce*, 642 N.E.2d 579 (Sup. Jud. Ct. Mass. 1994); *Commonwealth v. Cutts*, 831 N.E.2d 1279 (Sup. Jud. Ct. Mass 2005).

court held, it was entirely reasonable for the judge to refuse to offer an instruction on the defendant's claim that he acted in self-defense to repel a sexual advance. And it clearly was, but perhaps not because the amount of violence the defendant employed was so entirely excessive to his claimed objective. Rather, the defense ought not to have been allowed because the evidence of an advance on the part of the victim was itself fishy. By the defendant's own account, he had voluntarily gotten into the victim's bed with him just prior to the murder.

Other cases raising provocation defenses invite similar sorts of simplifying and rationalizing juridical strategies. Quite often, the prosecutor will seek to rebut the defense by offering evidence of the victim's heterosexuality.[122] The court's disposition of these cases leaves the impression that they are cases "about" animus and not desire, but what is sacrificed in this construction of the facts? We may be happy with the outcome of the *Bennett* case (after all, the defendant was unable to mitigate his own liability by blaming the victim for his own murder), but it comes at the price of an overly simplified understanding of sexuality. Did the defendant kill the victim out of a terrified rage (as he claimed)? Or was he perhaps feeling something else?

Even where it fails, the homosexual panic/sexual advance defense is infuriating—perhaps because it reminds us of the complex nature of sexual desire as a motivating emotion. As we saw in Chapter 3, desire is a simultaneously personal and social phenomenon. We are neither fully determined by it, nor are we

---

122. A particularly striking example of this may be found in *Parsons v. Galetka*. There, a federal district court considering a petition for *habeas corpus* rejected a claim of homosexual panic in part because the state trial court had "noticed there was no evidence of the victim being a homosexual and the evidence was of the victim's heterosexual relationships ... Actually, the record in this case also shows counsel had an autopsy examination report that showed no evidence of anal sexuality." 57 F. Supp. 2d 1151, 1157–8 (Utah Dist. Ct. 1999).

free to disregard it. Yet if this is so, what, then, can we say about the authority that we claim in order to punish the Aaron McKinneys[123] of the world? Without resorting to the logic of the predictive binary matrix of sex, gender, and sexuality, how can we know what "really" motivated McKinney to kill Matthew Shepard? If we take seriously the claims of contemporary theorists of sexuality, we may be forced to admit that, not only can we not know whether Aaron McKinney felt mostly hatred or mostly desire before he killed Matthew Shepard, we also cannot know that our own desires are free of unpleasantly aggressive and even violent impulses. Nor can we say which of the vast array of human emotions that is implicated in human sexuality may or may not be susceptible to volitional control.

None of this may matter if all we care about is the disposition of cases. On balance, courts' reliance upon the predictive binary matrix seems to be working in ways that advocates of anti-gay hate crime laws would welcome, making it more difficult to raise homophobic affirmative defenses and less difficult to secure convictions in cases alleging anti-gay hate crime. But both anti-gay hate crime discourse and these affirmative defenses raise similarly disquieting questions about how legal discourse may be participating in the construction of a sexual truth regime that is inimical to sexual freedom. Whether they succeed or fail, claims of anti-gay hate crime and sexual advance both require a fictive disarticulation of the emotive and cognitive dimensions of animus and desire. Of course it is true that law, as a set of structured institutions, must delimit the field of sexual and social possibility. But if we ask courts and juries to make determinations

123. McKinney was one of two men charged in the beating death of Matthew Shepard. His lawyers argued that Shepard made an advance toward McKinney which sparked a memory of childhood molestation suffered by McKinney at the hands of an older man. It was this relived sensation of vulnerability, they argued, that caused McKinney to lash out in violence.

of criminal liability and punishment based on impoverished conceptions of the nature of passion, we are virtually assured that they will do so in ways that replicate the models that lie at the heart of anti-gay violence and discrimination. Given that some people will go as far as murder in order to establish the boundary between heterosexuality and homosexuality publicly and conclusively, ought we to continue to participate in a project that repeatedly announces that same boundary as an essential signifier of identity?

# 5

## Same-Sex Sexual Harassment and the Categorical Imperatives of Identity[1]

*The queer project carries a brief for the weirdness of sex wherever it appears; it is (or should be) agnostic about where, when, and among or between whom the intensities of sex are possible.*

—JANET HALLEY, *"Sexuality Harassment"*[2]

Let's begin with a thought experiment. Imagine, for a moment, that you are a judge presented with the following sets of allegations. Which, if any, suggests to you that someone has been the victim of sexual harassment on the job, such that he or she might have a right to sue for legal redress?

(a) "In the first incident, Craft observed La Day sitting in a car with La Day's girlfriend and saw 'passion marks' on La Day's neck. According to La Day and his girlfriend, Craft approached them and stated, 'I see you got a girl. You know I'm jealous.' On a later date, La Day alleges that Craft approached him from behind while he was bending down and fondled his anus. La Day described the contact as similar to 'foreplay with a woman.' La Day turned around immediately and told Craft

---

1. Portions of this material have appeared previously in *Finding the Sex in Sexual Harassment: How Title VII and Tort Schemes Miss the Point of Same-Sex Hostile Environment Harassment*, *Michigan Journal of Law Reform* 39(3): 391–431.

2. Halley 2002: 98.

not to touch him that way because 'I don't play like that.' Craft laughed and walked away."[3]

(b) "The [conduct complained of consisted of], among other things, being grabbed in the crotch and poked in the anus on numerous occasions, being forced to look at pictures of naked men having sex while his coworkers looked on and laughed, being caressed, hugged, whistled and blown kisses at, and being called 'sweetheart' and 'Muneca.'"[4]

(c) "Jemison began, in view of Shepherd, to 'sit there and play with himself' (that is, to handle his penis) and 'to make it go down his leg.'...... On another occasion in December, Shepherd was lying face-down on a bench in his work area in an effort to alleviate a bout of stomach cramps. When Shepherd looked up, he saw Jemison 'rubbing himself into an erection,' watching Shepherd . . . Jemison told Shepherd, 'If you [don't] turn over, [I'm] liable to crawl up on top of [you] and fuck [you] in the ass.'"[5]

(d) "In June 2001 Dill, who earlier had remarked that Shafer had a 'cheerleader ass' that 'would look real nice on my dick,' forced Shafer's face down to his crotch (while clothed), moving his groin to give the impression that Shafer was performing fellatio. A few weeks later, in the same company, Dill grabbed Shafer's hand and moved it to his crotch (again while clothed) while moaning as if Shafer were masturbating him. The force was enough to put Shafer in fear that Dill would break his arm. The next month Dill approached Shafer in the locker room when Shafer was not wearing a shirt and pulled a handful of hair from Shafer's chest, causing considerable pain.

3. *La Day v. Versus Catalyst Technology, Inc.*, 302 F.3d 474, 476 (5th Cir. 2002).

4. *Rene v. MGM Hotels, Inc.*, 243 F.3d 1206, 1207 (9th Cir 2001). "Muneca" is idiomatic Spanish for "babydoll"—a term one might use for one's girlfriend.

5. *Shepherd v. Slater Steels Corp.*, 168 F.3d 998, 1001 (7th Cir. 1999).

Finally, in August 2001, Dill bit Shafer in the neck hard enough to raise welts, though not to penetrate the skin."[6]

The correct answers are (a) and (c). The other two cases failed at the summary judgment phase—and, indeed, the first and third cases did as well, initially.[7] That is, a court decided that each of these cases could not go forward because no reasonable jury or judge could interpret the facts as stating a legally sufficient claim of sexual harassment on the job.

This seems counterintuitive given what we think we know about what we call "sexual harassment." After all, in each of these cases, a person engaged in apparently unwelcome touching, innuendo, and/or solicitation of another person; and in each case, this conduct was either literally sex-specific, involving primary or secondary sex organs, or it was undertaken using gendered and sexed language ("bitch," "Muneca"). Several of the cases allege sexual batteries. It seems hardly a stretch to suggest that most people would, on the facts as alleged, find these work environments "hostile" and inappropriately sexualized. And yet these cases were dismissed because numerous federal courts found such conduct did not—indeed, *could* not—amount to "sexual harassment." To be precise, they found the alleged conduct could not be deemed "sexual harassment" because it did not occur "because of sex."[8]

6. *Shafer v. Kal Kan Foods, Inc.*, 417 F.3d 663, 665 (7th Cir. 2005).

7. The complaints filed by Shepherd and La Day were both dismissed at the district court level. These decisions were later overturned by appellate courts. *Shepherd*, 168 F.3d at 1000; La Day, 302 F.3d at 476.

8. Even the most cursory examination of the case law of courts adjudicating claims of same-sex harassment reveals that courts vary wildly in their analysis of whether or not the alleged behavior at issue was *caused* by sex. In-depth analyses bear out these surface appearances. *See, for example,* Diefenbach 2007; Zylan 2006.

As perplexing as this might seem at first glance, it is explicable—at least in the sense that the judicial finding becomes understandable—once we reach beyond our everyday understanding of words like "sex", "harassment", "sexual" and "caused", and locate them in their institutional context. What might have looked like an irrational, incoherent same-sex sexual harassment jurisprudence[9] is revealed to be a very particular sort of social construct, the product of juridical *habitus*. Faced with a need to make sense of confusing human behavior, courts and litigants addressing claims of sexual harassment engage in some of their most earnest social scientific projects. Unfortunately, they do so within an impoverished (and frankly idiosyncratic) policy environment. They muse aloud about gender roles, desire, animus, and the unavoidable difficulties of working in the kinds of all-male workplaces that conjure images of a modern day *Lord of the Flies*. They strive to infer sexual identity from behavior and, worse still, motivation from identity. They do all this because they are impelled to do so by the institutional location and doctrinal environment within which sexual harassment claims are brought, heard, and decided. As a result, same-sex harassment adjudications are sites deeply inflected by the reinscription of the categories and presumptions that constitute the binary matrix of sex, gender, and sexuality.

## I. Prohibiting Sexual Harassment Via Title VII of the 1964 Civil Rights Act (It Seemed Like a Good Idea at the Time)

There is no federal statute expressly prohibiting sexual harassment in the workplace, and until very recently, such conduct was

9. See, for example, Diefenbach 2007.

essentially unregulated at the federal level. However, during the early 1980s, the United States Supreme Court issued a series of opinions holding that Title VII of the Civil Rights Act of 1964 prohibits workplace sexual harassment.[10] First, the Court affirmed the right of employees to sue in federal court when they have been subjected to *"quid pro quo"* harassment—that is, when they have been required to submit to sexual contact in order to obtain, hold, or advance in employment.[11] Later, in *Meritor Savings Bank v. Vinson*, the Court extended Title VII protection to include employees subjected to other forms of sexual harassment that are "severe and pervasive" enough to create a hostile work environment.[12] As a consequence of these decisions, the primary mechanism by which employees may seek redress for harm suffered as a result of sexual harassment is a statute that says exactly nothing about the subject:

> It shall be an unlawful employment practice for an employer—
> (1) to fail or refuse to hire or to discharge any individual, or otherwise to discriminate against any individual with respect to his compensation, terms, conditions, or privileges of employment, *because of such individual's race, color, religion, sex, or national origin.*[13]

10. Leeser 2003: 1753–55.

11. *Williams v. Saxbe*, 413 F. Supp. 654 (D.D.C. 1976), *vacated sub nom. Williams v. Bell*, 587 F.2d 1240 (D.C. Cir. 1978); *Barnes v. Costle*, 561 F.2d 983 (D.C. Cir. 1977); *See* Leeser 2003.

12. *Meritor Savings Bank FSB v. Vinson*, 477 U.S. 57, 66 (1986) (protection under Title VII includes protection against "severe and pervasive" harassment that creates a hostile or offensive workplace environment). Leeser points out that claims alleging hostile environments far outpace claims alleging quid pro quo harassment. Leeser 2003:1757 (citing Juliano and Schwab 2001).

13. 42 U.S.C. § 2000e-2 (a)(1) (1994) (emphasis added).

The phrase "because of such individual's. . . sex" establishes the so-called "causation requirement" of Title VII. Courts interpreting the statute in light of claims of harassment return to this phrase again and again as a central limiting principle embedded within the legislation. The causation requirement is, they contend, one of the ways in which courts can weed out legitimate claims of actionable harassment from the potentially endless stream of complaints concerning workplace behavior that might be unpleasant, unsavory, and even illegal under state tort or criminal law, but which is not prohibited by Title VII.

Yet legal scholars, philosophers, social and physical scientists, and many others have long known that determining "causation" is rarely a simple task. What does it mean to say that someone or something caused a certain outcome or effect? It is apparent that any particular event might be understood as having been caused by relatively more or less (and often different) causal factors depending upon how far back in time and how wide in scope one wishes to cast the net of inquiry. In law, this ambiguity is only amplified because analyses of causation are investigations into the proper attribution of responsibility. For example, let's say that an oil company drills in very deep water off the American coastline, the consequence of which is an oil rig explosion and spill that kills 11 of the company's employees, impacts local businesses, and produces lasting harm to the ecosystem in the water and on coastal lands.[14] Let us further imagine that we can identify all of the possible elements, events, and activities that came together in the moments, hours, days, and weeks before the explosion. We might consider human actions, the functioning of a host of interoperative technologies, weather, tides, gravity, the comings and goings of things and creatures that inhabit

14. Robertson and Krauss 2010.

the sea, etc. If it is true—as it likely is—that the absence of any one of these events or elements would have led to a different (better) outcome, and if it is further true that the company was able to exercise control over only a tiny fraction of them, then does it make sense as an empirical matter to say that the company *caused* the disaster? Physicists, chemists, and engineers would almost certainly argue otherwise, but the law is quite likely to say just that.

Perhaps this is best thought of as a policy judgment. Law may embody a social or moral view that the company ought to be held responsible for culpable recklessness or negligence. Attributing causation signals that it was wrong for the company to have been drilling when it couldn't guarantee the safety of the enterprise. Alternatively, law may embody the principles of behavioral economics. In that case, requiring the company to bear the costs of the disaster is a way of encouraging others to take the sort of precautionary measures that might prevent or mitigate future calamities. In fact, it is difficult to view law's various notions of causation as anything other than a set of policy judgments because (language and appearances to the contrary notwithstanding) not only do legal inquiries into causation never consider the full array of possible influences or factors leading to an event or outcome, but such inquiries are attended by little coherence or rigor.[15] This is true for many reasons (none of which we can engage here); as a practical matter, we can simply observe that legal causation emerges as the product of a variety of rules, practices, and devices that have evolved over time and in site-specific ways.

For analytical philosophers H.L.A. Hart and Tony Honore, legal causation is a complex animal, sprawling across a multitude of legal domains and clustering around the notion of intentional,

15. Jones and Goldsmith 2005.

voluntary, human action.[16] In their book *Causation in the Law*—first published in 1959, but still perhaps the most comprehensive examination of the subject—Hart and Honore argue for an institutionally specific understanding of legal causation. As Nicola Lacey summarizes it, their position is constituted by four subclaims:

> First, causal explanation is not the same as causal attribution. The explanatory statement that a fire came about through the combination of naked flame, combustible material, and oxygen in the air employs a notion of cause different from the attributive statement that the person holding the match caused the fire. Secondly, the point of view from which a statement is made will affect the causal account given. For example, a political activist might attribute a drought to a governmental failure to address environmental concerns, while a meteorologist might attribute it to weather. Thirdly, the detailed factual context will affect the causal account given. While normally we would not cite the presence of oxygen in the air as a causal factor in a fire, we would do so if the fire occurred in a factory where the productive process was such that oxygen had to be specifically excluded. Finally, the disciplinary context in which a causal statement is made will affect its meaning. Causation in law is not the same as causation in morals, and it is very different from causation in science.[17]

For Hart and Honore, law's approach to legal causation is structured and limited by notions of harm, intentional action,

16. See Lacey 2006: 963–94.

17. *Ibid*: 967.

and the connections that may legitimately be established between them:

> All forms of legal responsibility have a limited scope. Rules of law determine expressly or implicitly what is the harm for which punishment or compensation may be exacted, and how it must be connected with the defendant's conduct in order for responsibility to arise.[18]

The facts that will be deemed relevant and material, the rules that permit some sorts of relationships to be considered (but not others), and the disciplinary perspectives that may be entertained as bearing on the questions at hand are circumscribed by, and themselves define, the parameters of legally cognizable harms. Plainly, policy preferences—as they have been determined through processes of political mobilization and political mediation—have a role to play here. For example, the very notion that sexual harassment on the job ought to constitute a legally redressable harm at all is a fact of very recent origin, the result of feminist political activism in and around the state's core institutions.[19]

Law's identification of the specific nature of the harm posed by sexual harassment may be understood as partly the result of political mobilization and partly the result of institutional innovation. But once sexual harassment was identified as something that works a *discriminatory* harm, it was confined within a specifically limited universe of legal inquiry. Locating sexual harassment law within the larger body of anti-discrimination law was a principled choice, given a certain understanding of feminist theory and practice. It was also strategically clever and

18. Hart and Honore 1985: xlvii.

19. *See* Marshall 2005.

effective. But because a given notion of compensable harm serves to organize legal inquiries into causation, it was also materially consequential in ways that Hart and Honore's theory would, perhaps, have predicted.

As Lacey suggests, Hart and Honore's account implies a sociological perspective on causation.[20] By emphasizing the location of causation requirements in factual, perspectival, and disciplinary contexts, Hart and Honore draw attention to the ways in which a singular concept—attribution of causality—can be the product of a variety of analyses. They also vigorously distinguish legal concepts of causation from non-legal analogues. Law's notion of causation is not, they argue, the same as morality's notion, nor is it the same as a claim of causation from science or metaphysics. For Hart and Honore, confusion can only result from the mixing of science and law in causation inquiries. At the same time, they contend that legal causation is susceptible to precise empirical and analytical definition, even as they seek to retain the perspective of "common sense" in legal analyses of causation. Hart and Honore recognize that there are layers of incoherence and confusion embedded in social practices of assigning and understanding causal relationships, but they also understand that courts are committed to using "the ordinary man's conception of cause" as a way of assigning legal responsibility.[21]

---

20. Lacey 2006: 955–58.

21. Hart and Honore at xxxiii–xxxiv ("For though in everyday life we make a distinction between conditions and causes and, with the help of the distinction, explain puzzling events, control our environment, and assign praise or blame, we are often unable to explain the principles on which we do so. Hence lawyers in particular, when called upon to give an account of the causal principles they apply, often resort to obscure metaphors of 'causal potency,' the "exhaustion" of causes, and the "breaking of causal chains." Though in legal contexts [the concept of causation] has to be refined and modified in various ways, the clarification of the structure of ordinary causal statements was and is an indispensable first step towards understanding the use of causal notions in the law.").

Other legal scholars and practitioners find intra-judicial variation in notions of causation deeply problematic. Some critics think law ought to import more behavioral concepts and theories into its evaluations of causation and responsibility. If, as they contend, the point of law's attributing causal power to someone or something is to ensure the proper assignment of risk or to develop sanctions that are maximally calibrated to "induce people to behave more constructively,"[22] then inviting lawyers and judges to partake of the most rigorous and well-developed insights of behavioral science makes good sense.[23] Other critics—those described by Hart and Honore as "causal minimalists"—contend that legal actors and institutions ought to be more humble in their aspirations. For them, only inquiries into "actual" causation are institutionally legitimate. Most first-year law students are familiar with the notion of "actual" (or "but for") causation. The test for actual causation posits that the causal force of an action or characteristic is established if, *but for* that action or characteristic, the outcome in question would not have occurred.[24] As we shall see, Title VII causation inquiries frequently revolve around this "but for" language. However, there is nothing "minimal" about it; courts expend considerable effort to reduce the complexity of sexualized and gendered workplace interactions to the mechanical imperatives of actual causation. In this effort, they depend upon and repeatedly invoke the predictive binary matrix of sex, gender, and sexuality, reproducing what Berger and Luckmann might call a "recipe knowledge" of sexual desire.

22. Jones and Goldsmith 2005: 408.

23. *Ibid.*

24. Many scholars and practitioners consider "but for" causation the only legally sustainable notion of causation; they contend that all other understandings of causation fall into the (to them, unprincipled) category of "policy" decisions. This "policy" notion of causation is generally referred to as "proximate causation."

## II. Because of Sex

As noted above, Title VII prohibits "discrimination . . . because of . . . sex."[25] The spareness of this formulation means that causation inquiries in Title VII sexual harassment cases are plagued by at least two sources of ambiguity. First, what does the term "sex" mean? In popular usage, it can refer to one's biological sex—to the fact that an individual is either male or female. It can also refer to sexual activity or sexual organs.[26] Complicating matters considerably, feminist theory has added the insight that "sex" (maleness/femaleness) is better understood as a constellation of socially constructed features collectively termed "gender."[27] Indeed, to say that the multiple nature of the word "sex" has produced a problem or two within feminist theory and practice would be a profound understatement. Within contemporary feminist scholarship, sex is sometimes gender.[28] Other times, sex is sexuality.[29]

25. 42 U.S.C. § 2000e-2 (a)(1) (1994).

26. Webster's Collegiate Dictionary defines "sex" as: "1: either of the two major forms of individuals that occur in many species and that are distinguished respectively as female or male 2: the sum of the structural, functional, and behavioral characteristics of living things that are involved in reproduction by two interacting parents and that distinguish males and females 3 a: sexually motivated phenomena or behavior b: sexual intercourse 4: genitalia." *Merriam-Webster's Collegiate Dictionary* 1073 (10th ed. 1998).

27. *See* Lorber 1994; Connell, 1987; Butler 1990. As Butler puts it: "If gender is the cultural meanings that the sexed body assumes, then a gender cannot be said to follow from a sex in any one way. Taken to its logical limit, the sex/gender distinction suggests a radical discontinuity between sexed bodies and culturally constructed genders.". Butler 1990: 6. Note that—unlike many feminist theorists—Butler does not claim that "gender" is inscribed upon an anatomical "sex." Instead, she claims that "sex" and "gender" are equally constructed by social and cultural forces, with one function of "gender" being the perpetuation of the idea that "sex" is fundamental, or "prediscursive." *Ibid*: 6–7.

28. Butler 1990; Lorber 1994. *See also* Lorber and Farrell, 1991.

29. *See* MacKinnon 1989; Dworkin 1987. For a foundational, nuanced treatment of the relationship between biological sex, sexuality, and the social identities associated with them as gender, see Beauvoir 1953.

For Catharine MacKinnon, a crucially important contributor to sexual harassment jurisprudence, gender vs. sexuality is a distinction without a difference. In MacKinnon's epistemological framework, gender is sexuality, which is the product of male domination and the essence of power itself.[30] (More on this in a bit.)

Even if one is able to adequately define "sex," a second question arising from the causation requirement immediately follows: what does it mean to say something is "caused" by sex? In the early days of sexual harassment litigation, one seemingly straightforward answer was that the harassing behavior was the result of the harasser's unreciprocated sexual desire for the target.[31] This was because most early harassment cases involved female targets and male harassers, and because heterosexuality is the presumed orientation of most people.[32] As Justice Scalia noted in *Oncale v. Sundowner Offshore Oil Services*:

> Courts and juries have found the inference of discrimination easy to draw in most male-female sexual harassment situations, because the challenged conduct typically involves explicit or implicit proposals of sexual activity; it is reasonable to

30. *See* MacKinnon 1989.

31. Note that this can be an issue even in cases not alleging *quid pro quo* harassment: a demand for sexual contact that either promises tangible job benefits in return for compliance or threatens adverse economic consequences in return for lack of compliance, or both. Many cases alleging hostile environment harassment assert that repeated, unrequited demands for sexual contact from a coworker or supervisor—while not leading to specific employment consequences in terms of compensation or advancement—make the workplace an abusive setting.

32. It is indisputable that this is the fundamental assumption held by most Americans. However, there has long been empirical evidence of a high incidence of homo-, and bisexuality in the population, placing this truism in doubt (even when evaluated according to purely behavioral criteria). *See, e.g.,* Kinsey 1948; Bell, et al, 1978. A prior question—of even greater import—is what it means to "count" one as homo-, hetero-, or bisexual. To quote Kinsey's observation of over a half-century ago: "[t]he world is not to be divided into sheep or goats," Kinsey 1948: 639.

assume those proposals would not have been made to someone of the same sex.[33]

In this formulation, sexual desire solves both the "sex" and "because of" problems; the behavior is discriminatory, in the sense contemplated by the statute, because women have to endure it and men do not, and because this differential experience of the workplace is the result of the woman's sex or gender or both (it doesn't really matter which one—or it does, but it is the woman's gender that makes her desirable and a target in the first place).

In same-sex harassment cases, however, courts have had enormous difficulty in assessing the role of sexual desire in motivating harassment.[34] This difficulty does not emerge because the cases are factually more complex; if anything, the behavior alleged in many of the same-sex harassment cases is more explicitly sexualized, more expressly focused on sexual organs, and more clearly evocative of sexual acts.[35] Instead, courts' inability to say with certainty what causes same-sex sexual harassment

33. *Oncale v. Sundowner Offshore Svcs., Inc.* 523 U.S. 75, 80 (1998).

34. *See Oncale,* 523 U.S. 75; *McWilliams v. Fairfax County Supervisors,* 72 F.3d 1191 (4th Cir. 1996), *cert. denied,* 117 S. Ct. 72 (1996); *Hampel v. Food Ingredients Specialties, Inc.,* 729 N.E.2d 726 (Ohio 2000); *Johnson v. Hondo, Inc.,* 125 F.3d 408 (7th Cir. 1997). Because courts assume sexuality is dichotomous (persons are either homo- or heterosexual, but either way, orientation is fixed and certain), they are hard pressed to make sense of cases alleging demonstrably sexual forms of harassment that appear to fall outside the expected sexual behavior of the litigants. Instead of relying on an examination of the acts, *per se,* courts nonetheless attempt to divine the purpose of the acts in assessing whether or not they were sexual *enough* to be actionable.

35. More to the point, the unique difficulty in assessing motivation in same-sex cases is not traceable to the fact that cases alleging different-sex harassment are factually *less* complex than those alleging same-sex harassment. As the discussion *infra* makes clear, there is no simple answer to the question of what motivates sexually aggressive behavior in the workplace.

results from a fundamental flaw in existing sexual harassment jurisprudence: its conflation of sexuality with gender in service of what Janet Halley has described as "sexual subordination feminism."[36] More specifically, same-sex harassment litigation has led courts to reconsider and redefine the harm that Title VII's prohibition on harassment is designed to punish and prohibit, and then to apply that regulatory paradigm in light of "common-sense" notions of why gay and straight people do the things they do. Because a finding of discrimination both proves too much and too little in these cases, courts engaged in Title VII causation inquiries produce a deeply regressive sexual truth regime: one that insists on clear categorization while inviting homophobic practices in both the workplace and the courtroom.

## A. Sex as Harm: Catharine MacKinnon and the Structuring of Causation Inquiries in Sexual Harassment Litigation

As an anti-discrimination statute, Title VII targets conduct that disadvantages one group of people versus another: the law expressly prohibits discrimination on the basis of race, color, religion, sex, or national origin. Thus, the harm that is the object of the statute is the harm of discrimination—of being treated differently, and less well, than others with respect to core social functions and institutions, for the reason that you are a member of a particular social group. In her landmark study of the phenomenon, Catherine MacKinnon argued convincingly that sexual harassment in the workplace works such a discriminatory harm

36. Halley 2002: 81.

upon women.[37] Note, however, that other sorts of harm might also issue from harassment that takes a sexual or sexualized form. For example, many people would find an oversexualized workplace harmful, whether or not it was designed or intended to treat one group of workers better or worse than another.[38] Unwelcome or inappropriate sexualization of a person or a work environment might constitute a generalized dignitary harm—perhaps a common law tort.[39] Harassment might also be experienced by an individual as demeaning or physically abusive, whether or not there was any discriminatory impact such as is contemplated by Title VII.[40] Being subjected to unwanted poking, grabbing, and touching by creepy coworkers may be identifiable harms that take on a particular quality and raise particular concerns because they occur in the workplace. But they need not be discriminatory harms.

Nonetheless, most workplace harassment claims are brought under the auspices of Title VII and so must allege discrimination. To understand why, we must look to the influence of feminist legal scholar Catharine MacKinnon. As Janet Halley has written, MacKinnon's landmark 1979 book, *Sexual Harassment of Working Women*, "did more than anything else to provide the theoretic basis for sex harassment law."[41] MacKinnon also participated in some of the early litigation establishing sexual harassment as a cognizable

37. MacKinnon 1979.

38. As Halley demonstrates convincingly, others may find sexualized workplaces deeply pleasurable. Halley 2002: 95–98.

39. Ehrenreich 1999.

40. In addressing claims brought under Title VII, courts frequently consider the alternative theory that the individual is being harassed because he or she simply isn't well liked, or is perceived as psychologically or physically vulnerable, or is particularly sensitive to sexual innuendo or humor. If the court finds this likely, the plaintiff cannot recover.

41. Halley 2002: 82.

harm under Title VII of the 1964 Civil Rights Act.[42] Both the Equal Employment Opportunity Commission and the United States Supreme Court largely adopted the logic and overall framework of MacKinnon's theory of sexual harassment in determining that claims of harassment could be brought pursuant to Title VII.[43]

In MacKinnon's account, sexuality, gender, and power are mutually constitutive: "men in particular, if not men alone, sexualize hierarchy; gender is one."[44] For MacKinnon, sexuality and violence are virtually indistinguishable; both are created by men to ensure the perpetuation of male dominance.[45] Women, in this view, are the objects of male domination, with no independent sexual identity of their own.[46] Even more important for sexual harassment analysis, in MacKinnon's account, the word "sex" no longer has three separate meanings[47]; instead, the three meanings

42. MacKinnon was co-counsel on Meritor Savings Bank v. Vinson, which held that a plaintiff could establish a viable Title VII claim via allegations of a sexually hostile work environment. *See Meritor Savings Bank v. Vinson*, 1986 WL 728234 (U.S.) (Appellate Brief).

43. *See generally* Schultz 2003: 2077–2087.

44. MacKinnon 1989: 127.

45. As MacKinnon puts it: "In this light, the major distinction between intercourse (normal) and rape (abnormal) is that the normal happens so often that one cannot get anyone to see anything wrong with it." *Ibid*: 146. This may be one of MacKinnon's most controversial claims. Few feminists—even those who generally agree with MacKinnon's view that sexual harassment is a form of sex-based discrimination— would also subscribe to her view that sex and rape are barely distinguishable. For our purposes, it is enough to note that this assertion forms an important part of MacKinnon's theory of sexuality as male power.

46. ". . . there is no such thing as a woman as such; there are only walking embodiments of men's projected needs." MacKinnon 1989: 119. Note that MacKinnon uses the term "woman" to mean a socially constructed woman; this being the case, it matters not whether the parties are biologically male or female. What matters is the social position occupied. If this sounds confusing, it is because the account may be tautological.

47. The three meanings are: sexuality, biological/anatomical sex, and gender.

are collapsed into one signifier of male domination.[48] While even the Supreme Court has acknowledged the role of MacKinnon's scholarship in shaping the jurisprudence of sexual harassment,[49] no court has expressly recognized or embraced the theoretical conception of sexuality that is central to her perspective and therefore underlies the jurisprudence. It seems unlikely that most courts analyzing harassment claims understand that, in adopting the "because of sex" formulation as it has been derived from MacKinnon's analysis of harassment as a form of sex-based/gender discrimination, they are also subscribing to the following theory of that connection:

> To be clear: what is sexual is what gives a man an erection. Whatever it takes to make a penis shudder and stiffen with the experience of its potency is what sexuality means culturally. Whatever else does this, fear does, hostility does, hatred does, the helplessness of a child or a student or an infantilized or restrained or vulnerable woman does, revulsion does, death does. Hierarchy, a constant creation of person/thing, top/bottom, dominance/subordination relations, does.[50]

If one subscribes to MacKinnon's view of sexuality, it becomes easy to see how any sort of sexual harassment of women by men—sexual imagery on the walls, uninvited, or even invited, sexual advances, invasive touching—could constitute discrimination on the basis of sex, whether or not sex is defined as gender, biological sex, or sexuality. In adjudicating what might be deemed the "first wave" of sexual harassment claims, many courts simply

48. "To be rapable, a position that is social not biological, defines what a woman is." *Ibid*: 178.

49. *Burlington Indus. v. Ellerth*, 524 U.S. 742, 752 (1998).

50. MacKinnon 1989: 137.

assumed (and naturalized) the relationship between these concepts.[51]

However, the statute itself was hardly limited to the male harasser/female target fact pattern. And so lawyers did what lawyers do: they brought different kinds of cases that seemed to be "about" sexual harassment, even as they were factually variant from MacKinnonesque scenarios of male sexual domination. As new forms of harassment—particularly cases of same-sex harassment—came to the courts' attention, the presumed relationship between sex, gender, and sexuality was gradually exposed to analysis.[52] Because they had not adopted (nor even, in all likelihood, understood) MacKinnon's full theory of harassment, courts struggled to fit the diversity of sexual harassment cases within the existing framework. To do so, they had to delve more deeply into the motivating forces in harassment cases. For example, many cases—like *Oncale*—involved the harassment of assertedly heterosexual men by other assertedly heterosexual men.[53] Others involved the sexually explicit harassment of self-identified gay men or lesbians by heterosexual coworkers or supervisors.[54] In some cases, this harassment included what

51. In short, while MacKinnon provided a theory of how sex, sexuality, and gender were interconnected—with this interconnection most obvious in cases of sexual harassment or rape—those who subscribed to her claim that sexual harassment is a form of sex-based discrimination largely assumed a *natural* connection between the three. Courts typically refer to this assumption as a "natural" or "reasonable" inference. It should be readily apparent why advocates of gender and sexual equity ought to resist this reflexive inferential gesture.

52. *Wrightson v. Pizza Hut of Am., Inc.*, 99 F.3d 138, 142 (4th Cir. 1996); *Quick v. Donaldson Co.*, 90 F.3d 1372, 1378 (8th Cir. 1996); *Hopkins v. Baltimore Gas & Elec. Co.*, 77 F.3d 745, 751 (4th Cir. 1996), *cert. denied*, 117 S. Ct. 70 (1996); *English v. Pohanka Chantilly, Inc.*, 190 F. Supp. 2d 833 (E.D. Va. 2002).

53. *Oncale v. Sundowner Offshore Svcs., Inc.*, 523 U.S. 75 (1998); *Breitenfeldt v. Long Prairie Packing Co.*, 48 F. Supp. 2d 1170 (1999); *McWilliams*, 72 F.3d 1191.

54. *Dillon v. Frank*, 952 F.2d 403 (6th Cir. 1992); *Simonton v. Runyon*, 2000 U.S. App. LEXIS 21139 (2d Cir. 2000); *Higgins v. New Balance Athletic Shoe, Inc.*, 194 F.3d 252 (1st Cir. 1999).

were, on their face, invitations to sexual contact.[55] In other cases, self-identified or presumed gay/lesbian co-workers or supervisors harassed assertedly heterosexual people of the same sex, frequently by subjecting them to uninvited sexual advances or contacts.[56]

These incidents of same-sex harassment seem either to fall outside MacKinnon's theory of the harm of sexual harassment or to call the harassment-as-discrimination theory itself into question. After all, the harassment of women by men on the job was first deemed actionable because it represented a kind of condensation point of gender-based power: men, as a class, exert their power over women in part through masculinity as it is expressed in sexual dominance. For her part, MacKinnon has claimed that the biological sex of the harasser and the target are immaterial to the gendered dimensions of sexual harassment, and therefore irrelevant to whether same-sex harassment claims should be actionable under Title VII (they should).[57] For MacKinnon, the essential

55. The most common advances include a request or demand for fellatio or anal sex. *See, e.g., Simonton*, 2000 U.S. App. LEXIS 21139 at 3. Note that the vast majority of same-sex harassment cases that have been brought—prior to and after the *Oncale* decision—involve male litigants.

56. *See Kelly v. City of Oakland*, 198 F.3d 779 (9th Cir.1999); *Merritt v. Del. River Port Auth.*, LEXSEE 1999 U.S. Dist. LEXIS 5896 (E.D. Penn. 1999); *Shepherd v. Slater Steels Corp.*, 168 F.3d at 998; *Carney v. City of Shawnee*, 38 F. Supp. 2d 905 (D. Kan. 1999); *Brewer v. Hillard*, 15 S.W.3d 1 (Ky. Ct. App. 1999). *But see Smith v. USA Truck, Inc.*, 1998 U.S. Dist. LEXIS 3455 (W.D. Ark. 1998) (construing Ark. Law with reference to Title VII to hold that "one instance" of unwelcome act of fellatio does not give rise to employer liability).

57. MacKinnon 1989. This is because, according to MacKinnon, biological sex is itself socially constructed. What it means, socially, to be a woman is what is important to her theory of sexual power, not the particular assemblage of anatomical parts. Although she has spent little time explicating the point, MacKinnon has said that gay men and lesbians are not exempt from the oppressive dynamics of sexuality. *See also* Janet Halley's analysis of MacKinnon's briefing of the *Oncale* case to the Supreme Court. Halley convincingly argues that MacKinnon may have invited the Court to articulate a homophobic standard of causation—one that equates a finding

feature of sexuality is gendered power, whether it is expressed between men and women, men and men, women and women, or a man or woman alone in his/her most private moments.

Critics of the MacKinnon approach have tended to argue a different tack but on similar anti-discrimination terrain. In a widely read and influential law review article, Katherine Franke argued that same-sex harassment should be actionable under Title VII not because men and women are interchangeable in the MacKinnon sense[58] but because sexual harassment is a "technology of sexism."[59] According to Franke, what men are doing when they are grabbing the genitalia of other men is not seeking sexual gratification but engaging in a form of gender discipline. Franke's argument is appealing because it satisfies the demands of Title VII causation, while avoiding some of the more totalizing gestures of MacKinnon's structural account. On the other hand, Franke's argument, which has been embraced and pursued by a good number of litigators, has run into its own trouble as it has been taken up by courts determined not to allow Title VII "sex" discrimination claims to turn into "sexual orientation discrimination" claims. I discuss this further, below.[60]

Vicki Schultz—while generally approving of MacKinnon's view that sexuality and gender are intricately connected—blames

of "homosexuality" in the perpetrator with an adequate showing of but for causation. Halley 2002: 80.

58. By this, I mean that MacKinnon imagines a totalizing structure of male domination. Within this structure, biological males and females may occupy or play different roles but the structure itself is hierarchically male. In other words, a lesbian woman may be the boss, but when she harasses her female secretary, she is objectifying her as any male boss would. Sexuality is imprinted with gender domination, whether it is heterosexual or homosexual. *See* MacKinnon 1989.

59. Franke 1997: 693.

60. *See* the discussion, *infra* at pp. 190-195.

what she calls the "desire-dominance paradigm" for misinterpreting the basic function of sexual harassment.[61] For Schultz, desire often has little to do with sexual harassment; instead, it is about undermining worker competence in an effort to assert male privilege and the exclusivity of male occupational domains.[62] Schultz goes further than Franke and others in her critique of the sexuality-gender framework[63] by noting that there may be an arena of sexual harassment that has nothing to do with efforts to assert gender inequality at all. Noting that "some discussions and overtures—and perhaps even some forms of outright discrimination based on sexual orientation—are not gender-based attempts at denigration,"[64] Schultz underscores her point that her approach goes beyond that of MacKinnon and others by declining to "conflate harassment on the basis of gender with harassment on the basis of sexual orientation."[65]

Nonetheless, the thrust of Schultz's account remains embedded within a framework defined by discriminatory harm and, like Franke's, it continues to define sexual harassment in largely instrumental terms. Sexual harassment serves a "function" or is a "technique." This framing of the conduct is entirely sensible, given that each theorist is trying to make a claim about harassment as a form of discrimination subject to the state's legal and disciplinary power.[66] Because each is trying to meet the institutional demands of the causation requirement, she produces an account that conceives of the behavior at issue in these cases as issuing from actors subject

61. Schultz 1998: 1687–89.

62. *Ibid*: 1687.

63. Abrams 1998: 1213–14.

64. Schultz 1998: 1787.

65. *Ibid*.

66. Foucault, et al, 2007: 277.

to categorization by gender, sex, and sexual identity. As Todd Brower has written, "law requires clear distinctions. Title VII in particular requires neat categorization of sexuality and gender and sex."[67] Still, Franke and Schultz offer ways to understand same-sex harassment that do not reduce to MacKinnon's conflation of desire and dominance. Indeed, they seem to agree that desire is largely peripheral to incidents of sexual harassment.

Not so, according to the United States Supreme Court. In 1998, the Court took up a same-sex harassment case called *Oncale v. Sundowner Offshore Svcs., Inc.* Prior to that case, federal courts had been noticeably split on the question of whether allegations of same-sex harassment were actionable under Title VII.[68] In deciding *Oncale*, the Court answered that question clearly (they are), but its cutely worded opinion invited new trouble, most of it circulating around the causation requirement. One thing the Court did make clear, however, is that evidence of homosexual desire by the defendant would satisfy the statute's causation requirement. As a consequence, courts now pointedly engage in processes of classification and identification of motive forces, relations, and persons. In so doing, they draw upon and authorize "commonsense" understandings of the binary nature of sex, gender, and sexuality.

## B. The Common Sense of Oncale v. Sundowner Offshore Oil Svcs.

As a roustabout on an oil rig stationed in the Gulf of Mexico, Joseph Oncale was subjected to the sort of harassing behavior

67. Brower 2009: 76.

68. Storrow 1998: 689–716.

that is alleged with some frequency in same-sex harassment suits arising from all-male workplaces.[69] Oncale was regularly teased, poked, threatened, and assaulted by his coworkers. They held him down and rubbed their genitals against his body in view of each other, threatened him with rape, and penetrated him with a bar of soap. When he complained, his supervisor brushed off the conduct, noting that Oncale's alleged harassers had "picked on him all the time too" including calling him a "faggot."[70] Oncale eventually quit, noting on his pink slip that he was doing so because he could no longer endure the "harassment and verbal abuse."[71] He then sued in district court, which dismissed his claim on the grounds that "Mr. Oncale, a male, has no cause of action under Title VII for harassment by male coworkers."[72] Oncale appealed, lost again in the 5th Circuit, and appealed to the U.S. Supreme Court. The Court granted *certiorari* to clarify the status of same-sex harassment claims under Title VII, which had been inconsistently handled by the courts below.

In its opinion, the *Oncale* Court established three nominal routes by which a plaintiff could make out a same-sex harassment case under Title VII:

> [An inference of erotic attachment] would be available to a plaintiff alleging same-sex harassment, if there were credible evidence that the harasser was homosexual. But harassing

69. Because of the procedural posture of the case, the Supreme Court treated Oncale's allegations as true. The case was never tried, so the facts may have been subject to dispute. (Oncale settled after issuance of the Supreme Court's opinion in the case, having determined he was unlikely to prevail on remand.) Whether or not Oncale's allegations were true, the point is that the Supreme Court decided his case as though they were.

70. *Oncale v. Sundowner Offshore Svcs., Inc.*, 523 U.S. at 77.

71. *Ibid.*

72. *Ibid.*

conduct need not be motivated by sexual desire to support an inference of discrimination on the basis of sex. A trier of fact might reasonably find such discrimination, for example, if a female victim is harassed in such sex-specific and derogatory terms by another woman as to make it clear that the harasser is motivated by general hostility to the presence of women in the workplace. A same-sex harassment plaintiff may also, of course, offer direct comparative evidence about how the alleged harasser treated members of both sexes in a mixed-sex workplace.[73]

Regardless of the route a plaintiff might choose to pursue, however, the *Oncale* court made clear that s/he "must always prove that the conduct at issue was not merely tinged with offensive sexual connotations, but actually constituted 'discrimina[tion]. . . because of. . . sex.'"[74] This language was important because it served to re-fix the boundaries of harassment litigation within the policy environment of anti-discrimination law. Reiterating that the harm covered by the statute was the harm of discrimination—not the dignitary harms associated with unwanted or inappropriate sexualization of the individual or the workplace—the Court refocused litigation practice on the categorical relations between persons (and persons-as-members-of-groups) that constitute the *sine qua non* of discrimination.

While the Court was not particularly clear in defining the causation requirement, its focus on discrimination as the harm of actionable harassment specified the evidentiary boundaries and the factual and legal questions that could and would frame future litigation. To begin with, the Court clarified that it would

73. *Ibid*: 80.

74. *Ibid*.

be entirely legitimate—indeed, almost *de rigeur*—for plaintiffs to seek discovery bearing on the sexual orientation of the harasser in same-sex harassment cases. Why? The Court seemed to think its erotic attraction theory was so plain as not to require explanation, but the presumptions embedded within its first proposed "evidentiary route" seem to multiply upon inspection, suggesting that the Court was operating with (and authorizing) a radically reduced conception of sexuality and sexual interaction. For the *Oncale* court (and its progeny), a judicial finding of erotic attraction would satisfy the causation requirement of Title VII because, as the Court suggested with respect to different-sex harassment, such a finding would provide strong evidence that the conduct at issue would not have been directed at members of the "other" sex.

This theory has a surface plausibility, but when examined further, it is revealed as a set of rules that rig the game in advance. Remember that the operative question in a hostile environment sexual harassment case is why did coworker (or supervisor) X engage in certain sexualized conduct toward coworker (or subordinate) Y? Perhaps, the Court is saying, X wished to have sex with Y and so was using his or her position or proximity to subject Y to advance unwanted, repeated, and (at best) socially awkward solicitations. If the conduct was ambiguous—and by definition it was in a hostile environment case[75]—how can we tell if desire was at work here? One obvious way, in the Court's view, would be to line up the categories of sex and sexuality and

---

75. A "quid pro quo" claim alleges a direct solicitation of sexual contact. Of course, it is not uncommon for cases brought under Title VII to allege both kinds of violation. Where the solicitation was either ambiguous on its face, or ambiguous because it was accompanied by other sorts of conduct (perhaps evincing animus or violence), a hostile environment claim may seem more promising. As the *Oncale* Court's instruction suggests, there is a variant of quid pro quo theory embedded within hostile environment theories of harassment.

see what they would predict with respect to an underlying motivation. If X is categorically gay, and Y is categorically a member of the *same sex* as X, then it is reasonable to read X's conduct as being driven by sexual desire and, further, to assume that—had Y been of a categorically different sex—X would not have desired Y. Thus, but for causation would be persuasively (if not conclusively) established, and the case should go forward.

Not long after *Oncale* was announced, legal scholar Janet Halley predicted that the Court's suggestion that plaintiffs seek "credible evidence" of the alleged harasser's sexual orientation constituted an invitation to courts to "[*implicitly*] declare open season on gay men and lesbians, leaving us unprotected from lawsuits that threaten our very ability to work and learn."[76] She was right. Justice Scalia's suggestion in *Oncale* that courts use "common sense" in interpreting whether sexualization practices in the workplace amounted to actionable harassment or mere coworker ribbing led to a "commonsense" pattern of judgments finding sexual behavior by allegedly gay employees actionable, while similar behavior by allegedly straight employees was often deemed a brand of juvenile horseplay.[77]

But, as Halley understood, the threat posed by the Court's articulation of this first evidentiary route was considerably more pernicious. Not only did the Court invite homophobic bias to play an authorized role in defining the nature of ambiguous acts and words as either sexual or not, desire-based or not, it also encouraged litigants to engage in specific practices of categorization that both deploy and reinforce the predictive binary matrix of sex, gender, and sexuality. In holding that evidence of an alleged harasser's homosexual orientation would go far toward establishing

76. Halley 2002: 81.

77. Zylan 2006.

desire and (therefore) causation, the Court constructed sexuality as fixed, stable, and mechanical. By repairing to categorical sexual identity, the Court both assumed and demanded that desire be understood as a univocal drive emerging from prediscursive bodies arrayed near and around one another, drawn to or repelled from one another in predictable ways based on the primary sex organs possessed by each of them. Does X desire Y? For the *Oncale* court, the material facts might be reduced to this: X is a gay man, Y is a man; there is some sort of sexualized language or contact between them. The inference that may then be drawn is straightforward: X engaged in this behavior because he desired Y. And because sexual orientation is dichotomous, it is reasonable to assume that had Y been of the "other" sex, X would not have desired him. Therefore, X has discriminated because of sex.

Clearly, this story simultaneously proves too little and too much. Why does the but for causation claim follow naturally on the heels of the court's determination that desire was at work here? This can only be true if sexual desire is fully contained within categorical identifications. The fidelity to categories means that we "know" that X would not have found Y desirable had Y been a woman. But while this counts as truth within the parameters of this social construct, it is not necessarily the only, or even the most, plausible reconstruction of what transpired between X and Y. Consider a different hypothetical—one in which X is categorically heterosexual and male, and (again) Y is male. Similar sexualized language or conduct ensues. But because X is heterosexual, he could not have desired Y, and so causation cannot be established under this theory. But perhaps this is wrong. Perhaps X did desire Y, but simply did not (and does not now) recognize it as such, living (as he does) in a sexually binarized social world. Clearly that would not mean that desire was not operative, nor that we ought not to describe the evidentiary traces of that relationship as suggesting the presence of sexual longing. Indeed, one way to make sense of the odd and conflictual behavior often observed in these cases is as a scene of gender and sexual confusion, as desire in contestation with efforts to make sense of one's own identifications. And if that is at least partly accurate, then troubling our authoritative accounts of what passes between men may create the space for future contestations to be undertaken without violence, coercion, or humiliation. This is one compelling reason why sexual progressives ought to "carr[y] a brief for the weirdness of sex wherever it appears."[78]

But it is also true that the claim proves too little because it suggests that while X was "discriminating," he was doing a fairly lazy job of it. He was simply dividing his coworkers into two groups, men and women, and setting his sexual sights on one or the other half. Now, this may be true in some cases, but it is an odd view of how people experience or pursue sexual desires. On the other hand, it does resonate with a long-standing homophobic understanding of gay sexuality as uncontrollable and predatory: gay men seek any and all men, and lesbians prey on any and all women.[79]

## III. The Imperatives of Identity: Categorizing Desire

It is also worth noting that, in the *Oncale* universe, Y exists as a passive object of X's drives. (Halley's counterfactual hypotheticals of the *Oncale* case illustrate this dramatically.[80]) Narratives

78. Halley 2002: 98.

79. Brower 2009: at 15–16.

80. Halley 2002: 95. Halley's piece suggests several thought experiments: what if Joseph Oncale was performing his sex/gender/sexuality to "signal his willingness to be mastered"? What if Oncale was performing a "perfectly masculine man" in order to produce a particularly male and masculine sexual interaction? What if Oncale's coworkers were performing a kind of bitchy femininity such that he operated as the henpecked husband or lesbian partner or the sexual bottom? What if all of the above

of the kind invited by the first evidentiary route produce and partake of doubly reified conceptions of desire. Each party to the interactions at issue exists as a discrete, fully formed corporeal self with a sex, a gender, and a sexual identity. One acts (as a desiring subject) while the other is acted upon (as a desirable object). The bodies stand apart, in a particular, determinate stance toward one another based on their categorical relationship, which locates and defines the quality of the force that drives the conduct between them:

> The only alleged harasser whose conduct is relevant to the "homosexual harasser" inquiry is Ms. Hinkle, who the record reveals to be one of the most physically and verbally demonstrative harassers. Ms. Dick herself does not allege that Ms. Hinkle was homosexual, and, as discussed more fully below, has conceded that she "[didn't] know [Ms. Hinkle's] true sexual preference." Under the [Fifth Circuit's] test, Ms. Hinkle's conduct—specifically her attempts to pinch Ms. Dick's breasts on two occasions—was certainly. . . "sexually demeaning." But the evidence does not show that Ms. Hinkle had a sexual interest in Ms. Dick, as required to satisfy the first prong of the test. Ms. Hinkle's conduct falls within the category of "mere humiliation."[81]

were in play? None of these scenarios depends, as the Court's scenario does, on the image of Oncale as passive object to his bullying or sexually predatory coworkers.

81. *Dick v. Phone Directories Comp., Inc.*, 265 F. Supp. 2d 1274, 1279–80 (W.D. Utah 2003). *See also Russell v. University of Texas of the Permian Basin*, 234 Fed. Appx. 195, 201 (5th Cir. 2007 [unpublished opinion]. ("In this case, Dr. Russell has created a fact issue that the sexual harassment was discrimination because of sex since Dr. Russell put on evidence that Dr. Watson made sexual advances to her and it is undisputed that both Dr. Russell and Dr. Watson are lesbians.")

The categorical relations can also be read in reverse: where the court thinks it sees conduct evincing desire, it may then infer the sexual orientation of the harasser accordingly:

> It is not possible for us to specify all the possible ways in which a plaintiff might prove that an alleged harasser acted out of homosexual interest in him. Nonetheless, there are two types of evidence that are likely to be especially "credible" proof that the harasser may be a homosexual. The first is evidence suggesting that the harasser intended to have some kind of sexual contact with the plaintiff rather than merely to humiliate him for reasons unrelated to sexual interest. *The second is proof that the alleged harasser made same-sex sexual advances to others*, especially to other employees.[82]

Sometimes, however, the evidence of conduct is difficult to square with the sex, gender, and sexual identifications of the case's primary actors. Within the framework established by the interplay of anti-discrimination law and the recipe knowledge constituted by the predictive binary matrix, teasing (or "horseplay") functions as a kind of residual grouping, where cases go to die on summary judgment when the fit between categorical identity and conduct is simply too awkward to make sense of. Having confounded predictions, such cases are deemed not really sexual at all, despite any and all evidence to the contrary. This is not an entirely surprising result, given that courts are ill equipped by their reflexively formal institutional practices to examine sexuality explicitly, directly, and in its full complexity. In cases that test the limits of their sexual imagination, courts simply avoid sex entirely, replacing it with

82. *La Day*, 302 F.3d at 480 (5th Cir. 2002) (emphasis added).

a scenario sounding in "juvenile provocation" or "horseplay" or "roughhousing."[83]

A particularly strained example of the judicial gymnastics that may be required to avoid sex in a sexual harassment case is offered in the case of *McWilliams v. Fairfax County Board of Supervisors,* discussed by Richard F. Storrow in his analysis of the pre- and post-*Oncale* landscape.[84] In McWilliams, the plaintiff was a cognitively disabled man who was subjected to a variety of sexually charged contacts by his coworkers. At one point, McWilliams was fondled to the point of erection by one of them. Yet the McWilliams court pronounced the behavior by plaintiff's coworkers to be "horseplay." In the absence of evidence that any or presumably all of the harassing workers were actually homosexual, the court seemed unable to view the harassment as being caused by McWilliams's [male] sex. (In this case the court plainly implied that by "sex," it meant biological sex.) Was the court suggesting that the fact that McWilliams had a penis was irrelevant to the conduct of his coworkers? Perhaps. But what seems plain is that it was unable to pronounce the conduct sexual because, having determined that McWilliams's harassers were not gay, it could not imagine any sexual reason why they would have been fondling his penis.

Another method by which courts locate sexual desire in these cases is through identifying evidentiary traces of the emotion that, as we saw in Chapter 4, stands as its binary opposite: animus. This particular grammar of motives[85] may also be traced, in part, to the *Oncale* court's instruction. While the Court established that either a finding of animus or a finding of desire would satisfy

83. *See* generally Storrow 1998. *See, for example, Shafer,* 417 F.3d at 663; *McWilliams,* 72 F.3d at 1196; *English,* 190 F. Supp. 2d at 845.

84. Storrow 1998.

85. Burke 1969.

the causation requirement, the language and structure of its opinion marked these routes as operating in the alternative. As should be evident by now, the conduct alleged in these cases is frequently weird, unruly, and susceptible to multiple and even conflicting interpretations. Defendants are by turns nasty and solicitous, brutal and tender, clueless and attentive. In one especially poignant case, a plaintiff alleged that she was first mercilessly ridiculed about her obesity by a coworker, then relentlessly pursued by the same coworker after she, the plaintiff, had undergone gastric bypass surgery. As the dissent in the case noted, whether teased or pursued for sex, the plaintiff should have been able to proceed with the case because either or both would have occurred "because of" her sex(ed) body.[86] However, working with their own recipe knowledge of the nature of desire, the majority of the court interpreted the evidence of animus as weighing against a finding of desire and vice versa. The predictive matrix of sex, gender, and sexual identity categories served to rationalize disparate facts within a simple master narrative of desire or teasing or animus. Desire precludes animus, and insult precludes desire:

> Love alleged that before and after her surgery, co-worker Jeanne Sirey subjected her to sexual harassment through inappropriate comments, gestures, and physical contact. She concedes that Sirey never made explicit proposals for sexual activity but argues that Sirey's actions were implicitly suggestive proposals for sex. The district court held, *inter alia*, that Love's evidence, while showing rude and humiliating behavior by Sirey, failed to establish that Sirey had a sexual interest in Love because Sirey's conduct was generally accompanied by

86. *Love v. Motiva Enterprises LLC*, 349 Fed. Appx. 900, 908 (5th Cir. 2009) (unpublished opinion).

derogatory comments about Love's appearance and character. We agree.[87]

## IV. Going Another Way (But Feeling the Sting of the Bootstrap)

The mechanics of causation analysis also thwart efforts by plaintiffs to ground their claims in a "sex-plus"[88] theory of sexual harassment, pursuant to Katherine Franke's suggestion that same-sex harassment may best be understood as a technique of gender discipline.[89] The problem emerges because of yet another categorical imperative of sexual harassment jurisprudence: as is required of any Title VII claimant, a same-sex harassment plaintiff must first prove membership in a "protected class."[90] Because neither gender identification nor sexual orientation is included in the list of protected classes, this first procedural move necessarily anchors the case in a set of ideas about binary anatomical sex. These ideas then structure the subsequent analysis via the social logic of the predictive binary matrix: a gay or lesbian plaintiff who asserts that s/he was harassed because of gender nonconformity invites a rebuke from the court for

87. *Love,* 349 Fed. Appx. at 902.

88. Courts have used this term to denote gender-based discrimination to distinguish it from sex-based discrimination. In other words, it applies where the discrimination is alleged to result because of plaintiff's perceived failure to sufficiently match his/her masculinity/femininity to his/her biological sex. *Price Waterhouse v. Hopkins,* 490 U.S. 228, 250–52 (1989).

89. Franke 1997: 739, 758, 764–70.

90. Boso 2009: 64.

attempting to "bootstrap" a sexual orientation claim to a sex discrimination claim.

For example, in *Vickers v. Fairfield Medical Center*, the plaintiff, a private police officer for a medical center, claimed that he was targeted for harassment by two coworkers after he befriended a gay doctor at the Center. Vickers argued that the harassment—which included, *inter alia*, being repeatedly called a "fag" and having a sanitary napkin shoved in his face—was caused by his failure to adhere to gender norms as manifested by his perceived sexual practices:

> Vickers contends that in the eyes of his co-workers, his sexual practices, whether real or perceived, did not conform to the traditionally masculine role. Rather, in his supposed sexual practices, he behaved more like a woman.[91]

The court added in a footnote that Vickers supported his theory with evidence that "he was only teased about giving, not receiving fellatio, and about receiving anal sex."[92] Vickers contended that his claim was merely a variation on the argument advanced and upheld in *Price Waterhouse v. Hopkins*, in which a female executive claimed she was discriminated against by her colleagues for what they viewed as her excessive masculinity.[93]

The Sixth Circuit rejected Vickers's claim, finding that "the harassment of which Vickers complains is more properly viewed as harassment based on Vickers' perceived homosexuality, rather than based on gender non-conformity."[94] Yet there was plainly

91. *Vickers v. Fairfield Medical Center*, 453 F.3d 757, 763 (6th Cir. 2006).

92. *Ibid*: n. 2.

93. *Price Waterhouse*, 490 U.S. at 228.

94. *Vickers*, 453 F.3d at 763.

evidence that Vickers was subjected to explicitly gendered harassment—the sort that Franke would likely identify as a performative technique of aggressive and punitive resocialization into normative masculinity. Why did the court feel the need to elevate the dimension of the conduct that appeared to circulate around Vickers's sexual orientation, to the point of occluding the gendered quality of the harassment itself? Because Congress has expressly and repeatedly refused to add sexual orientation to the list of protected classifications:

> Ultimately, recognition of Vickers' claim would have the effect of *de facto* amending Title VII to encompass sexual orientation as a prohibited basis for discrimination. In all likelihood, any discrimination based on sexual orientation would be actionable under a sex stereotyping theory if this claim is allowed to stand, *as all homosexuals, by definition, fail to conform to traditional gender norms in their sexual practices.*[95]

The court appears to be attempting to hew to a narrow judicial role here, to divine and protect Congress's legislative intent in enacting and amending (and refusing to subsequently amend) Title VII. But in so doing, it is also actively participating in a particular construction of homosex—one that ties gender to anatomy to sexual practices. Vickers is not claiming that he is being harassed for effeminacy—for queening it up at work. He purposely (strategically?) leaves unanswered the question of his own sexual orientation[96] and directs the court's attention to his coworkers' apparent belief that *he has sex like a woman*. One is reminded here of Leo Bersani's claim that the image of a man

95. *Ibid*: 764 (emphasis added).

96. *Ibid*: 759.

being penetrated, legs high in the air, is both the specter that haunts the straight mind and the fantasy that instantiates a specifically gay desire.[97]

The court minimizes this aspect of Vickers's claim by reducing it to a footnote and then repurposes it as a judicial finding about all gay and lesbian sex—a finding that leads the court to hold that Vickers's argument amounts to an impermissible attempt to "bootstrap" sexual orientation discrimination to sex discrimination. Having sex "like" a woman (if one is a man) or "like" a man (if one is woman) is, for the court, equally a marker of sexual orientation and a manifestation of gender because to be gay is *per se* to fail to conform to gender norms. The court deploys and reinscribes the predictive binary matrix in its most reflexive, self-proving form and finds that any allegations concerning the failure of a gay or lesbian plaintiff to evince gender conformity must really be allegations about the plaintiff's sexual orientation.

The *Vickers* court has hardly been alone in embracing and elaborating upon this construction. A Seventh Circuit court was equally forceful in its conclusion that a gender-stereotyping claim brought by a gay plaintiff would not be actionable under Title VII. In *Hamner v. St. Vincent Hospital*,[98] the court refused to rule on plaintiff's claim of homophobic harassment consisting of gender-specific mockery[99] because it was not raised in the court

97. See the discussion, *supra*, at chapter 3.

98. *Hamner v. St. Vincent Hosp. and Health Care Ctr., Inc.*, 224 F.3d 701 (7Cir. 2000).

99. In this case, plaintiff alleged, in part, that a supervisor lisped and "flip[ped] his wrists" at him. *Ibid*: 703.

below. But in dicta, the court felt compelled to offer its position on the viability of such a claim, stating:

> this argument has no merit. We have already established from Hamner's testimony that he believed that Edwards's gestures evinced his "homophobia," and thus pertained only to Hamner's sexual orientation, and not to his sex. And the record contains no evidence to indicate that Edwards's gestures were motivated by a general hostility to men, which would be an example of the type of evidence necessary in this case to sustain Hamner's [claim].[100]

The court cited *Oncale* in reaching this position.[101]

The Second Circuit has been even more decisive and expansive. In *Dawson v. Bumble & Bumble*, the court rejected a gender stereotyping claim brought by a lesbian salon employee who alleged harassment by her sexually diverse crew of coworkers on the grounds that it was an improper attempt to bootstrap a sexual orientation claim to a sex discrimination claim.[102] Dawson claimed that she was disciplined at work not for failing to conform to gender norms broadly (she conceded that the salon was hardly a model of gender normativity), nor for being gay (there were other gay and lesbian stylists), but for being too butch of a lesbian. For Dawson, the two were deeply connected. Her identity as a particular kind of lesbian was what seemed to cause problems

---

100. *Ibid*: 707.

101. *Ibid*. The *Hamner* court's citation of *Oncale* appears to indicate that it took the "three evidentiary routes" to proving sex-based discrimination to be exclusive of the ways in which a plaintiff could satisfy the "because of. . . sex" requirement. *See also* Samborski v. West Valley Nuclear Svcs. Co., Inc., 2002 U.S. Dist. LEXIS 12745 (W.D.N.Y. 2002).

102. *Dawson v. Bumble & Bumble*, 398 F.3d 211 (2nd Cir. 2005).

for her at work. It wasn't that she was a lesbian that made her a target; it was that she was a *dyke*.[103] But the court was incapable of understanding this intersectional claim.[104] Dawson's contextual knowledge and experience of the harassment as sexuality-inflected gender discipline was recast as evidence of the impossibility of segregating gender stereotyping claims from sexual orientation discrimination claims, particularly where the plaintiff is openly gay:

> When utilized by an avowedly homosexual plaintiff. . . gender stereotyping claims can easily present problems for an adjudicator. This is for the simple reason that stereotypical notions about how men and women should behave will often necessarily blur into ideas about heterosexuality and homosexuality. Like other courts, we have therefore recognized that a gender stereotyping claim should not be used to bootstrap protection for sexual orientation into Title VII.[105]

## V. Add Gay and Stir

Todd Brower cites the *Dawson* case as an example of how courts inevitably use "cognitive schemas" of sex, gender, and sexuality to make sense of disparate or confusing fact patterns in sex discrimination cases brought under Title VII.[106] For Brower, courts and litigants rely extensively on schemas to match such facts to settled understandings of how their gendered, sexed, and

103. *Dawson*, 398 F.3d at 215.

104. On intersectionality generally, *see* Crenshaw 1991.

105. *Dawson*, 398 F.3d at 219.

106. Brower 2009: 58–60.

sexual worlds work. He argues that schemas are more or less indispensable—both within and beyond juridical domains. As a general matter, we all need them because, "if we had to constantly analyze each piece of information, event, or situation anew, we would either be swamped by minutia or paralyzed into inactivity."[107] But courts and litigants rely on them even more heavily because they operate within law's *habitus*.[108] Legal reasoning—with its constant movement between distinction and analogy—is largely a process of formalized "schema-matching."[109]

Problems are just as inevitable however, because schemas are inherently reductive, and may distort information through the rationalizing process that lies at the core of schema-matching. Brower notes that law's specific character may exacerbate these limitations:

> The problem is that the law requires clear distinctions. Title VII in particular requires neat categorization of sexuality and gender and sex. On the other hand, social cognition strongly suggests that we may not truly be able to classify those characteristics cleanly or that we can only classify them idiosyncratically depending on our underlying schemas. That tension is exacerbated because legal doctrine assumes that people are aware of, and can access and understand, their cognitive processes ... complete consistency and clarity in legal doctrine is an expectation in which we are fated to be disappointed.[110]

107. *Ibid*: 3.

108. Bourdieu 1987.

109. Bower 2009: 4.

110. *Ibid*: 76. Brower also suggests that law is more demanding of sex/gender/ sexuality schemas than either social scientists or people engaged in everyday encounters: "The law requires strict separation between sexual orientation and gender; litigants and judges are forced to classify in ways that social scientists often do not and that empirical research shows people generally may not." *Ibid*.

For Brower, the solution is to add sexual orientation to the list of protected classifications and to explicitly recognize that schemas are imperfect, overly neat renderings of more complex social realities.[111] He takes a practical, instrumental view of the problem; were Congress to add sexual orientation to the list of protected classifications, the fact that courts and litigants might sometimes mistake gender discrimination for sexual orientation discrimination, or vice versa, would be rendered a distinction without a difference. Gay and lesbian plaintiffs would no longer shoulder an additional burden in their efforts to bring Title VII claims. Other critics have similarly suggested that statutory reform offers the potential for courts and legislatures to develop more workable alternatives. Yet even were such a bill to be enacted into law—at present, efforts to pursue such reform have stalled in the midst of the gay marriage juggernaut—it would closely track the language of Title VII; the "because of" language remains intact in proposed legislation.[112] As a result, there is little reason to believe that an employment nondiscrimination law would effect much of a shift in the substance of existing sexual harassment jurisprudence. To the contrary; by adding the categorical identifiers "sexual orientation" and "gender identity" to the list of protected classifications, the bill might in fact strengthen law's reliance upon the binary matrix.[113]

111. *Ibid*: 76–77.

112. Employment Non-Discrimination Act of 2009 (Sec. 4)., 3017 111th Cong. (2009). Note, however, that recent revisions of the bill have inserted express prohibitions of quotas and preferential hiring treatment for gay men and lesbians, as well as an express exemption for religious organizations.

113. Interestingly, the bill prohibits discrimination against persons undergoing "gender transition," but still allows employers to require dress and grooming in conformity with *the* gender to which the person is transitioning. *Ibid*: Sec. 8(a)(5). The causation requirement remains in force, thus necessitating an inquiry into whether the conduct at issue was undertaken "because of" plaintiff's sexual

Ultimately, the problem of sexually hostile work environments is so deeply embedded in the psychology of work and sexuality[114] that its source is probably beyond the reach of judicial action. The dysfunctional quality of the work-sex nexus is endemic to advanced capitalist societies, and I remain pessimistic that workplaces will ever become desexualized, as long as they remain (at bottom) routinized, sterile environments where nobody is enjoying his or her job very much. The true solution to sexual harassment in the workplace lies in a transformation of the workplace, not a transformation of the law.

That said, Brower may be right with respect to the instrumental politics and tactics of the matter. It seems plain that, within the current policy environment, openly or apparently gay or lesbian plaintiffs are radically disadvantaged in their efforts to bring Title VII claims. Because courts imagine desire to issue in predictable ways based on categorical identity assignments, they are unwilling or unable to view harassment of gay plaintiffs by assertedly or impliedly heterosexual harassers as evidence of unwelcome sexual desire.[115] Moreover, as *Dawson* and *Vickers* illustrate, they are structurally resistant to "sex-plus" claims brought by gay and lesbian plaintiffs, viewing them as impermissible efforts to judicially amend Title VII to prohibit sexual orientation discrimination. Were sexual orientation to be added to the list of protected classifications, the effort to isolate conduct as being primarily "about" sex or gender or sexual orientation would perhaps whither away, and gay and lesbian plaintiffs might find

orientation. *See* Employment Non-Discrimination Act of 2009, H.R. 3017, 111th Cong. § 4(a)(1) (2009).

114. Elsewhere, I have proposed a theory of workplace sexual harassment that attempts to move beyond the categorical predictions of the binary matrix. *See* Zylan 2006.

115. Zylan 2006.

themselves in a less disadvantageous starting position in Title VII litigation.

But what happens in Title VII courts does not stay in Title VII courts, and this fact raises the stakes of sexual harassment litigation strategies. It might be imagined that the discursive effects of same-sex sexual harassment litigation remain confined to judicial institutions, for unlike the campaigns for hate crime laws and same-sex marriage, same-sex harassment litigation is relatively opaque to non-legal audiences. As a consequence, decisions rendered in faraway courthouses and arguments advanced in esoteric pleadings would seem to have little opportunity to seep into the vernacular. But of course they do. Few employees today—whether they work for large employers or small, public or private—are likely to escape at least some instruction in the rules prohibiting sexual harassment in the workplace. Such rules are published in employee handbooks (which may become part of the employee's contract) and discussed in orientation procedures, and many modern workplaces also set aside staff and other resources to respond to sexual harassment complaints as they arise.

Most employees probably spend little time thinking about why this particular issue is given such focused attention relative to other potential workplace issues and the message might seem to be that sexual harassment is simply a bigger problem than other conflicts that arise at work. But the prominence of sexual harassment policies can instead be traced to its provenance in a number of important legal opinions. Law and society scholar Anna-Marie Marshall's examination of the subject demonstrates that, while the process by which legal rules and categories work their way into social practices is neither simple nor unidirectional, the development of a widespread commitment to combatting sexual harassment in American workplaces is traceable to action first undertaken in the courts.[116] A series of important decisions (litigated by politically committed attorneys such as Catharine MacKinnon) established both the impetus for, and the original form of, organizational rules and policies prohibiting harassment. Certainly, such rules were not enough, nor were they adopted whole by employers; Marshall expressly rejects the notion that law simply implants its own categories in social practices. Instead, she argues that workers elaborate upon legal categories in developing a consciousness of what counts as wrongful workplace conduct,[117] often broadening their analyses to include political and cultural themes. Still, Marshall's account makes clear that legal categories are centrally and foundationally important in this interactive process.[118]

Equally as important, because LGB political and cultural strategies are increasingly subsumed to the imperatives of litigation, there may be less and less to distinguish legal from political and cultural discourses. Litigation strategies require participation in a process by which sex, gender, and sexuality are socially constructed and reconstructed in conformity with an overly narrow, profoundly constrained conception of human behavior—one that cannot fully consider desire, longing, aggression, pain, mastery, subordination, *jouissance* and hostility in their complexity and concatenation. The categorical processing that is the *sine qua non* of Title VII causation analysis simply and decisively forecloses the legal possibility that bodies, genders, identifications, and intrapsychic and intersubjective experiences might be fluid or indeterminate. One might not be so concerned about legal im/possibility *per se* if LGB advocates were expending time,

116. Marshall 2005: 39.

117. *See also* McCann 1994; Edelman 2002.

118. *Ibid*: 22.

effort and money on progressive campaigns outside the law in an enthusiastic effort to open spaces for fluidity and indeterminancy in progressive (and maybe even fun) ways. But in the near total conflation of the legal and the cultural (*see e.g.* the same-sex marriage campaign discussed in Chapter 6), one can't help but be afraid that categorical processing in the legal context means the dramatic othering—if not erasure—of indeterminate bodies, genders, identifications, and experiences in the cultural context as well.

# 6

## Aspiring to Be Iowan: Same-Sex Marriage and the End of Gayness As We Know It

*At its best, queer politics has fought the stigmatization of sex, in all the ramifications that stigma has for people, from queer youth to sex workers and single mothers. But in its newest manifestation, the lesbian and gay movement threatens to become an instrument for the normalization of queer life. Nowhere is that more visible than in the presentation of the gay marriage issue.*

—MICHAEL WARNER[1]

The same-sex marriage movement is a bona fide political and cultural juggernaut. A search of the Lexis-Nexus database revealed that, in one month last year, there were 55 articles in American newspapers on the topic of same-sex marriage.[2] References to same-sex marriage crop up everywhere—sometimes in the

---

1. Warner 1999: 80.

2. Based on a keyword search for articles containing five or more references to "same-sex marriage," "same sex marriage," or "gay marriage," conducted on March 10, 2010. Expanding the search to include articles with at least one mention of one of these phrases results in 494 hits. Some of this volume may be attributed to the enactment of a gay marriage ordinance in the District of Columbia, which led to the granting of licenses beginning on March 9. But random searches conducted on different dates led to similar results (perhaps because there is, as of this writing, nearly always some big thing happening on the same-sex marriage front).

weirdest places[3]—suggesting that the issue is fast becoming one of the central political fault lines in the country. And LGB movement and lobbying organizations have almost uniformly embraced "marriage equality" as one of their top agenda items.[4] Indeed, one would be hard pressed to contend that it is not *the* top agenda item for just about every national LGB movement organization in existence and most local organizations as well.

The rise of this campaign is stunning for its rapidity and because it has now been almost universally embraced among American LGB activists and community members. This is in spite of the fact that marriage as a political, economic, and social institution was, until quite recently, the object of a sharp and sustained critique by feminists and progressives within and

3. For example, Republican Senator Bob Bennett of Utah sought to introduce a ban on same-sex marriage in the District of Columbia as an amendment to a budget reconciliation bill designed to make changes to the Patient Protection and Affordable Care Act (the "health care reform" law). *New York Times* 3/23/10 http://prescriptions.blogs.nytimes.com/2010/03/23/senate-republicans-add-health-care-amendments/ (accessed 3/26/10). The amendment (which failed) was offered as a "poison pill," intended to force supporters of health insurance reform to vote against the "right" of the people of the District of Columbia to define marriage for themselves.

4. *See, for example,* Human Rights Campaign Web site http://www.hrc.org/issues/marriage.asp ("Only marriage can provide families with true equality."); Lambda Legal Web site http://www.lambdalegal.org/issues/marriage-relationships-family/ (We also fight to establish the rights of people in same-sex relationships to obtain benefits and protections as we work toward the goal of marriage equality."); National Gay and Lesbian Task Force Web site http://www.thetaskforce.org/issues/marriage_and_partnership_recognition; NCLR Web site http://www.nclrights.org/site/PageServer?pagename=issue_marriage ("NCLR is committed to assuring that LGBT couples who wish to marry are free to do so. As the past few years have dramatically illustrated, the battle to win this freedom will have a lasting impact on the pace and progress of all LGBT civil and human rights in this country—for generations."); American Civil Liberties Union LGBT Rights Project http://www.aclu.org/lgbt-rights/relationships ("Since the first marriage lawsuit for same-sex couples in 1972, the ACLU has been at the forefront of both legal and public education efforts to secure marriage for same-sex couples and win legal recognition for LGBT relationships."); see also Gay & Lesbian Advocates and Defenders Web site http://www.glad.org/rights/c/marriage/. (all sites accessed 5/16/10)

around LGB communities.[5] Such critics found much to dislike in marriage. Feminists of many different philosophical and political provenances have long understood marriage to be at best problematic for, and at worst deeply oppressive to, women as a class. A generation of radical and socialist feminist lesbians understood marriage to be an institution predicated on men's exchange of women as objects.[6] Egalitarian and liberal feminists, too, have criticized marriage, seeing in today's formally equal institution a legacy of coverture, male privilege, and long-standing legal and social disabilities afflicting wives, ex-wives, and widows.[7] Because the modern LGB movement emerged in and around the second wave of the American feminist movement,[8] feminist positions on marriage were deeply influential in the construction of LGB identity politics.

Nor have feminists been alone in critiquing marriage from within the LGB movement and community institutions. Radicals, progressives, and sexual outlaws—Faeries, hippies, separatists, lesbian feminists, leather queens, twinks, and others—have been able to draw upon a long and varied genealogy of socialists, free lovers, and communitarians in constructing a notion of sexual identity and practice that disarticulates marriage (and/or monogamy) from sexuality, and affirms sexuality as a different modality of kinship and relationship or a form of expression that eschews the very notion of relationship.[9]

5. *See* Polikoff 2008; Warner 1999. See also Chauncey 2004: 93–94.

6. Rubin 1975.

7. Hoff-Wilson1991: 128.

8. *See generally* D'Emilio and Freedman 1997: chapter 13.

9. On early American sexual political movements, *see* D'Emilio and Freedman 1997. On the production of alternative conceptions of sex and relationship, *see* Warner 1999.

Nevertheless, as Michael Warner has documented, the LGB movement's current political leadership class has largely disavowed this earlier critique. Some have claimed that it was never more than a marginal perspective and that it was a product of a naive, 1970s-style, liberationist idealism. On this view, the anti-marriage critique has simply withered in the face of bracing realism, its remnants merely a reminder of the rank immaturity of the movement during that period of time. Public figures like Andrew Sullivan, Jonathan Rauch, and Michaengelo Signorile have all argued that the LGB community's embrace of marriage represents the coming of age or maturation of the movement.[10] Much as a young gay man might grow up, stop his clubbing ways, and settle down with a boyfriend/husband, they have suggested, the movement simply (and by their lights, happily) grew out of its pleasure-seeking, hedonistic youth and got serious about sharing property, raising children, and becoming integrated into normative social institutions. Marriage advocate and Lambda Legal Defense and Education Fund attorney Evan Wolfson famously declared that whatever dissent may have once existed on the subject of marriage within the LGB community, "that ship has sailed."[11]

But why? How? And where did it go? George Chauncey, noted historian and a frequent expert witness in same-sex marriage litigation,[12] has argued that changes in the nature of American marriage over the course of the past century "have made the right

10. Sullivan 1996; Warner 1999: 110.

11. Wolfson 1994: 611.

12. Chauncey was one of the first witnesses to appear for the plaintiffs in *Perry v. Schwarzenegger*, the constitutional challenge to Californians' effort to repeal judicial recognition of same-sex marriage, a case heard in early 2010. *Perry v. Schwarzenegger*, United States District Court for the Northern District of California, case no. 3:09-cv-02292, Trial Transcript 1/12/2010.

to marry seem both more imaginable and more urgent to lesbians and gay men."[13] While acknowledging that, until very recently, "support for marriage was a distinctly minority position in the lesbian and gay movement,"[14] Chauncey contends that broad institutional, legal, and cultural changes have led 'progressively' toward the emergence of same-sex marriage as the issue of our time. He argues that, over time, marriage has become more open to individual choice, more egalitarian, less dominated by religious institutions, and more tightly imbricated with state mechanisms of distribution. For Chauncey, these four broad changes opened up the possibility of marriage to gay people, while two shorter-term changes worked to sway gay people to the position that they ought to fight for marriage: the tragic sequelae of AIDS and the rise of the "gayby boom," which (together) brought to light the particular vulnerabilities that appear at the beginning and end of the life cycle. Chauncey contends that media coverage of certain high-profile cases of blatant (and especially mean-spirited) discrimination against gay couples who were left exposed by inadequate or unrecognized legal instruments underscored the ways in which marriage provides encompassing and seemingly unassailable protections. Thus, he seems to say,[15] the argument for marriage simply became

13. Chauncey 2004: 59.

14. *Ibid*: 93.

15. Chauncey also suggests that the internal debate was never particularly important in the first place: "We shouldn't overstate the strength of any of these cultural or political tendencies in the 1970s. They were especially characteristic of young white lesbians and gay men living in certain places, although they had disproportionate political significance because those same people formed the core of the organized gay movement. The sexual revolution in San Francisco, New York, and a few other cities far outpaced that occurring in most of America. Most lesbians and gay men still looked for a steady relationship, and across the country, thousands of couples asked the MCC to bless their relationships as holy unions." Putting aside certain empirical questions that immediately come to mind—i.e., weren't a disproportionate share of gay people living in those super sexy cities Chauncey names? Aren't there ways of celebrating or codifying "steady relationship[s]" other than marriage? And

more compelling, essentially crowding out liberationist and feminist arguments against the institution. As gay men and lesbians became more convinced of the utility and desirability of marriage, they became ever more demanding of marriage as a collective aim, and gay political and legal advocates merely, and sometimes reluctantly, responded to this rising demand.

This seems plausible, given the near unanimity that now attends marriage as a goal of the LGB movement.[16] But Chauncey's claims about short-term changes may misstate the relationship between legal and social advocacy in this case. The emergence

ought we not to consider the efforts of some couples to secure religious or cultural affirmation as distinguishable from efforts to secure inclusion within state-sanctioned marriage?—the claim is odd for another reason. Chauncey minimizes the importance of the anti-marriage critique by suggesting it was limited to LGB political and cultural elites. But what we want to understand is the complete turnaround of precisely these elites—the ones leading the organizations that Chauncey claims had "disproportionate political significance" and which "mostly ignored the issue [of marriage]" during the 1970s. *Ibid*: 94.

16. *See generally* Schacter 2009. All of the significant national LGB organizations have not only embraced marriage, but have placed it at or near the top of their legislative and litigation priorities. A wide and deep array of feminists, progressives, and queer theorists have also endorsed same-sex marriage. Even Judith Butler, whose work might lead one to expect her to display a deep suspicion of (if not antipathy to) the constitutive risks posed by the marriage program, has said that "[o]f course, if marriage exists, then homosexual marriage should also exist; marriage should be extended to all couples irrespective of their sexual orientation; if sexual orientation is an impediment, then marriage is discriminatory." Butler 2009. One might contend that the "if" that appears near the beginning of Butler's statement negates (or dramatically tempers) her endorsement of the liberal legal project of "marriage equality." But Butler's further comment underscores the instrumentalism her argument presumes: "I agree that the right to homosexual marriage runs the risk of producing a conservative effect, of making marriage an act of normalisation, and thereby presenting other very important forms of intimacy and kinship as abnormal or even pathological. But the question is: politically, what do we do with this? I would say that every campaign in favour of homosexual marriage ought also to be in favour of alternative families, the alternative systems of kinship and personal association. We need a movement that does not win rights for some people at the expense of others. And imagining this movement is not easy. The demand for recognition by the state should go hand in hand with a critical questioning: what do we need the state for?"

of AIDS care communities during the 1980s and 1990s could just as easily have led LGB organizations to reject as to embrace policies rewarding heternormative kinship arrangements. Indeed, AIDS activism produced a radicalization of grassroots politics and a dramatic expansion (and transformation) of community institutions—often conceived and understood to constitute new forms of kinship.[17] And while it is true that lesbians and gay men with children have long sought ways to safeguard and codify their parenting and co-parenting relationships, many (if not most) of them employed strategies and tactics falling outside the ambit of marriage. Indeed, nascent "gayby boom" organizations embraced an inclusive philosophy that eschewed the privileging of certain family forms, claiming that "love makes a family, nothing more, nothing less."[18] It is far from obvious that these creative,[19] ad hoc, and disparate strategies and activities were preordained in the span of a decade at most, to transmogrify into a collective call for marriage.

In truth, the community of LGB-identified people did not lead the way on marriage; lawyers did.[20] And lawyers did so for

17. *See* Hilderbrand 2006; Crimp 2002; Andriote 1999; Kayal 1993; Padgug and Oppenheimer 1992; Harney 1999. *And see generally* Valocchi 2009.

18. This slogan was proudly displayed at the 1987 National March on Washington for Lesbian and Gay Rights. *See* Weston 1991.

19. It is undoubtedly true that much of this creativity was born of necessity—sometimes forged in undeniable human tragedy. To say this, however, is not to raise an argument against creativity. To the contrary, the history of organic, disparate, and local strategies of care in the LGB community demonstrates how vital creativity can be; it keeps us alive and flourishing when the state would just as soon see us disappear. All the more reason, I think, to jealously guard the non-normative spaces within which such strategies might arise.

20. Eskridge 2002: 5: "Thus, at the very point when activists were deliberating over the kind of politics gay liberation ought to emphasize and what ought to be its stance toward marriage, lawyers and their gay and lesbian clients were engaging in a preemptive strike." Eskridge notes that the marriage litigation in Hawaii and D.C. was also not endorsed by the national "gaylegal" organizations. He suggests

the reason that lawyers often do things: they thought it made sense as an instrumental matter.[21] Lawyers are duty-bound to select strategies that advance the interests of individual clients, even if those strategies come at the expense of community interest(s).[22] As Chauncey's own research makes clear, individual lawyers representing gay and lesbian clients were aware of political and intellectual debates over the wisdom of pursuing marriage, but many took an "above my pay grade" approach to them; they neither ignored the debate nor felt inclined to try to resolve it. Instead, they looked for as many tools as they could find with which to help their clients. Entry into marriage (or civil unions) offered one increasingly appealing choice among many. Chauncey quotes Mary Bonauto, one of the lead attorneys in *Baker v. State* (the Vermont same-sex marriage case that many view as having launched the contemporary marriage movement) as saying that, for her, it was a matter of "puzzl[ing] it through and [seeing] the number of rights associated with marriage that are otherwise categorically denied . . ."[23] Bonauto saw marriage

that upstart local attorneys and their clients simply resisted the disciplining efforts of the national gaylegal leadership, and filed their cases anyway—as a kind of local "activism." But it is important to note the extent to which this activism was confined within *judicial* domains. The point here (and it is one that Eskridge acknowledges) is that the modern same-sex marriage movement issued from within the narrow terms of legal doctrine and institutional practice. *See also* Warner 1999: 85 (marriage campaign launched by cadre of leader/litigators, "not by a consensus among activists").

21. *See supra*, chapter 5. *See, for example*, Marshall 2005: 38.

22. It is true that often the judge (either by invitation or by intuition) will be called upon to balance the individual's interests against those of the 'community', but in the context of same-sex marriage that balance has been constructed as occurring between the individual LGB person's right to marry and the heterosexual community's right to exclude LGB people from the institution. To the extent that the interests of the LGB community *qua* community are factored in, they have been assumed to be co-extensive with the individual litigant's dream to be married.

23. Chauncey 2004:128.

for the instrumental goodie bag that it undoubtedly was and is: by undertaking a single transaction, couples could sign on to hundreds of rights, benefits, obligations, and duties.[24] Convinced that there was sufficient demand from her clients for a marriage "choice," and satisfied that marriage was sufficiently "gender-neutral," Bonauto put to one side any concerns she might have harbored about the political debates that percolated around her and got to work.[25]

Seen in light of this evidence, Chauncey's argument about changes in the nature of marriage appears less convincing as a historical account of why and how the anti-marriage critique failed or dissipated than as a normative argument for why we need not be too concerned about its demise. And today, few advocacy organizations evince any conflict over whether or not to pursue marriage as a goal. On this point, Wolfson was correct: that ship has sailed. Indeed, as Warner predicted more than ten years ago, perhaps the marriage movement's greatest consequence thus far is its normalizing effect on LGB politics itself.[26] The grassroots did not push the legal and political leadership of their movement toward marriage, but now that it is in full swing, it enthusiastically and uncritically supports the effort.[27]

24. The actual number is subject to some debate. Marriage advocates usually put it over one thousand, although that number probably refers to the number of statutory mentions of the word "marriage" or "spouse." Actual benefits, rights, obligations, and duties are a subset of that. *See, for example,* http://mpetrelis.blogspot.com/2010/03/1138-federal-provisions-not-benefits_23.html (accessed 4/7/10). There are strategic reasons why advocates often cite the bigger number, but there is no denying that marriage is a package deal.

25. I want to reiterate that I am not here critiquing Bonauto or any of the attorneys who litigated those early cases. They were doing what skilled lawyers ought to do as a matter of professional imperative: they were pursuing their clients' interests as effectively and efficiently as possible.

26. Warner 1999: 80.

27. There can be little doubt about the breadth or depth of this enthusiasm. Members of the community are mobilizing around marriage to an extent unmatched

## I. Same-Sex Marriage Litigation Comes Out

In 1979, the first National March on Washington for Lesbian and Gay Rights concluded its opening program with this statement of purpose:

> Today in the capital of America, we are all here, the almost liberated and the slightly repressed; the butch, the femme and everything in-between; the androgynous; the monogamous and the promiscuous; the masturbators and the fellators and the tribadists; men in dresses and women in neckties; those who bite and those who cuddle; celebates[sic] and pederasts; diesel dykes and nelly queens; amazons and size queens, Yellow, Black, Brown, White, and Red; the short-haired and the long, the fat and the thin; the nude and the prude; the beauties and the beasts; the studs and the duds; the communes, the couples, and the singles; pubescents and the octogenarians. Yes, we are all here! We are everywhere! Welcome to the March on Washington for Lesbian and Gay Rights![28]

The tenor of the March is clearly in evidence here: inclusive, overtly sexual, and celebratory of gay and lesbian specificity. By 1987, the March's list of demands had grown to include a

by their mobilization around any other issue. *See, for example*, Taylor et al, 2009. And each time a state or municipality initiates the granting of marriage licenses to same-sex couples, long lines of betrothed couples appear with truly remarkable speed. When Mayor Gavin Newsom ordered the granting of such licenses to couples in San Francisco in 2004, thousands of couples rushed to snap them up before a court injunction put a halt to the practice. *Lockyer v. City and County of San Francisco*, 33 Cal. 4th 1055, 1070 (Sup. Ct. Calif. 2004). After the California Supreme Court declared that state's marriage ban unconstitutional, over 18,000 couples married in the span of just four and one half months. Taylor, et al, 2009: 870.

28. National March on Washington Official Souvenir Program at 3. Available at http://www.rainbowhistory.org/mowprogram.pdf.

call for "legal recognition of gay and lesbian relationships." But in the context of deepening threats from the New Right and a nascent push toward radical, direct action activism borne of state indifference to the AIDS pandemic,[29] the critical edge of the movement was still very much in evidence. Calls for an end to discrimination and legal recognition of relationships were still couched in inclusive terms that celebrated racial, class, and sexual difference.[30] The winnowing of "relationships" to "marriage" had not yet made its appearance on the national LGB agenda.[31] Even as late as the 1993 March on Washington, the demand for marriage was not yet on the program.[32] Instead, the March organizers explicitly called for a change in the legal definition of

29. See Fetner 2008; Ghaziani 2008: chapter 5.

30. Ghaziani 2008: chapter 5.

31. Chauncey and others note that there was a community wedding ceremony associated with the 1987 March, seeing this as evidence of a significant level of community interest in legal marriage. But the community wedding in Washington was, as its name suggests, a *community*-based ritual, distinguishable in kind and purpose from a drive for legal marriage "recognition."

32. "We demand passage of a Lesbian, Gay, Bisexual, and Transgender civil rights bill and an end to discrimination by state and federal governments including the military; repeal of all sodomy laws and other laws that criminalize private sexual expression between consenting adults.

We demand massive increase in funding for AIDS education, research, and patient care; universal access to health care including alternative therapies; and an end to sexism in medical research and health care.

We demand legislation to prevent discrimination against Lesbians, Gays, Bisexuals and Transgendered people in the areas of family diversity, custody, adoption and foster care and that the definition of family includes the full diversity of all family structures.

We demand full and equal inclusion of Lesbians, Gays, Bisexuals and Transgendered people in the educational system, and inclusion of Lesbian, Gay, Bisexual and Trans-gender studies in multicultural curricula.

We demand the right to reproductive freedom and choice, to control our own bodies, and an end to sexist discrimination.

We demand an end to racial and ethnic discrimination in all forms.

family so that it would "includ[e] the full diversity of all family structures."[33] It was not until the highly criticized 2000 "Millenium March" that marriage emerged on the national LGB political scene and, even then, it was not universally embraced.[34]

The situation within legal advocacy organizations was quite different. In 1992, Lambda Legal Defense directors Tom Stoddard and Paula Ettelbrick publicly debated the merits of pursuing marriage versus a more inclusive "family recognition" agenda.[35] In 1993, the Hawaii Supreme Court ruled that Hawaii's ban on same-sex marriage might be violative of that state's constitution, concluding a case that was begun in 1991.[36] By 1997, and inspired by events in Hawaii, Bonauto and two other lawyers were initiating the litigation that would result in the Vermont Supreme Court's determination that excluding gay men and lesbians from marriage was a violation of Vermont constitutional law.[37]

We demand an end to discrimination and violent oppression based on actual or perceived sexual orientation, identification, race, religion, identity, sex and gender expression, disability, age, class, AIDS/HIV infection." Official Program of the 1993 March on Washington for Lesbian and Gay Rights (available through the Queer Resource Directory at http://www.qrd.org/qrd/events/mow/mow-full.platform (accessed 4/10/2010).

33. *Ibid.*

34. The March was widely viewed as a study in what ailed the LGB movement at that time. Critics argued that it was not democratically organized, that it was insufficiently political, and that it had been co-opted by corporate interests. *See* Ghaziani 2008, chapter 9; Sandalow 2000. A 2000 article in the San Francisco Chronicle which describes the content of the March (as well as the criticism it engendered) makes no mention of marriage until the last paragraph, when it quotes comedian Margaret Cho, whose advocacy for legal marriage was couched within her trademark irreverence: "A government that would deny a gay man a bridal registry is a fascist state," Cho said. "I urge love without restraints, unless you are into leather, and then by all means use restraints." Sandalow 2000.

35. *See* the discussion in Polikoff 2008: chapter 3.

36. *Baehr v. Lewin,* 852 P2d 44 (Sup. Ct. Hawaii 1993); Eskridge 2002: 26.

37. Chauncey 2004:127.

Thus, well before the Massachusetts Supreme Judicial Court issued its instantly famous ruling on same-sex marriage in 2003,[38] American lawyers had been actively pursuing equal protection and substantive due process claims for marriage in courts around the country for at least a decade.

The Massachusetts case plainly accelerated this process. While several states affirmed their same-sex marriage bans in the immediate wake of *Goodridge v. Dept. of Public Health* (including Arizona, New York, and Washington), in recent years, the trend has reversed: five states have struck down their bans judicially—California, Connecticut, Vermont, New Jersey, and Iowa[39]—and two state legislatures have acted to extend marriage to same-sex couples (Maine and New Hampshire).[40] The momentum now appears to be in the direction of opening marriage to same-sex couples.[41]

38. *Goodridge v. Dept. of Public Health*, 798 N.E.2d 941 (Sup. Jud. Ct. Mass. 2003).

39. *Standhardt v. Superior Court*, 77 P.3d 451 (Ariz. Ct. App. 2003); *Hernandez v. Robles*, 855 N.E.2d 1 (Ct. App. NY 2006); *Andersen v. State of Washington*, 138 P.3d 963 (Sup. Ct. Wash. 2006); *In re Marriage Cases*, 43 Cal. 4th 757 (Sup. Ct. Calif. 2008); *Kerrigan v. Commisioner of Public Health*, 957 A.2d 407 (Sup. Ct. Conn. 2008); *Baker v. State*, 744 A.2d 864 (Sup. Ct Vermont 1999); *Lewis v Harris*, 908 A.2d 196 (Sup. Ct. New Jersey 2006); *Varnum v. O'Brien*, 763 N.W.2d 862 (Sup. Ct. Iowa 2009).

40. Maine's same-sex marriage law was passed by the state legislature and signed by the Governor in 2009, but was overturned by a state ballot referendum later that year. *See* Cover 2009; *see also* "An Act To End Discrimination in Civil Marriage and Affirm Religious Freedom", Maine revised statutes Title 19A § 650 et seq., as of May 6, 2009. "An Act Relative to Marriage and Civil Unions" was passed by the New Hampshire state legislature and signed by the governor in 2009. *See* http://www.gencourt.state.nh.us/legislation/2009/HB0436.html.

41. Most of the litigation has been intentionally directed at the state level. National gaylegal organizations have (almost certainly correctly) anticipated that any marriage ban challenge that were to make it to the United States Supreme Court would lose, given the current conservative makeup of the Court. *See* ACLU, et al 2009. Nonetheless, events in California enticed or pushed two renowned American lawyers, David Boies and Ted Olson, to file suit in federal court challenging the constitutionality of California's "Proposition 8": the state constitutional amendment reversing the California Supreme Court's holding in *In re Marriage Cases*

Tracing the marriage movement to its roots in legal advocacy draws our attention to its original, narrowly defined, purposive instrumentalism. As Bonauto and other attorneys "puzzled through" the best way to protect the interests of their lesbian and gay clients, they imagined that they would, if successful, be establishing a greater array of choices for structuring and codifying intimate relationships and kinship arrangements. In short, they believed they would be expanding their legal toolkits. Today, however, the movement's posture is decidedly more ambitious and the narrow instrumentalism of the early litigation is largely forgotten. Instead, the most striking thing about the current marriage movement is its full-throated commitment to the notion that marriage is desirable because of its unique *constitutive* power.[42] Political and legal discourse has shifted in focus from a claim for enjoyment of the "no less than 1049 federal rights granted to heterosexuals"[43] to a claim for the right to be stamped with the dignifying and normalizing power of the word "marriage." Yet even as they espouse the power of marriage as a normative institution

(43 Cal. 4th 757 (Sup. Ct. Calif. 2008)). Prop 8, which passed by referendum in 2008, was upheld by the California Supreme Court in 2009 as a lawful amendment to the state constitution. *Strauss v. Horton*, 46 Cal. 4th 364 (Sup. Ct. Calif. 2009). Boies and Olson's suit is a high-profile effort to essentially go over the heads of the California court and constitution and to have a federal court strike down the marriage ban on Fourteenth Amendment grounds. National gay rights advocates strongly—and publicly—pressured Boies and Olson not to file the suit, arguing that the time was not right for a federal challenge. *See* ACLU 2009. Boies and Olson were undeterred, however, and the suit is going forward in the 9th Circuit.

42. *See* National Center for Lesbian Rights 2010, "Marriage" http://www.nclrights. org/site/PageServer?pagename=issue_marriage ("The freedom to choose whether and whom to marry is a fundamental human right. Being excluded from this right not only deprives same-sex couples of critical legal protections, it also demeans and stigmatizes same-sex relationships and encourages anti-LGBT discrimination."). *See also* Perry v. Schwarzenegger, Case No. C 09-2292-VRW, U.S. Dist. Court, Northern Dist. of California, Transcript of Proceedings, Jan. 11, 2010: 22 ("[Marriage] means something to them. It means something to society. And it means something to the State of California.")

43. Kotulski 2004.

and contend that no word other than "marriage" will suffice to convey the gravitas of committed same-sex relationships, marriage advocates evince a high degree of faith in the voluntarism of relationship "choice."[44] The movement advances what might be described as an instrumental theory of linguistic constitutionalism: advocates simultaneously claim that (1) marriage has unmatched power and authority to constitute identity, and that (2) this power can be embraced or abjured at will.

The second claim is actually two related, but distinguishable, claims. First, there is the relatively straightforward proposition that, once it is available, marriage can become one choice among many from which gay and lesbian (and presumably heterosexual) couples might draw in describing and ordering their relationships. Second, there is the idea that once "inside" the legal definition of marriage, lesbian and gay couples can throw off its normative strictures and reinvent the institution. This latter claim reflects, and emerges from, the lingering discomfort that many gay men, and especially[45] lesbians, appear to feel about the institution of marriage. The belief that "gays will change marriage" and that marriage will not change gays is a balm to that discomfort. It permits the movement to grow beyond those who embrace marriage

44. *See* National Center for Lesbian Rights 2010, "Marriage" http://www.nclrights. org/site/PageServer?pagename=issue_marriage ("The freedom to choose whether and whom to marry is a fundamental human right.); Lambda Legal 2010, "Marriage", http://www.lambdalegal.org/issues/marriage/ ("Lambda Legal will continue to seek an end to discrimination in access to civil marriage so that same-sex couples in this country have the same choices other couples have, including whether or not to marry.").

45. There undoubtedly is, and has been, a gendered component to the internal LGB debate on marriage. Gay men have been the loudest and longest-standing proponents of marriage among the ostensible leaders of the LGB movement, while lesbians have been its most persistent critics (even as some have eventually come to believe that pursuing marriage is a good thing). Of course there are exceptions to this rule, but the gendering of the debate should not be surprising given the influence of feminist thought on lesbian culture and praxis.

uncritically to include many gay men and lesbians who can now understand their participation in the marriage movement as a radical, transgressive act.[46]

From a social constructionist perspective, these claims are perplexing. Basic sociology teaches us that norms are hardly choices—one option among a cafeteria of social possibilities. Norms have power and significance precisely because they constrain and channel human action.[47] Moreover, norms are backed by sanctions, making compliance something far less than voluntary in nature. In the case of marriage, particularly in the United States, the cultural and social imperatives toward marriage are exceptionally powerful.[48] In 2008, only about 7 percent of Americans 55 years old or older had never been married.[49] And despite changes in the timing of first marriage, a 2002 survey of 15- to 44-year-old Americans found that the odds of a man marrying by the age of 40 remained over 80 percent, while women had an 86 percent probability of being married at least once by that age.[50] The percentage of "never marrieds" drops precipitously after age 40, so that ultimately, about 90–95 percent of Americans will have married at least once in their lives before death.[51] A leading proponent of same-sex marriage, columnist Dan Savage, has written an entire

46. *See* Taylor, et al, 2009.

47. *See generally* Durkheim 1952; Parsons 1961; Giddens 1984.

48. *See, for example*, Ingraham 2008. Anyone who doubts the power of marriage as a cultural imperative simply hasn't been to the movies lately. Or watched television. Or passed a newsstand. And, as Ruthann Robson has argued, marriage's centrality as an economic institution which privatizes dependency renders it "compulsory" in the sense of the word as it was deployed by Adrienne Rich. *See* Robson 2009.

49. United States Bureau of the Census 2010. See also Cherlin 1992.

50. U.S. Dept. of Health and Human Services, National Center for Health Statistics 2009: 2.

51. United States Bureau of the Census 2010.

book on his own experience considering marriage that forcefully asserts the "marriage can be a choice" claim, while endlessly detailing the powerful pressures to marry that are brought to bear upon him by family, friends, and the culture at large.[52] (Savage eventually capitulates, marrying his boyfriend in Canada.)

Law plainly participates in this normative push toward marriage. As Michael Warner has argued (and the case law makes clear) marriage is inherently an institution of privilege and, as such, requires the inscription and reinscription of the line dividing the privileged from the unprivileged.[53] Courts participate in this inscriptive process by denying marriage-like protections and benefits to those who are eligible to marry but who choose not to.[54] Same-sex marriage proponents readily recognize the ways in which law favors the married over the unmarried but fail to project this observation onto a future, post–same-sex marriage world. Once we are eligible to marry, however, it seems plain that we, too, will be eligible for this sort of sanctioning.[55]

The more nuanced claim, however, is the one that proposes that, once allowed to marry, gay men and lesbians will "change

52. Savage 2005.

53. Warner 1999: 117.

54. *See, for example*, Elden v. Sheldon, 46 Cal.3d 267 (1988). *See generally* Robson 2009.

55. The same can be said with some confidence about the redisciplining of parenting relationships within marriage. There has been significant movement in the law in the direction of recognizing parent-child relationships on their own terms, outside of presumptions based on marital status. Polikoff 2008: chapter 3. Yet the focus on parenting in the cases that have affirmed same-sex marriage makes clear that the availability of marital status to same-sex couples may work against this trend. See the discussion, *infra*, pp. 249–50. As a result, it will make increasing sense as an instrumental matter for same-sex couples to marry as a way of ensuring the legal recognition of their parenting relationships, thus increasing the pressure to marry and decreasing the incentive to create alternative kinship structures and legal instruments designed to codify and protect those structures.

marriage."[56] This claim is, in turn, predicated on two assumptions: that marriage can both retain its cultural and discursive power and submit to radical reformulation, and that marriage and gayness can coexist in the same construct. The first assumption amounts to an oxymoron, and as we shall see, it is manifestly rejected in same-sex marriage legal discourse. The second assumption requires us to ask: is "gay marriage" possible and, if so, what would it look like? Here, we come up against the conservative incarnation of the same question—the one that sees "gay marriage" as a definitional impossibility because it conceives of marriage as essentially heterosexual in nature: a union of one man and one woman.[57] But as a discursive construct, the institution of marriage is not hetero*sexual*, even though it does remain hetero*normative*.[58] Marriage is not fundamentally sexual at all: monogamous love, commitment, cohabitation, economic interdependency, and the creation of a privatized family unit have precious little to do with sexuality (and indeed are often defined as the antithesis of sexuality). To the extent that marriage (as it is constituted in these cases) has anything to do with sexuality, it is as an institution dedicated to a particular sociobiological program: directing and minimizing men's procreative sexual drives in service of the

56. *See*, for example, Poirier 2008a.

57. *See* 1 U.S.C. § 1 ("In determining the meaning of any Act of Congress, or of any ruling, regulation, or interpretation of the various administrative bureaus and agencies of the United States, the word "marriage" means only a legal union between one man and one woman as husband and wife. . ."").

58. Heteronormative is a term of underdetermined meaning. Here, I use it to describe a binarized conception of gender norms that is thought to derive from heterosexuality, but which can and does exist apart from it. *See generally* Warner 1991.

privatization of dependency.[59] But marriage is, fundamentally, a marker of *not*-sexuality.

Certainly, marriage cannot be reconciled with a specifically gay or lesbian sexuality. In constituting the figure of marriage as a legal concept, courts—even where they explicitly reject the "one man, one woman" formulation—nonetheless define it as a distinctly not-gay social institution. That is, they install marriage as a modality which is orthogonal to gayness as a specific set of sexual experiences and practices, the decidedly *homo* gender/sex/sexuality performances described by Leo Bersani and Teresa DeLauretis.[60] Moreover, they do this while upholding a key feature of the predictive binary matrix: its reliance upon the notion of a stable, prediscursive sexual identity. In adjudicating the same-sex marriage cases, courts simultaneously recognize gay identity as an aspect of individual personhood and establish that entry into marriage requires a relinquishing and denunciation of gayness as lived experience. Gay *people* may now marry in some states. But this does not mean that *gay marriage* exists anywhere.

## II. A *Loving* Inquiry into the Nature of Marriage

In all of the modern same-sex marriage cases, courts have been faced with a surprisingly difficult task: describing what marriage is. On one hand, marriage is ubiquitous, and most Americans[61]

---

59. *See Hernandez v. Robles*, 855 N.E.2d 1 (Ct. App. N.Y. 2006). *See generally* Franke 2006.

60. *See supra* chapter 3.

61. I should underscore that I am limiting my focus to the American same-sex marriage debate. While the drive to extend marriage to same-sex couples is evident in many other countries as well, it should go without saying that marriage (as a cultural, social, and legal set of practices) is likely to mean different things in different places.

can readily rattle off several of its defining features: commitment, monogamy, shared child rearing, cohabitation, permanence, a widely acknowledged reason for having a big party to which people will feel compelled to travel long distances, etc. But these are all cultural dimensions, and marriage is simultaneously cultural and legal in nature. And as diverse and multivalent as it is as a cultural institution, marriage's legal dimensions and implications are perhaps even more so. Indeed, marriage fits so awkwardly within existing American legal frameworks that it may be *sui generis*. Civil marriage straddles status and contract (with special rules on the contract side); it exceeds the boundaries of substantive law categories (finding its way into property law, rules of evidence, criminal law, trusts and estates, the tax and bankruptcy codes, family law, and so forth); and it comes perilously close to stamping religious authority with the imprimatur of the state. To make matters even more complicated, as both a cultural and a legal matter, marriage may be variously understood as a system of distribution—organizing the flow of benefits, obligations, duties, and rights between the married couple and between the state and individuals—and as a conferrer of privileged status.[62] Thus, through marriage, the state has the power to order economic and legal relationships and to confer "dignity" upon particular kinds of relationships and, by definition, not others.[63]

Typically, these internal tensions and complications remain concealed from view. In everyday life and in most judicial settings, marriage can be experienced and described in situationally appropriate ways, permitting holistic inquiries into the nature of the institution to remain in abeyance or to recede to the background.

62. Cott 2000: Polikoff 2008; Robson 2009; Cherlin 2009; West 2007.

63. Warner 1999. *See, for example, In re Marriage Cases*, 43 Cal. 4757 (Sup. Ct. Calif. 2008).

But this sort of backgrounding is simply not possible in contemporary same-sex marriage litigation. Here, the question of what marriage is and what marriage does is thrust to the foreground. And so courts address same-sex marriage in grand and sweeping terms, opining on the nature of marriage as an institution, on sexual identity, and on the relevant qualifications of gay men and lesbians for admission into the institution of marriage. Yet they do so from within a specified and narrow organizational and discursive field.[64]

The delimiting of the field upon which marriage is considered in the same-sex marriage cases may be traced to the imperatives of constitutional analysis and the structuring influence of prior doctrine. First, whatever the specific basis of the claim—equal protection, equal enjoyment of benefits, privacy, a "right to marry," etc.—in order to pursue a constitutional attack on same-sex marriage bans, advocates must craft their arguments in such a way as to implicate the rights of individuals, not of groups (LGB people, collectively), or of couples.[65] The effect of this strategy, once it is taken up by opponents and the court and redeployed in specific doctrinal analysis, is to entrench a discourse of fixed

64. On organizational fields, *see generally* Suchman and Edelman 1996.

65. Although they are not identical to the federal Constitution, the state constitutions at issue in the marriage cases track it closely, and they, too, conceive of the right to be treated equally and to enjoy certain fundamental rights as rights held by the individual. Courts do remark upon the need to individualize the claim, but often elliptically and frequently in a footnote. See *Lewis v Harris*, 908 A.2d at 422; *Kerrigan*, 957 A.2d at 413, n. 2. *See also In re Marriage Cases*, 43 Cal. 4th 757 at 726, n. 34. Having noted the requirement that the right be described in individual terms, most then go on to treat the couple as, in essence, holding a summation of the rights held by each constituent member. It should be noted that equal protection analysis nonetheless often relies on a comparison of groups—here it will be heterosexual people vs. homosexual people. But the right to be treated equally is not a right held or enjoyed by a group. Rather, it is the right of a person to be treated *as an individual* just like any other individual, *regardless of one's actual or perceived membership in a group*. If this sounds a bit circular, that may be because it is.

and permanent sexual identity driving predictable, sex-specific desires and behaviors.

Second, because the substantive claims in the marriage cases include a mixture of equal protection and substantive due process claims to "privacy," "autonomy," "liberty," or some variation on the "right to marry,"[66] marriage discourse circulates around certain doctrinal fence posts. As we saw in the context of anti-gay hate crime and sexual harassment law, these fence posts typically include a consideration of the appropriate level of scrutiny to apply to the challenged law, and of how to classify the rights and the people in question. But whereas in the anti-gay hate crime cases the question of status versus conduct was explicitly engaged, here it is largely bracketed. Homosexuality is decidedly a quality of being and not doing in the marriage cases.[67] The inquiry instead focuses on what *sort* of quality it is: Is it "immutable"? Is it relevant, especially with respect to the dictates of married life? Immutability is ever present in the marriage cases, and relevancy is increasingly

66. *See Dean v. District of Columbia*, 653 A.2d 307 (D.C. Ct. App. 1995) (equal protection); *Goodridge v. Dept. Of Public Health*, 798 N.E.2d 941 (Sup. Jud. Ct. Mass. 2003) (equal protection and privacy/liberty); *In re Marriage Cases*, 43 Cal. 4757 (Sup. Ct. Calif. 2008) (equal protection and substantive due process/privacy); *Kerrigan v Commissioner of Public Health*, 957 A.2d 407 (Sup. Ct. Conn. 2008) (equal protection); *Lewis v. Harris*, 908 A.2d 196, (Sup. Ct. N.J. 2006) (equal protection and "fundamental right to marry"); *Hernandez v. Robles* (equal protection and substantive due process); *Varnum v. Brien*, 763 N.W.2d 862 (Sup. Ct. Iowa 2009) (equal protection).

67. One way of understanding this shift is to see it as an outcome of *Lawrence v. Texas*, which not only decriminalized homosexual conduct but (in so doing) removed a critique of gay sexual practices from the repertoire of arguments that might be effectively raised against assertions of gay rights. *See* Franke 2004. Take, for example, *Dean v. District of Columbia*, a pre-*Lawrence* case that delves deeply (and awkwardly) into the possibility of using marriage to "redeem" sodomitical sexual practices. (The dissent suggests that heterosexuals are permitted such redemption, while homosexuals are not.) Today, one searches in vain for explicit references to sodomy in same-sex marriage cases. At most, courts may refer to "sexual attraction" or "non-procreative sexual activities." More often than not, however, they refer only to love and (even more frequently) commitment.

salient. As the equal protection strategy emerges with particular force in jurisdictions that have already extended civil unions to LGB couples,[68] advocates are increasingly required to demonstrate that gay and straight couples are "similarly situated."[69] As a result, gayness itself is increasingly subject to erasure from same-sex marriage discourse.[70]

## A. Stabilizing Sexual Identity and Desire

Three cases substantially generate and define the same-sex marriage field of inquiry: *Loving v. Virginia* (*Loving*),[71] *United States v. Carolene Products* (*Carolene Products*),[72] and *City of Cleburne v. Cleburne Living Center, Inc.* (*Cleburne*).[73] *Loving* is easily the most recognizable of the three cases; it is the 1967 case that declared state anti-miscegenation statutes unconstitutional. In so holding,

68. *See* Klein and Redman 2009 (stating that passage of a civil union law in Connecticut rendered LGB couples "similarly situated" to heterosexual couples with respect to marriage).

69. A different sort of "similarity" inquiry runs through these cases as well: the effort to analogize sexual identity to racial identity. *See* the discussion *infra* at 226–27. *See generally* Halley 1998.

70. Although the numbers are too small to establish this definitively, there is a strong *prima facie* case to be made for the influence of policy diffusion in these early cases and therefore their proportionately greater influence. *See generally* DiMaggio and Powell 1983. That is, each court appears to be looking directly at the actions of courts in sister jurisdictions for guidance. Citations to like-minded courts are plentiful, and specific language is repeated in such a way as to belie the possibility of mere coincidence. (*See, for example,* citations to Ronald Dworkin's poetic musings about the transcendental qualities of marriage in both *Lewis* and *Kerrigan*.) Also, the framing of the constitutional issues is so similar across jurisdictions as to suggest the influence of institutional diffusion, especially since each jurisdiction is governed by its own, distinct state constitution.

71. 388 U.S. 1 (1967).

72. 304 U.S. 144 (1938).

73. 473 U.S. 432 (1985).

the *Loving* Court issued language that is frequently repeated (and disputed) in same-sex marriage litigation:

> The freedom to marry has long been recognized as one of the vital personal rights essential to the orderly pursuit of happiness by free men. Marriage is one of the "basic civil rights of man," fundamental to our very existence and survival.[74]

Within the terms of Fourteenth Amendment analysis, if marriage is a "basic civil right," then it is a fundamental one (an unenumerated substantive right) and cannot be denied or abridged in the absence of a compelling state interest.[75] But is marriage a basic civil right, or did the *Loving* Court have in mind only *heterosexual* marriage when it made that assertion?[76] This is where much of the action happens in same-sex marriage cases, and *Loving* therefore serves as a pivot point in adjudicating the substantive due process claims that arise therein.

For our purposes, however, there is a more important aspect of *Loving's* influence. In order to bring her challenge within the purview of the Fourteenth Amendment, Mildred Loving first had to establish that her claim was grounded in a notion of individual rights. That is, she had to describe her right to marry as located within herself as an individual, even as the state's infringement of the right was intelligible only in relational terms (i.e., in order to know what was being prohibited, one had to know something about both would-be spouses). And so she argued that she was being denied her right to marry on the basis of an individual,

74. *Loving v. Virginia*, 388 U.S. 1, 12 (1967).

75. *See Kramer v. Union Free School District*, 395 U.S. 621 (1969); *Griswold v. Connecticut*, 381 U.S. 479 (1965); *Roe v. Wade*, 410 U.S. 113 (1973).

76. *Dean v. District of Columbia*, 653 A.2d at 363 (Steadman, J., concurring); *Conaway v. Deane*, 932 A.2d at 620; *Hernandez v. Robles*, 855 N.E.2d at 5–6.

ascribed characteristic—namely, race (either hers or that of her would-be husband). In response, the state of Virginia claimed that the statute was not discriminatory because it was applied equally to white and black individuals: none was permitted to marry across the color bar.[77] In a break with precedent, the *Loving* Court rejected this defense, looking behind the formally equal application of the statute, and declaring that it had been "designed to maintain White Supremacy."[78]

For reasons that should be plain, plaintiffs in same-sex marriage cases often try to leverage *Loving* by analogizing same-sex marriage bans to anti-miscegenation statutes.[79] This strategy is sometimes effective, but the process by which it occurs works a reinscription of sex/sexuality binary categories, further hardening them as descriptors of identity tethered to specific expectations of desire and behavior. The arguments that circulate around and through the *Loving* precedent take a number of forms, but because of the individualizing nature of the inquiry, all converge to constitute sexuality as sexual *orientation*: as a stance assumed from the position of one anatomical sex toward another. Thus, in a direct parallel to *Loving*, some plaintiffs argue that the ban on same-sex marriage discriminates on the basis of sex (mine or my partner's),[80] while defenders of the ban contend that, because there is no prohibition on gay people marrying people of the opposite sex, there is no discrimination of

77. Virginia's statute treated white and "colored" persons formally equally: "*Punishment for marriage.*—If any white person intermarry with a colored person, or any colored person intermarry with a white person, he shall be guilty of a felony and shall be punished by confinement in the penitentiary for not less than one nor more than five years." *Loving v. Virginia*, 388 U.S. 1, 4 (1967).

78. *Loving*, 388 U.S. at 11.

79. *See generally* Halley 1998.

80. *See, for example, Hernandez*, 855 N.E.2d at 6-7; *In re Marriage Cases*, 43 Cal. 4th at 837-839; *Kerrigan*, 957 A.2d at 414; *Andersen*, 138 P.3d at 48.

any kind.[81] Some courts have accepted this defense,[82] but even where they have not, the response has been equally individualizing and binarizing. The opinion of the California Supreme Court on this issue is revealing:

> In arguing that the marriage statutes do not discriminate on the basis of sexual orientation, defendants rely upon the circumstance that these statutes, on their face, do not refer explicitly to sexual orientation and do not prohibit gay individuals from marrying a person of the opposite sex. . . In our view. . .[b]y limiting marriage to opposite-sex couples, the marriage statutes, realistically viewed, operate clearly and directly to impose different treatment on gay individuals because of their sexual orientation. *By definition, gay individuals are persons who are sexually attracted to persons of the same sex and thus, if inclined to enter into a marriage relationship, would choose to marry a person of their own sex or gender.*[83]

All of this is hard to argue with, and one can readily see why the California Supreme Court has endeared itself to proponents of same-sex marriage. But note that what the court is doing here is solidifying a notion of gayness as a characteristic of the individual that drives sexual attraction to persons of the same sex. Marriage, in turn, is posited as a straightforward codification

81. *See In re Marriage Cases*, 43 Cal. 4th at 839-840; *Kerrigan*, 957 A.2d at 431, n.24.

82. *Conaway*, 932 A.2d at 599 (sex discrimination claim fails because there is no evidence that the legislature intended "to differentiate between men and women as classes on the basis of some misconception regarding gender roles in our society"); *Andersen*, 138 P.3d at 988-989 (no violation of state Equal Rights Amendment because discrimination on basis of "sex" and on basis of "sexual activities or interests" are distinguishable).

83. *In re Marriage Cases*, 43 Cal. 4th at 839 (emphasis added). This formulation appears more than once in the opinion.

of this naturalized drive. Same-sex marriage opponents dispute the claim that discrimination or animus against gay people is at work, but they, too, advance a notion of fixed, prediscursive sexed and sexual identity. They contend that the traditional definition of marriage is simply and clearly related to heterosexual drives—those that lead to reproduction.[84] Whether or not courts side with opponents or proponents of same-sex marriage on this issue, then, sexuality is installed as a categorical descriptor of identity—one that is linked in predictive ways to desire. The formulation is both untroubled and untroubling. There are two sexes and two sexual orientations in this account, ontological facts established in such offhand fashion and converging in the arguments advanced by both sides, that their taken-for-granted qualities are confirmed.

Indeed, it is where courts have aligned with proponents of same-sex marriage—that is, where the legal campaign for same-sex marriage has been successful—that they have demonstrated a particularly forceful commitment to this ontology:

> In our view, it is sophistic to suggest that [the marriage ban does not discriminate] by reason of the circumstance that the marriage statutes permit a gay man or a lesbian to marry some-

---

84. Again, there are variations on this argument. Most frequently, opponents of same-sex marriage contend that limiting marriage to male/female couples is necessary to offer the proper encouragement and incentives to them to ensure procreation within stable, economically interdependent nuclear family units. This is, in essence, a sociobiological argument about the unruly quality of heterosexual men's desire to spread their DNA as far and as wide as possible. (It is hard to imagine a more mechanical conception of sexuality than this.) *See, eg., Hernandez*, 855 N.E. at 17–18. Others make a more cultural argument, contending that marriage has always signaled the state's sanctioning of a particular family form: sexed and gendered parents providing care and sustenance for their biological issue. Sexuality is definitively tied to procreation in these accounts, which renders them somewhat awkward, given the rather undeniable de-linking of marriage, sex, and procreation over the course of American history. *See* D'Emilio and Freedman 1997.

one of the opposite sex, because making such a choice would require the negation of the person's sexual orientation.[85]

The question of what gayness is and how it might operate is bracketed; the parties and the court converge in an understanding of homosexuality as a feature of identity, one that is stable and predictable, and which drives the desire to join with someone of the same sex (also conceived as a prediscursive property of the person) to create a family. Thwarting this drive results in a "negation" of identity. Thus described, (through a set of deductive and inductive gestures that apparently require no explanation or justification) sexuality immediately recedes. Its retreat is further hastened in the "winning" cases by certain specific doctrinal requirements of equal protection analysis which establish preconditions to heightened scrutiny.

As we saw in Chapter 4, determining the level of scrutiny is an important threshold inquiry in equal protection analysis. In contemplating this question, courts often begin with *United States v. Carolene Products*, in which the United States Supreme Court mused about

> whether similar considerations [should] enter into the review of statutes directed at particular religious or national or racial minorities: whether prejudice against discrete and insular minorities may be a special condition, which tends seriously to curtail the operation of those political processes ordinarily to be relied upon to protect minorities, and which may call for a correspondingly more searching judicial inquiry.[86]

---

85. *In re Marriage Cases*, 43 Cal. 4th at 840. The *Kerrigan* court adopted precisely the same reasoning, and quoted this passage from *In re Marriage Cases* at length, summarizing it this way: "In other words, this state's bar against same sex marriage *effectively* precludes gay persons from marrying; to conclude otherwise would be to blink at reality." *Kerrigan*, 957 A.2d at 431, n.24.

86. *Carolene Products*, 304 U.S. 144, 152, n. 4. (1938) (citations omitted).

*Carolene Products* was about "filled" milk: not the stuff of gripping equal protection analysis. But the Court's observation about "discrete and insular minorities" has nonetheless served as an important clarification of at least one justification for applying heightened scrutiny to certain legal classifications. According to the Court, statutes that are directed at such minoritites may warrant closer scrutiny because we can assume that such groups face political vulnerabilities that make it difficult for them to resist the majority's imposition of legal disabilities. In short, some groups are, by their nature, politically weak (if not powerless) and courts may wish to look especially carefully at laws that seem to be aimed at disadvantaging them.

As Susan Schmeiser has documented, this initial consideration of political vulnerability "metamorphosed into efforts to identify the precise nature of the group alleging prejudice," leading courts to refine the analysis, emphasizing "the conditions for entry and exit" from the group.[87] In an ever narrowing inquiry, the word of consequence became "immutable." In a sex discrimination case, *Frontiero v. Richardson*, the Supreme Court described the significance of immutability this way:

> [S]ince sex, like race and national origin, is an immutable characteristic determined solely by the accident of birth, the imposition of special disabilities upon the members of a particular sex because of their sex would seem to violate 'the basic concept of our system that legal burdens should bear some relationship to individual responsibility.[88]

Later, in *Lyng v. Castillo*, the Supreme Court added the idea that immutability might be important because it could serve to identify

87. Schmeiser 2009: 1508.

88. *Frontiero v. Richardson*, 411 U.S. 677, 686 (1973).

the targets of discriminatory legislation "as a discrete group."[89] The *Lyng* formulation plainly derives from the *Carolene Products* focus on a group's status as a "discrete and insular minority," while the *Frontiero* formulation appears to be an effort to define footnote 4's "prejudice" component.

In *City of Cleburne v. Cleburne Living Center, Inc.*, a case that considered an equal protection challenge brought on behalf of a group of developmentally disabled people, the Court expanded on the *Frontiero* language, indicating that the immutability inquiry was simply a way of determining whether a statute's targeting of a group was likely based on prejudice, rather than a good faith effort to advance the interests embodied in the statute. Thus, the *Cleburne* court noted, most laws are given a relatively low level of scrutiny, but some laws—those distinguishing on the basis of race, alienage, or national origin—are subject to heightened review because such aspects of identity

> are so seldom relevant to the achievement of any legitimate state interest that laws grounded in such considerations *are deemed to reflect prejudice and antipathy*–a view that those in the burdened class are not as worthy or deserving as others. For these reasons *and because such discrimination is unlikely to be soon rectified by legislative means*, these laws are subjected to strict scrutiny and will be sustained only if they are suitably tailored to serve a compelling state interest.[90]

In the wake of what many have viewed as the *Cleburne* Court's elucidation of the *Carolene Products* footnote, the inquiry into immutability now often focuses on the twin notions of prejudice

89. *Lyng v . Castillo,* 477 U.S. 635 ( 1986 ).

90. *City of Cleburne v. Cleburne Living Center,* 473 U.S. 432, 440 (1985) (emphasis added).

and political powerlessness. However, *Frontiero*'s reference to "accidents of birth" continues to animate a nascent biologism that courses through the jurisprudence.

Schmeiser notes that immutability has never been an entirely satisfactory test, frequently devolving into circular investigations of the nature of group identity and animus, with a finding of animus depending on the specific juridical definition of the group or vice versa.[91] Sometimes, courts have focused on only one element of the *Carolene Products/Cleburne* heuristic while, at other times, they have required a finding of immutability *and* obviousness *and* involuntary membership in the class, slavishly (if erroneously) following a satisfaction-of-the-elements method of inquiry. (The incoherence of these analyses illustrates how easily the tail of doctrine can come to wag the dog of judicial fact finding.)

Recognizing this, many legal scholars have long advocated the abandonment of immutability as an analytical device entirely, and Schmeiser notes that such efforts found some success until the notion of immutability was revived by LGB legal scholarship and practice.[92] Indeed, all of the modern marriage cases engage the issue of immutability. Moreover, each court's resolution of the immutability inquiry tends to signal its ultimate holding on the merits. For example, in Washington and Maryland, state appellate courts held that equal protection claims predicated on sexual orientation failed the immutability test, did not give rise to strict scrutiny of the marriage bans at issue, and did not warrant striking down the challenged laws.[93] Neither court defined

91. Schmeiser 2009: 1507–8.

92. *Ibid*: 1512.

93. *Andersen*, 138 P.3d at 974 ("The plaintiffs do not cite other authority or any secondary authority or studies in support of the conclusion that homosexuality is an immutable characteristic"); *Conaway*, 932 A.2d at 615 ("Appellees point neither to scientific nor sociological studies, which have withstood analysis for evidentiary admissibility, in support of an argument that sexual orientation is an immutable characteristic.").

the term "immutable," but the Maryland high court's long, foot-noted literature review makes clear that its working definition turned on biology and the question of whether homosexuality might properly be classified as an accident of birth.[94]

Despite a sustained and energetic investigation into the matter, however, science has yet to find a solid and infallible biological basis for homosexual desire.[95] As a consequence, where courts have affirmed a right to marriage for same-sex couples, they have generally described homosexual orientation as *virtually* immutable in the sense of being so closely tied to selfhood as to be indistinguishable from an ascribed characteristic.[96] This is an approach that trades on the normative power of biology, while satisfying specific doctrinal requirements. As we have seen, immutability in the *Lyng/Carolene Products* sense is important because it has functional significance within a certain concept of legal ordering. That is, a particular characteristic of a person matters only if one could say that it is not something that s/he could change for the purpose of avoiding the discriminatory impact of the law at issue. The legal phrase of note here is "self-help," as it was described with unusual clarity by a dissenting judge in *Dean v. District of Columbia*:

> Under these circumstances, I cannot say as a matter of law that homosexuality is not as immutable as race or gender for purposes of equal protection analysis, for I am not willing to

94. *Conaway* 932 A.2d at 615, n. 57 (citing studies of genetics, brain structure, twin studies, etc.). One of the more interesting aspects of the Conaway court's footnote is its inclusion of Janet Halley's critical analysis of the concept of immutability. *See* Halley 1994. But the court seems to be offering it as a kind of methodological and evidentiary critique of the genetics/brain study literature, rather than what it plainly is: an effort to displace that very inquiry.

95. *See* Halley 1994.

96. *In re Marriage Cases*, 43 Cal. 4at 842; *Kerrigan*, 957 A.2d at 432; *Varnum*, 763 N.W.2d at 892–3.

> say that traumatic, possibly emotionally destructive self-help, rather than constitutional protection, is the price homosexuals must pay (assuming such self-help would be effective, which I strongly doubt) to avoid pernicious discrimination. Indeed, the increasing use of gene therapy and drugs to manipulate health and human behavior suggests the quite scary spectre of enforcing a public policy for "curing" homosexuals—an Orwellian road not to be traveled.[97]

In spite of its vigorous rejection of the idea that the state might require gay men and lesbians to either submit to reparative therapy or cease complaining about anti-gay legislation, this language keeps the debate firmly on the ground of what could be changed. And in this account, sexual orientation is fixed.

In recognizing the limitations of a biological argument, the California, New Jersey, Iowa, and Connecticut courts relied instead on the quasi-psychological notions of personhood and identity to advance the claim that sexual orientation is foundational. The California Supreme Court, for example, addressed the immutability inquiry by emphasizing sexual orientation as a quality of identity:

> Because a person's sexual orientation is so integral an aspect of one's identity, it is not appropriate to require a person to repudiate or change his or her sexual orientation in order to avoid discriminatory treatment.[98]

Here, the discussion of drugs and gene therapy gives way to consideration of the foundational qualities of identity, signaling a more interpersonal and psychological approach. At the same

97. *Dean,* 653 A.2d at 352.

98. *In re Marriage Cases,* 43 Cal. 4th at 842.

time, however, biology and genetics do not disappear entirely. Rather, the California court, like the New Jersey, Iowa, and Connecticut courts, moves back and forth between what may be the possible biological basis of homosexuality to its undeniable fixity and priority in determining human behavior: "whether or not sexual orientation is based on biological or physiological factors, which may be a matter of some controversy, it is a deeply personal characteristic that is either unchangeable or changeable only at unacceptable personal costs."[99] In so doing, the court reinscribes the predictive matrix of sex, gender, and sexuality by defining sexual orientation as both a characteristic of the person and a driver of desire and sexual conduct:

> As explained in the amicus curiae brief filed by a number of leading mental health organizations . . . Sexual orientation is commonly discussed as a characteristic of the individual, like biological sex, gender identity, or age. This perspective is incomplete because sexual orientation is always defined in relational terms and necessarily involves relationships with other individuals. Sexual acts and romantic attractions are categorized as homosexual or heterosexual according to the biological sex of the individuals involved in them, relative to each other. Indeed, it is by acting—or desiring to act— with another person that individuals express their hetero- sexuality, homosexuality, or bisexuality.[100]

On this view, sexual orientation is a characteristic of the person that can be "expressed" (or not), while desire and identity

99. *Ibid.*

100. *Ibid*: 840, n. 59.

are defined by the "biological sex" of the parties involved.[101] What at first appears to be a relational discourse of homosex ("sexual orientation is always defined in relational terms") is quickly revealed to instead emerge from the logic of the predictive binary matrix. Sexuality is not a doing, but an interior quality of the person that can be divined from the biological sex configuration of a given couple. And to the extent that it is a doing, the performance is expressive of an underlying, already constituted sexual orientation ("*their* heterosexuality, homosexuality, *or* bisexuality").

101. The *Kerrigan* court is in accord: "In view of the central role that sexual orientation plays in a person's fundamental right to self-determination, we fully agree with the plaintiffs that their sexual orientation represents the kind of distinguishing characteristic that defines them as a discrete group for purposes of determining whether that group should be afforded heightened protection under the equal protection provisions of the state constitution. This prong of the suspectness inquiry surely is satisfied when, as in the present case, the identifying trait is 'so central to a person's identity that it would be abhorrent for government to penalize a person for refusing to change [it]. . . .'" *Kerrigan*, 957 A.2d at 438.

Schmeiser notes that the *Kerrigan* court seems to move away from this focus on immutability as a fixed characteristic of the person, and in the direction of a social constructionist view, which emphasizes the ways in which sexual orientation is deployed as a social and legal category in service of legal and social discrimination:

"But the [*Kerrigan* opinion] offers yet another reading of immutability, one that turns not on the significance of individual self-definition or the question of volition, but rather on the persistence of 'social and legal ostracism' as the relevant aspect of group definition. . . This conception of identity underscores its social and legal dimensions rather than stressing the significance of internal self or group-definition. In other words, it reminds us that equal protection analysis is centrally concerned with status-not in the sense of one's stable identity, but in the sense of one's access to the rights and protections afforded the majority." Schmeiser 2009: 1518.

I'm not entirely convinced this reading is supported by the language of the opinion itself, but if true it would be a welcome departure from standard immutability inquiries, which relentlessly serve the aim of anchoring and solidifying sexual identity and desire in the body or psyche.

## B. The Polysemic Qualities of Immutability

The biological conception of sexuality is reinforced and extended in public discourse through the force of polysemy. Even as immutability has emerged and functions as a term of art from within equal protection analysis, it resonates culturally and politically with a different, yet related, sort of inquiry about homosexuality. As Schmeiser notes, in the context of identity politics broadly conceived, immutability is understood as the diacritical counterpart to "choice": one does not choose to be gay (according to the Human Rights Campaign), gayness chooses you.[102] Whereas the equal protection analysis variant of the immutability concept considers the notion of sexual fixity as it concerns the ability of gay men and lesbians to access democratic institutions, the cultural and political notion of immutability is deployed as a normative argument designed to foreclose a discussion of eradicating or curing gayness itself.[103] Describing one's sexuality as "innate" or otherwise biologically determined can be an effective cultural and political argument—one as effective in marshaling public opinion in favor of policies of inclusion as in convincing

102. Quoted in Schmeiser 2009: 1504.

103. Despite the American Psychological Association's decision in 1973 to remove homosexuality from its list of mental disorders, there remain a number of practitioners who advocate "conversion" or "reparative" therapies, which purport to change homosexual orientation to heterosexual orientation. *See, for example*, Socarides 1978. The APA has roundly rejected such approaches as ineffective and potentially harmful (APA Task Force on Appropriate Therapeutic Responses to Sexual Orientation 2009), but the "ex-gay" discourse retains a fair degree of cultural resonance. It is important to note here that the juridical discourse is not at all immunized from these cultural and political discourses. Recall the dissent in *Dean v. District of Columbia*, in which a plainly well-intentioned Judge Ferren jumps from the notion of political self-help (informed by *Carolene Products*) to the question of whether a state might reasonably require gay people to undergo reparative therapy as a means of solving the "problem" posed by gay rights demands. *See Dean*, 653 A.2d at 346–49.

your parents that your gayness is not an indictment of their chil-drearing practices.

As a strategic matter, there seems to be reasonably good evidence that this approach has, over time, led to increased tolerance of gay people and, in turn, to increased tolerance of gay "lifestyles" writ large.[104] But its risks and costs are equally self-evident. Biology often moves in uncomfortable proximity to pathology.[105] Moreover, as Schmeiser persuasively argues, ceding sexual choice can amount to ceding the idea that gay men and lesbians are capable of full participation in democratic institutions of governance and self-governance.[106]

But there are larger problems. First, the *sotto voce* implication of the choice/immutability debate, and the reason why choice is abjured by LGB advocates, particularly in the marriage cases, is the implication that if one could choose one's sexual orientation, one would check the "heterosexual" box every time. Schmeiser's call to abandon the immutability trap is premised on an explicit rejection of this discursive predicate.[107] Second (and more pertinent to the claims of this project), the distinction between

104. Saad 2007 (cited by Schmeiser 2009: 1499, n.12). Of course, the Gallup poll hardly proves causation (i.e., that acceptance of gay people causes acceptance of gay "lifestyles"). But Gallup's decision to posit "born that way"/"caused by environment" as the independent variables seeking to explain variation in "acceptance of homo-sexual lifestyle" tells us that this is how the relationship is generally conceived.

105. See Schmeiser 2009 at 1520–21. This has been true at least as long as there has been a notion of homosexuality as (in Foucault's words) a distinct "personage." Foucault 1990: 43. *See also* Weeks 1985.

106. Schmeiser 2009: 1521–22.

107. Schmeiser quotes Ed Stein on this point: "[A] more promising and important project would be to try to convince [people] that a person's sexual orientation is not something one should want to change. Rather than trying to convince people that sexual orientations are immutable, I would prefer to try to convince them that we should change the legal and social norms regarding lesbians, gay men, bisexuals and others whose sexual desires make them social pariahs." *Ibid*: 1522.

"choice" and "biology" is never revealed in juridical discourse to be what it surely is: a cultural ruse.

The choice/biology debate revolves around the question of whether sexual orientation is, through the influence of biology, brain matter, or early psychosexual development, the sort of personal feature that one can or cannot contain or thwart or redirect. It asks: just how resistant to the force of individual will is "attraction to members of the same sex"? Law adopts a normative (straight) posture toward this question, producing a lose/lose calculation for the homosexed. Either sexual orientation is biological (and hence perhaps pathological) or it is a choice (and evidence of suspect morality). But a specifically and culturally gay answer to this question has a lot of fun at its expense positing a homosexual desire that is considerably more tenacious than its counterpart. So, for example, evidence of irrepressible gayness is titillating and satisfying wherever it appears: in the specter of a famous "ex-gay" spokesman hitting a gay bar[108] or a list of avowedly anti-gay legislators who have been caught having or soliciting same-sex sex.[109] While it undoubtedly trades on a notion of prediscursive (and even biological) gay essence, this cultural discourse has the power to draw attention to the performative quality of *straightness* (especially virulently anti-gay straightness) by inviting the gay- or lesbian-identified audience to view it as excess or supplement. This parodic technique resonates for culturally specific reasons. Looking for the hidden gay subtext, and reading between and against straight surfaces are subcultural practices of long standing in the gay and lesbian community.[110] Thus, even as they incorporate references to gay essentialism, these practices may have

108. Lawson 2000

109. Spaulding 2010.

110. *See* Fuss 1991 (especially Part II); De Lauretis 1984, 1994; De Lauretis and White 2007.

destabilizing effects on the hetero/homo binary when they emerge from specifically gay cultural contexts.[111]

But the legal discourse of immutability eschews such playfulness. It leaves in place a notion of relentlessly serious and unswerving commitment to categorical placement. It denies a notion of sexuality as a way of being and moving through the world, as a modality of desire that both partakes of and plays with gender, sex, and sexual referents. And because of legal discourse's polysemic qualities, this notion of sexual identity is both empowered and authorized as it informs social and cultural discourses of sex, gender, and sexuality. In its translation to these contexts, immutability sheds its doctrinal roots, appearing as a simple and naturalized conception of biology (or psychology) as destiny. Homosex is reduced and confined to a characteristic of gay/lesbian personhood, disciplining the self and reinforcing the taken-for-grantedness of binary sexual categories. But why does the juridical discourse prevail over, infect, and ultimately subordinate the gay subcultural discourse? Simply put, it is because the state enjoys a monopoly on "symbolic violence,"[112] a monopoly authorized by its reputation for "dispassionate, reasoned, communicative action,"[113] and by our willing submission to its authority.

## III. Erasing Gayness, Take One: *Cleburne* and Relevancy

Same-sex marriage litigation strategies produce and partake of a self-governance project that not only confines unruly sexuality to binary sexual categories but also works to erase and disparage

111. Sedgwick 1990.

112. Bourdieu 1987; Bourdieu and Thompson 1991.

113. Habermas 1996.

gayness itself. This occurs, in part, through legal actors' pursuit of the institutional mandate to consider a second dimension of equal protection analysis, one I refer to broadly as *relevancy*. It also results from a second set of dynamics that emerge from the expressly constitutive claims of the campaign.

Recall that in *Cleburne* the United States Supreme Court noted that immutable characteristics are often the basis for exaggerated, unfounded, and negative generalizations about a group's abilities or characteristics. This, the Court noted, is precisely why laws targeting certain classes of people ought to be subjected to greater judicial scrutiny. Of course, some identifying characteristics may, under certain circumstances, warrant differential legal treatment. But many—perhaps most—will not. In such cases, a law's effort to classify people likely signals a constitutionally impermissible level of animus or prejudice toward that group.

Courts can examine a statutory classification's relevance in a number of different ways. First, they can pursue a general line of inquiry into whether the classifying trait ought to matter at all to a group's legal or social status. The *Cleburne* court invited such an inquiry when it suggested that statutory classifications may indicate a legislative determination "that those in the burdened class are not as worthy or deserving as others." Second, courts may look more narrowly at the relationship between the classification at issue and the purpose of the challenged statute. The first and second inquiries differ in provenance (though it can sometimes be difficult to see this in the opinions themselves). The first operates as part of a court's determination as to the appropriate level of scrutiny to apply to the challenged statute, while the second arises within a court's analysis of whether the state's proffered interests in the statute can support its reliance on the classification. In practice, these inquiries are directly connected through the institutional mechanics of equal protection analysis: a finding of irrelevancy in the first inquiry will lead to heightened scrutiny of the statute, which will, in turn, make the court more skeptical about the state's justifications. Whatever the conceptual distinction between the two, the connection between them is fortified in these cases because the subject of the litigation is marriage. Marriage is so deeply entwined with cultural ideals concerning worth, maturity, citizenship, and kinship that establishing one's suitability for marriage may amount to establishing one's value as an American (and vice versa).[114] As a result, the marriage courts tend to move back and forth between discussions of the overall social worth of LGB people and the legal relevance of sexual identity to the purposes of marriage as an institution.

## A. First Comes. . .Babies

As they consider the nature and purpose(s) of marriage, courts are remarkably explicit and self-conscious about their social scientific aspirations. In previous chapters, we have observed courts demonstrating an almost blithe ignorance about the ways in which they interpose and hypothesize conceptions of human motivation, identity, and desire in an effort to adjudicate the truth of disputed events. By contrast, in the marriage cases, courts bring these processes into full view. They contrast "adjudicative" to "legislative" facts[115] and authorize themselves to undertake

---

114. Theda Skocpol's insight that—apart from soldiering—mothering may be the second most important path to full citizenship in the United States may help to explain this aspect of the discourse. Skocpol 1992.

115. *See, for example, Varnum v. O'Brien,* 763 N.W.2d 862 (Sup. Ct. Iowa 2009). As the *Varnum* court explained, "adjudicative" facts are facts bearing only on the parties to the litigation, while "legislative" or "constitutional" facts include additional political, economic, social, and scientific facts that provide a broader context within which to consider the dispute at hand. *Varnum* at 881. In determining the relevancy, materiality, and admissibility of adjudicative facts, the court notes, rules of evidence are vital in setting the "framework" within which factual disputes may

explicit inquiries into history, economics, and psychology (among others). They readily admit the complex and dynamic social and cultural environments within which they must insert themselves, and they take considerable care to mark off the limits of their interventions, usually by repairing to ideas about the separation of powers or democratic expressions of popular will.[116] Nonetheless, even as the marriage courts narrate a fact-finding process that intends itself to be more capacious than, for example, hate crime or harassment litigation, they fail to recognize the ways in which the institutional contours of adjudication have drastically limited their domains of inquiry. They may be setting out to engage in "independent research,"[117] but they are doing so within the confines of law's *habitus*.

be resolved. But legislative facts are not so bound by traditional and formal rules of evidence: ". . . constitutional facts are introduced into judicial decisions through independent research by judges and written briefs of the parties, as well as testimony of witnesses. . . Importantly, constitutional facts are not subject to the rules of evidence when presented by a party in the form of witness testimony. . ." This is not to say, however, that judicial inquiries into "legislative" facts are unbounded. Far from it.

116. *In re Marriage Cases*, 43 Cal. 4th at 759-60; *Varnum*, 763 N.W.2d at 874; *Goodridge*, 798 N.E.2d at 966.

117. *Varnum*, 763 N.W.2d at 881. *See also Perry v. Schwarzenegger*, Trial Transcript 1/11/10: 32 ("During the trial. . . *plaintiffs* and leading experts in the fields of history, psychology, economics, and political science will prove three basic fundamental points. . . Marriage. . . is vitally important in American society. . . [denying marriage to them] works a grievous harm on the plaintiffs and other gay men and lesbians throughout California. . . and [it] perpetrates this irreparable, immeasurable, discriminatory harm for no good.")(emphasis added). The *Perry* trial transcripts offer abundant examples of how slippery the distinction between plaintiffs' and experts' testimony can become. For example, plaintiffs were repeatedly asked to opine on whether or not they would be, or had been, subject to additional discrimination as a result of the marriage ban and Proposition 8—a question embodying a legal term of art and a theory of causation that cannot be determined as social scientific fact on the basis of anecdotal evidence. *See Ibid*: 83, 93–94, 114, 150–51.

While they sometimes make mention of external sources[118] bearing upon their evaluation of "legislative" facts, the marriage courts actually rely to a remarkable extent upon the findings of other courts. Is sexual identity immutable? Conflicting case law from the Ninth Circuit suggests we can't know.[119] Are LGB people "politically powerless"? Perhaps not power*less* but probably at least as politically weak as women were in 1973, which is the relevant benchmark because that's when the opinion in *Frontiero* was issued.[120] Perhaps more importantly, even when they are not relying solely or primarily upon case law, the courts adjudicating same-sex marriage claims clearly operate within a closed system, as when they look to "anti-gay hate crime" statistics for evidence of anti-gay animus.[121] As detailed in Chapter 4, "anti-gay hate crime" is itself a juridical construct, a concatenation of proxy-based determinations of motivation and emotion. But in the law of homosex, one substantive discourse cross-pollinates the others. The overall sexual truth regime is built on elusive, seemingly endless self-referentiality, made real by repetition across multiple juridical channels and by polysemic deployments by and to diverse, differently situated audiences.

And here again juridical institutions bracket certain questions as beyond the scope of the inquiry. None of the courts considering same-sex marriage claims seriously entertains the possibility that civil marriage might be modified to include more than two adults,[122] or that it might be preferable for the state to get out

118. *Kerrigan*, 957 A.2d at 433; *Lewis*, 908 A.2d at 223; *Varnum*, 763 N.W.2d at 899.

119. *Andersen*, 138 P.3d at 974.

120. *Kerrigan*, 957 A.2d at 452.

121. *Andersen*, 138 P.3d at 1030; *Conaway*, 932 A.2d at 611, n.48; *Kerrigan*, 957 A.2d at 433; *Varnum*, 763 N.W.2d at 889.

122. *See Goodridge*, 798 N.E.2d at 965.

of the marriage business entirely,[123] or even that their analysis of what marriage does and offers might include the perspective of people who prefer not to marry. In other words, at the moment that courts ask "why is marriage important?" they have already determined, *ex ante*, that marriage *is* important. Some simply repeat the invocations of the Supreme Court in *Maynard v. Hill* that marriage is "the most important relation in life" and "the foundation of the family and of society, without which there would be neither civilization nor progress."[124] Others offer statements of their own about the undeniable value of marriage:

> Marriage is a vital social institution. The exclusive commitment of two individuals to each other nurtures love and mutual support; it brings stability to our society.[125]

> It is beyond dispute that the State has a legitimate and longstanding interest in promoting a permanent commitment between couples for the security of their children. It is equally undeniable that the State's interest has been advanced by extending formal public sanction and protection to the union, or marriage, of those couples considered capable of having children, i.e., men and women.[126]

> [T]here are at least two grounds that rationally support the limitation on marriage. . . both of which are derived from the undisputed assumption that marriage is important to children.[127]

123. *Ibid.; In re Marriage Cases,* 43 Cal. 4th At 856; *Kerrigan,* 957 A.2d at 420, n.16. *Kerrigan,* 957 A.2d at 516 (Zarella, J., dissenting).

124. Cited in *Conaway v. Deane,* 932 A.2d at 620.

125. *Goodridge,* 798 N.E.2d at 948.

126. *Baker v State,* 744 A.2d 864, 881 (Sup. Ct. Vermont 1999).

127. *Hernandez,* 855 N.E.2d at 3. *See also Perry* Trial Transcript 1/11/10: 18–19 ("In short, in the words of the highest court in the land, marriage is 'the most important relation in life', and 'of fundamental importance for all individuals'.").

This last claim is particularly telling. Although there is some discussion of the romantic nature of marriage in these opinions,[128] what is perhaps most striking is the extent to which state courts inquiring into the nature of marriage focus on children: having them, rearing them, and (somewhat less explicitly) paying for them.[129] This is as true of the courts inclined to extend marriage to same-sex couples as it is of those that are not. The *Kerrigan* court describes same-sex couples as having the same interest in marriage as heterosexual couples, namely, an interest "in a committed and loving relationship . . . in having a family and raising their children . . . ,"[130] while the *Conaway* court (in denying same-sex couples' claim) notes that "virtually every Supreme Court case recognizing as fundamental the right to marry indicates as the basis for the conclusion the institution's inextricable link to procreation."[131]

This ineluctable focus on children means that what is relevant to the "similarly situated" inquiry in the marriage cases is

128. *See, for example, Andersen v. State*, 138 P.3d at 1035, n.84 (Fairhurst, J., dissenting) ("modern marriage is the result of that complex experience called being in love.").

129. Indeed, the *Andersen* court noted that "the right to marry is not grounded in the State's interest in promoting loving, committed relationships. While desirable, nowhere in any marriage statute of this state has the legislature expressed this goal." *Andersen*, 138 P.3d at 979, n.12. Similar language appears in *Kerrigan v. Commissioner of Public Health. Kerrigan*, 957 A.2d at 529, n.24.

130. *Kerrigan* 957 A.2d 424. See also *Baker*, 744 A.2d at 884. ("The laudable governmental goal of promoting a commitment between married couples to promote the security of their children and the community as a whole provides no reasonable basis for denying the legal benefits and protections of marriage to same-sex couples, who are no differently situated with respect to this goal than their opposite-sex counterparts.")

131. *Conaway*, 932 A.2d at 620. *See also Hernandez*, 855 N.E.2d at 3 ("there are at least two grounds that rationally support the limitation on marriage. . . both of which are derived from the undisputed assumption that marriage is important to the welfare of children.").

anything that might bear on an individual's (or couple's) fitness for producing or raising children. This, in turn, has the effect of discounting, if not negating, the significance of sexuality to same-sex couples' fitness for marriage and, more broadly, their claim to legal equality. Sometimes, this negation occurs indirectly, through an emphasis on the non-sexual elements of marriage and oblique references to stereotypes about the nature of gay relationships. For example, in striking down its state marriage ban, the California Supreme Court asserted (with little explanation) that same-sex and opposite-sex couples were similarly situated with respect to the marriage law,[132] noted pointedly the pernicious effects of "*outdated* social stereotypes,"[133] and stated unequivocally that "in contrast to earlier times, our state now recognizes that an individual's capacity to establish a loving and long-term committed relationship with another person *and to responsibly care for and raise children* does not depend upon the individual's sexual orientation. . . ."[134]

Other times, courts are more explicit:

The "marriage is procreation" argument singles out the one unbridgeable difference between same-sex and opposite-sex couples, and transforms that difference into the essence of

132. *In re Marriage Cases*, 43 Cal. 4th at 832, n. 54 ("both [heterosexual and homosexual couples] consist of pairs of individuals who wish to enter into a formal, legally binding and officially recognized, long-term family relationship that affords the same rights and privileges and imposes the same obligations and responsibilities. Under these circumstances, there is no question but that these two categories of individuals are sufficiently similar to bring into play equal protection principles. . ."). The *Kerrigan* court, as well, focused on raising children, accepting the rights and obligations of a codified, durable relationsip, and "participat[ing] fully in every important economic and social institution and activity that the government regulates" as the relevant qualifications for marriage. *Kerrigan* at 181.

133. *In re Marriage* at 843.

134. *Ibid.* at 782 (emphasis added).

legal marriage. Like "Amendment 2" to the Constitution of Colorado, which effectively denied homosexual persons equality under the law and full access to the political process, the marriage restriction impermissibly "identifies persons by a single trait and then denies them protection across the board.". . . In so doing, the State's action confers an official stamp of approval on the destructive stereotype that same-sex relationships are inherently unstable and inferior to opposite-sex relationships and are not worthy of respect.[135]

What the *Goodridge* court does in this brief passage is transform an argument about procreative sex (the "one unbridgeable difference" referred to in the "marriage is procreation" argument) into an argument about sexual identity ("a single trait") and stereotypical same-sex relationships ("unstable. . . inferior. . . not worthy of respect"). Buried in all of this is an unstated imagining about homosex: that it is degraded in some way, or ephemeral, or inferior to sex that has the capacity to result in pregnancy. These connections (or conflations) appear regularly in the marriage cases, the result of efforts to satisfy the "similarly situated" requirement and to establish that LGB people are fully contributing members of society.

Ultimately, this inquiry is structured by an explicit comparison: gay and lesbian couples who exist outside of the normative center of marriage are measured against heterosexual couples who constitute that normative center.[136] Plaintiffs seek to establish their

135. *Goodridge*, 798 N.E.2d at 962.

136. Make no mistake: this is the direction of the comparison. The essence of social, political, economic, and legal subordination is the privileging of a normative center over its subordinated margins. *See, for example*, hooks 2000. This is what leads Martha Nussbaum to conclude that perhaps the most important atttribute of an appellate court judge is his or her ability to imagine the lives and interests of others different from him- or herself. Nussbaum 2010: 80. ("Why, one might ask, do judges

similarity to heterosexual couples not only by eliding sexual differ-ence but by emphasizing their own procreative powers. Here, the effect of the gayby boom is striking, though not in the form sug-gested by Chauncey: where states have made institutional com-mitments to recognizing LGB parenting relationships, they have been less willing or able to entertain anti-marriage arguments predicated on an ostensible state interest in promoting opposite-sex parenting models.[137] Preexisting legislative and decisional law affirming same-sex parenting, itself the product of years of multi-faceted legal, political, and cultural efforts to promote awareness of diverse family forms,[138] nullifies the "gay people can't parent" argument before it can be made. In a very real sense, same-sex couples had to have children before they could get married.

But what the positive law gives, it may take away. In estab-lishing a constitutional mandate to open the institution of civil marriage to same-sex couples, the California Supreme Court repeatedly underscored the superiority of state-sanctioned marriage to unmarried cohabitation, citing two cases that affirmed the privileging of marriage by denying claims made by people whose relationships had not been officially sanctioned.[139]

need to use their imaginations?. . . judges have to consider relevant similarities and differences, and this means that they have to try to understand human aims and interests.")

137. *See Goodridge*, 798 N.E.2d at 962-3; *Lewis*, 908 A.2d at 212-13; *Kerrigan*, 957 A.2d. at 448.

138. Polikoff 2008.

139. *See In Re Marriage Cases*, 43 Cal. 4th at 815–18. In the first case, *Elden v. Shel-don*, the court denied a claim for tort damages to the unmarried partner of the dece-dent, reasoning that—because the (heterosexual) couple could have married but chose not to, they had actively eschewed the protections and rights that come with state recognition of an intimate relationship. *Elden v. Sheldon*, 46 Cal.3d 267 (Sup. Ct. Calif. 1998). In the second, *Dawn D. v. Superior Court*, 17 Cal. 4th 932 (Sup. Ct. Calif. 1998), the court denied the claim of a man seeking to establish paternity and visitation rights to a child he claimed to have fathered with a married woman while she was living apart from her husband, on the grounds that a child born to a married

In emphasizing the state's preference for marriage in these cases, the California Supreme Court betrays the incoherence of the "choice" argument for same-sex marriage. Once same-sex couples are also given the opportunity to enter into state-sanctioned marriages, courts will have, if anything, fewer incentives to recognize diverse intimate and kinship relationships. Seen this way, it becomes apparent that gay and lesbian couples are less likely to threaten marriage as a legal, cultural, and social norm than they are to save it.

## B. Redefining the Private in a Post-Welfare World

The debate over same-sex marriage is also embedded within a larger politics of welfare state retrenchment in the United States. As we have seen, marriage occupies an odd space within American law: it may implicate dignitary interests, but it also serves to structure and authorize mechanisms of social provision and "private"[140] ordering. In late capitalist America, this means that the debate over marriage is undertaken within the terms of

woman is presumptively the child of her husband. The *In Re Marriage Cases* court described the *Dawn D.* holding this way: "when biological mother was married at the time of a child's conception and birth, husband is the presumed father of the child, and another man who claims to be the child's biological father has no constitutional right to bring an action to establish a legal relationship with the child." *In Re Marriage Cases*, 43 Cal. 4th at 818.

140. While many married couples probably conceive of things like shared finances, child care arrangements, and expectations about medical decision making to be private matters, this is hardly the case. Law enforces some of these arrangements, refuses to enforce others, inserts proxy and default rules in the absence of specific, properly executed and witnessed documentation expressing other preferences, and may override even meticulously crafted contractual instruments signed by both parties. Whatever private content might be located within the ordering practices of married couples, it is the very fact of marriage that makes the state the final, public arbiter of the rules.

contemporary anti-welfare state discourse.[141] Marriage is offered ever more explicitly as the central institutional mechanism by which the United States privatizes the costs and burdens of caring for and reproducing the population, especially its most dependent and vulnerable members.[142] If one is attentive to it, this is hard to miss in the "winning" marriage cases, where same-sex plaintiffs are uniformly constructed as the discursive opposites of welfare "dependents"[143]:

> In terms of the value they place on family, career, and community service, plaintiffs lead lives that are remarkably similar to those of opposite-sex couples. Alicia Toby and Saundra Heath. . . have lived together for seventeen years and have children and grandchildren. Alicia is an ordained minister in a church where her pastoral duties include coordinating her church's HIV prevention program. Saundra works as a dispatcher for Federal Express. Mark Lewis and Dennis Winslow reside in Union City and have been together for fourteen years. They both are pastors in the Episcopal Church. In their ministerial capacities, they have officiated at numerous weddings. When Dennis' father was suffering from a serious long-term illness, Mark helped care for him in their home as would a devoted son-in-law.[144]

> Like most Iowans, [plaintiffs] are responsible, caring, and productive individuals. They maintain important jobs, or are retired, and are contributing, benevolent members of

141. *See generally* Zylan (in progress).

142. *See generally* the work of Martha Fineman and colleagues, Fineman 2004; Fineman and Dougherty 2005. *See also* Boyd 1997; Brush 2002.

143. Fraser and Gordon 1994: 324; Zylan 1996. *See generally* Soule and Zylan 1997; Zylan and Soule 2000.

144. *Lewis,* 908 A.2d at 424.

their communities. They include a nurse, business manager, insurance analyst, bank agent, stay-at-home parent, church organist and piano teacher, museum director, federal employee, social worker, teacher, and two retired teachers. Like many Iowans, some have children and others hope to have children. Some are foster parents.[145]

Indeed, equal protection analysis in the same-sex marriage cases is deeply inflected by the state's ever increasing interest in the privatization of care. Courts interrogate plaintiffs' ability to produce and contribute within the governing framework of marriage as a vaunted economic institution. They take up LGB

145. *Varnum*, 763 N.W.2d at 872. *See also Goodridge,*798 N.E.2d at 313–14 ("[T]he plaintiffs Maureen Brodoff, forty-nine years old, and Ellen Wade, fifty-two years old, had been in a committed relationship for twenty years and lived with their twelve year old daughter; the plaintiffs Hillary Goodridge, forty-four years old, and Julie Goodridge, forty-three years old, had been in a committed relationship for thirteen years and lived with their five year old daughter; the plaintiffs Gary Chalmers, thirty-five years old, and Richard Linnell, thirty-seven years old, had been in a committed relationship for thirteen years and lived with their eight year old daughter and Richard's mother; the plaintiffs Heidi Norton, thirty-six years old, and Gina Smith, thirty-six years old, had been in a committed relationship for eleven years and lived with their two sons, ages five years and one year; the plaintiffs Michael Horgan, forty-one years old, and Edward Balmelli, forty-one years old, had been in a committed relationship for seven years; and the plaintiffs David Wilson, fifty-seven years old, and Robert Compton, fifty-one years old, had been in a committed relationship for four years and had cared for David's mother in their home after a serious illness until she died. The plaintiffs include business executives, lawyers, an investment banker, educators, therapists, and a computer engineer. Many are active in church, community, and school groups."); *In re Marriage Cases*, 43 Cal. 4th at 786. ("According to declarations filed in the trial court, the named same-sex couples who are parties to these actions embody a diverse group of individuals who range from 30 years of age to more than 80 years of age, who come from various racial and ethnic backgrounds, and who are employed in (or have retired from) a wide variety of occupations, including pharmacist, military serviceman, teacher, hospital administrator, and transportation manager. Many of the couples have been together for well over a decade and one couple, Phyllis Lyon and Del Martin, who are in their 80's, have resided together as a couple for more than 50 years. Many of the couples are raising children together.").

litigants' invitations to focus on their work in caring for children and aged parents, and on their repeated representations that they are employed, taxpaying, church-going, durable, cohabiting households comprised largely of older men and women (grandparents, in many cases). This careful construction of same-sex coupledom operates to situate plaintiffs as not just similar, but perhaps superior, to opposite-sex couples with respect to marriage.[146] Same-sex couples are "like most Iowans"[147] and "remarkably similar to heterosexual couples" in these accounts in no small part because sexuality is nowhere to be found in them. Having constituted marriage as an institution that is child-centered and defined by its placement within a narrative of responsible economic citizenship, courts write sexual identity, experience, and practice out of the discourse. Sexuality appears only obliquely if at all, principally to suggest its own irrelevance:

> Plaintiffs' inability to contribute children to society by procreation through sexual intercourse with each other does not dictate the outcome of our consideration under this factor. The inquiry into gay and lesbian people's ability to contribute to society is a general one, designed to signal whether such classifications routinely risk elevating stereotype over ability. A person's ability to procreate is merely one of many ways in which the person can contribute to society. . . . the inability of gay and lesbian partners to contribute by procreation through sexual intercourse with each other does not indicate whether legislative classifications based on

146. *See Perry* Trial Transcript, 1/11/10: 142–43. Responding to a question about whether it mattered to her if the State of California sanctioned her relationship, one of the *Perry* plaintiffs stated: "I want it to happen for me because I do everything else I can think to do to make myself a contributing, responsible member of this state. And the state isn't letting me feel happy."

147. *Varnum*, 763 N.E.2d at 872.

sexual preference—which can conceivably occur in any legislative subject matter area—will generally be based on "stereotyped characteristics not truly indicative of their abilities."[148]

While sex may be dispensable, love, care, dependency, and permanence are all central to marriage. Indeed, the notion of permanence is invoked repeatedly and in multiple contexts to reinforce the suggestion that gay and lesbian couples are capable of committing to the sort of durable private ordering arrangements that civil marriage codifies for heterosexuals.[149] The self-selected plaintiffs[150] are rendered appealing and compelling as a direct function of the number of years they have devoted to one another. This emphasis on permanence is hardly surprising in a series of cases about marriage; after all, relationship permanence is a defining feature of marriage as a culturally, socially, and legally privileged institution. As the *Goodridge* court put it, marriage is an institution that "anchors an ordered society by encouraging stable relationships over transient ones."[151] But the repeated and multivalent invocation of permanence in same-sex marriage litigation achieves other aims as well. It counters the subtextual theme that gay sexuality is transient, hedonistic, and unmoored from deeper ethical values—the kind of sexuality that heterosexual marriage cannot incorporate. Fortunately for advocates of same-sex marriage, a strong case can be made that these are precisely the sorts of sexual practices and identifications that plaintiffs and the LGB movement have grown out of.

148. *Ibid.* at 892, n. 18.

149. *Goodridge*, 798 N.E.2d at 954, 961; *In re Marriage Cases*, 43 Cal. 4th at 815–16; *Kerrigan*, 957 A.2d at 474–5; *Lewis*, 908 A.2d at 200–201.

150. See Levit 2010.

151. *Goodridge*, 798 N.E.2d at 954.

## IV. Erasing Gayness, Take Two: Naming, Claiming, and Shaming

Increasingly, while earlier efforts to secure same-sex marriage privileged the language of "rights and benefits," recent legislative and judicial efforts have embodied an "only the word 'marriage' will do" approach, emphasizing its independent value and cultural significance. Partly, this is due to the juridical and legislative terrain upon which recent and current battles are waged: in California, Connecticut, and New Jersey, efforts to overturn marriage bans through the courts are being undertaken in the shadow of simultaneous or recent legislative enactments conferring upon domestic partnerships or civil unions all or most of the tangible benefits, rights, obligations, and duties afforded under state law via marriage. At its most ambitious, however, the drive to establish "marriage" as a word bearing constitutional weight is part of a broader, evolving understanding of the marriage campaign as a way of intervening in what Marc Poirier and others (citing the work of Louis Althusser) have referred to as social interpellation. In a classic essay, "Ideology and Ideological State Apparatuses," Althusser suggested that certain naming practices operate to subjugate individuals to state power. His classic example was of the policeman hailing a man on the street. When the man turns in response to "Hey, you there!" he is not only submitting to state authority, but in a very real sense submitting to the state's identification of him as a subordinate. Althusser's notion of "hailing" partakes of an Austinian conception of performative speech acts: by *speaking*, the state is *doing*. The man in the street is "interpellated" as a subject by the state.[152]

French theorist and Foucault scholar Didier Eribon has applied this idea in developing an account of gay identity and

152. Eribon and Lucey 2004: 56–57 (citing Althusser 2001).

politics that revolves around the politics and practices of insult. For Eribon, insult's "function is to produce certain effects—notably, to stabilize or to renew the barrier between 'normal' people and those [Erving] Goffman calls 'stigmatized' people and to cause the internalization of that barrier with the individual being insulted."[153] Insult is constitutive, a performative utterance in the Austinian sense. It "tells me what I am to the extent that it makes me be what I am."[154] Gay men and lesbians are called names, insulted, vilified, and stigmatized, and individual gay men and women "recognize" themselves in ways that partake of this stigmatized collective identity.[155]

Writing a decade ago and in the thick of a heated debate in France over same-sex marriage, Eribon positions himself squarely in the "gays will change marriage" camp. He is more troubled by the infighting within the gay community over marriage than he is by the normalizing tendencies of marriage. Reflecting a totalizing conception of anti-gay ideology, he views the internal debate as "one of the most pernicious traps set by a liberal form of homophobic discourse"[156] and asserts that the claim that the marriage campaign is assimilationist is simply wrong. "Were gay marriage to become a reality," he argues, "it would profoundly and permanently alter the institution itself."[157] What makes this argument curious, however, is his equally vigorous defense of

153. *Ibid*: 17.

154. *Ibid*.

155. Eribon echoes Foucault in understanding the individual to always be a product of the collective. But Eribon departs from Foucault in his decidedly top-down understanding of subject formation. "A 'subject' is always produced in and through 'subordination' to an order, to rules, norms, laws, and so on. This is true for all subjects. . . This is even more the case for those 'subjects' assigned to an 'inferiorized' place by the social and sexual order, as is the case for gay men and lesbians." *Ibid*: 5.

156. *Ibid*: 39.

157. *Ibid*.

the necessity of a specifically gay space from which LGB people might undertake practices of resignification in order to disrupt the politics of insult.[158]

Thus, there is a striking internal contradiction embodied in this account, though Eribon is hardly alone in failing to identify it. In fact, I think it is impossible to understand the wide and enthusiastic support of the same-sex marriage movement by members of the LGB community without recognizing this precise discursive gesture as a significant source of its multivalent appeal. Certainly, for some people who identify as gay or lesbian, the marriage campaign offers the possibility of normalcy that, according to Andrew Sullivan and others, is something "everyone" desires.[159] For others, however, same-sex marriage *feels* transgressive. Understanding homophobia and anti-gay animus to be pervasive and hegemonic, these marriage advocates trust in the radical potential offered by the juxtaposition of two sets of culturally incoherent signs: gayness and marriage.[160] Certainly this is what informs Eribon's perspective.[161]

On this view, what marriage promises is the possibility that homosex and the homosexed might move from a stigmatized, degraded, and shameful status to a status signaling "voice," inclusion, and "public acceptance."[162] Marc Poirier and others have

158. *Ibid*: 7 ("I try to reconstruct the ways in which gays are 'subjugated' by the sexual order, as well as the ways, different in different moments, in which they resist domination through the production of ways of life, spaces of freedom, a 'gay world.'")

159. Sullivan 1996.

160. *See* Taylor, et al, 2009; Poirier 2008a.

161. Eribon also embraces the generational account, saying that "One might also point out that what might seem to be two irrevocably opposed ways of life. . . can sometimes simply be different stages in the life of the same individuals." Eribon and Lucey 2004: 39.

162. Eribon and Lucey 2004; Poirier 2008a; Gabilondo 2006.

drawn upon similar notions in grounding their constitutive claims on behalf of civil marriage.[163] Poirier has suggested that marriage may be viewed principally as a naming practice and, as such, ought to be specifically and exclusively demanded by LGB couples so that they may strategically intervene in the interpellative practices that stigmatize them.[164] Adopting the insights of symbolic interactionism,[165] he contends that, once officially married, LGB couples' "microperformances" of married life will have the potential to produce dramatic social change, as heterosexuals are forced to confront their biases and unexamined assumptions about gayness in the face of the manifest ordinariness of the married same-sex couples they encounter:

> The basic engine of the piecemeal approach to wholesale recognition [of same-sex marriage] is an ever-increasing visibility of GLBT folks as normal, functional, decent human beings, capable of having normal, functional, decent familial relationships. It allows many people (both in the general population and in the legislature and judiciary) who may have been unfamiliar with GLBT folks to "get used to it," in the words of a well known queer slogan. "Getting used to it" takes the form of looking at a particular same-sex couple or same-sex parent-child relationship in a particular context and saying, "Well, that looks pretty healthy and normal, all things considered," over and over again.[166]

163. Poirier actually draws upon Jose Gabilondo who, in turn, draws upon Eribon. *See* Gabilondo 2006.

164. Poirier 2009.

165. *See generally*, Blumer 1969; Goffman 1969; Garfinkel 1967.

166. Poirier 2008b: 310.

Similar arguments have been advanced by Carlos Ball and Andrew Koppelman.[167] On this view, only marriage will do because the word itself is constitutive of the institution and its members. But wait, there's more: Poirier suggests that married same-sex couples will not only reassure heterosexuals with their normalcy and "decency," they will also unnerve "traditionalists" because they will "fail to follow the traditional, heteronormative structures and strictures of sexuality, gender, and family."[168] Same-sex marriage advocates not only enjoy the comfort of normativity in this account, they also partake of the subversive pleasures of troubling their neighbors with their non-normative practices.

Surely this promises too much. For one thing, the latter claim can only be true if gayness survives LGB couples' incorporation into marriage. This may or may not be possible in some hypothetical world, or as the result of cultural or political interventions. But juridical discourse renders homosex definitionally incompatible with marriage. Whatever the instrumental imaginings of same-sex marriage advocates (or the men and women who pay their salaries through political contributions), the constitutive claims of the marriage campaign depend upon the stability of the sign "marriage" over time and across space and, specifically, its distancing from gay practices and identity. The current marriage campaign demands marriage, and only marriage, precisely because of that institution's specific, constitutive power. Plaintiffs declare this in no uncertain terms: we wish to be married because marriage *makes* us the sorts of couples who *are* married.

The fundamental flaw in what must be viewed as an instrumental conception of constitutionalism—the idea that one

167. Ball 2006; Koppelman 2004.

168. Poirier 2008: 310.

might use the constitutive power of law strategically and at arm's length—is that it fails to take its own claims to heart. The state does indeed engage in interpellative practices: it *creates* subjects by naming them ("married," "single," "alien," "citizen," "mother," "Caucasian,"[169] etc.). But the desire for marriage expressed by the plaintiffs in the same-sex marriage cases is not a cynical desire to enter marriage in order to resist its subjugating force but, rather, an earnest desire to be constituted by it, to be created in its image of normalcy, ordinariness, and intelligibility.

> Q: When you said you wanted nothing more than to marry him, why?
>
> A: The word "marriage" has a special meaning. It's why we're here today. If it wasn't so important, we wouldn't be here today. I want to be able to share the joy and the happiness that my parents felt, my brother felt, my friends, my coworkers, my neighbors, of having the opportunity to be married. It's the next logical step for us.
>
> Q: Do you believe that if you are married, that that would change the relationship that you have, at all?
>
> A: Absolutely. I think—I think one's capacity to love can absolutely grow. I think one's capacity to be committed to another individual can absolutely expand. And I'm confident that that would happen with us.[170]

And, even more pointedly:

> Q: Do you think if you were able to get married, that that would in any way change your relationship with Mr. Zarillo?

---

169. On the nominative qualities of legal whiteness, *see* Haney-Lopez 1996.

170. *Perry,* Trial Transcript, 1/11/10: 80.

A: I think it would.

Q: In what way?

A: Being married allows us access to the language. Being able to call him my husband is so definitive, *it changes our relationship*. We currently struggle, in certain circumstances, about what to call each other. *We both dislike "lover."* You know, it's just—it's a challenge. *But "husband" is definitive. It's something that everyone understands.*[171]

As theorists of interpellation must understand, the state does not recognize relationships as marriage; it creates them.

In pursuing these constitutive claims, same-sex marriage advocates invite the erasure of gayness—their own and, by implication, that of all who identify as gay—by narrowing the field of possible sexual and affilial configurations that might be or become legally and culturally intelligible. The remedy discourse in the marriage cases establishes plaintiffs' belief that conventional marriage is the only possible cure to the constitutional harms suffered by same-sex couples. Gay and lesbian couples don't wish to change or "deinstitutionalize" marriage but to fortify it[172]:

It is important both analytically and from the standpoint of fairness to plaintiffs' argument that we recognize they are not seeking to create a new constitutional right—the right to "same-sex marriage"—or to change, modify, or (as some have suggested) "deinstitutionalize" the existing institution of marriage.[173]

171. *Perry*, Trial Transcript, 1/11/10: 88–89 (emphasis added).

172. *See also* Yoshino 2007.

173. *In Re Marriage Cases*, 43 Cal. 4th at 812; see also *Perry*, Trial Transcript, 1/11/10: 33 ("It won't change the institution. It will fulfill the institution."); *Goodridge*, 798 N.E.2d at 965 ("If anything, extending civil marriage to same-sex couples reinforces

Nor do same-sex couples challenge the right of the state to impose any other limitations on marriage, including consanguinity provisions and, especially, the requirement that it remain a binary institution:

> Here, the plaintiffs seek only to be married, not to undermine the institution of civil marriage. They do not want marriage abolished. They do not attack the binary nature of marriage, the consanguinity provisions, or any of the other gate-keeping provisions of the marriage licensing law.[174]

These are not incidental to the claim for marriage, they are integral to it. An essential element of the constitutive power of marriage is its ability to confer a specific and widely understood meaning upon a relationship through official solemnization practices. Gay and lesbian couples want the right to call themselves married and to be understood as constituting part of a particular sort of privileged relationship.[175]

> When we say that the Legislature cannot deny the tangible benefits of marriage to same-sex couples, but then suggest

the importance of marriage to individuals and communities. That same-sex couples are willing to embrace marriage's solemn obligations of exclusivity, mutual support, and commitment to one another is a testament to the enduring place of marriage in our laws and in the human spirit."). Accord, *Kerrigan*, 957 A.2d at 474.

174. *Goodridge*, 798 N.E.2d at 965. See also *Lewis*, 908 A.2d at 206.

175. See *In Re Marriage Cases*, 43 Cal. 4th at 830–31 ("The current statutes—by drawing a distinction between the name assigned to the family relationship available to opposite-sex couples and the name assigned to the family relationship available to same-sex couples, and by reserving the historic and highly respected designation of marriage exclusively to opposite-sex couples while offering same-sex couples only the new and unfamiliar designation of domestic partnership—pose a serious risk of denying the official family relationship of same-sex couples the equal dignity and respect that is a core element of the constitutional right to marry.").

that "a separate statutory scheme, which uses a title other than marriage," is presumptively constitutional . . . we demean plaintiffs' claim. What we "name" things matters, language matters ... Labels set people apart as surely as physical separation on a bus or in school facilities. Labels are used to perpetuate prejudice about differences that, in this case, are embedded in the law. By excluding same-sex couples from civil marriage, the State declares that it is legitimate to differentiate between their commitments and the commitments of heterosexual couples. Ultimately, the message is that what same-sex couples have is not as important or as significant as "real" marriage, that such lesser relationships cannot have the name of marriage.[176]

During the *Perry v. Schwarzenegger* trial, plaintiffs and their advocates repeatedly dismissed domestic partnerships as lacking cultural intelligibility.[177] The fight for same-sex marriage is a fight for cultural and social shorthand, and shorthand is only valuable to the extent that it predictably and faithfully signals its underlying referent.

Moreover, the flip side of the affirmative claim for "marriage only" is plaintiffs' active disparagement of the constitutive effects of domestic partnerships and civil unions.[178] Plaintiffs contend that these parallel legal systems of distribution are not simply inadequate to the task of sanctioning gay and lesbian relationships, but that they actually stamp those relationships with (in the parlance of equal protection jurisprudence) a badge of

176. *Lewis*, 908 A.2d at 226, 227 (C.J. Portiz, conccurring and dissenting).

177. *Perry*, Trial Transcript, 1/11/10: 38–9, 82–3, 153–4, 208.

178. *See generally* Eskridge 2002.

inferiority.[179] Why? Precisely because these institutions are associated with LGB people, practices, and kinship arrangements. Put simply, civil unions and domestic partnerships are tainted with homosex:

> Because of the widespread disparagement that gay individuals have historically faced, it is all the more probable that excluding same-sex couples from the legal institution of marriage is likely to be viewed as reflecting an official view that their committed relationships are of lesser stature than the comparable relationships of opposite-sex couples.[180]

Same-sex couples' claims for nothing-short-of-marriage thus brings to mind a well-known observation of Groucho Marx: "I don't care to belong to any club that will have me as a member."[181]

One final justificatory claim crystallizes all that is troubling about the constitutive thread of same-sex marriage discourse. Plaintiffs in the marriage cases increasingly offer a kind of inverted privacy argument in support of their claim that only marriage will do. A domestic partner, they contend, is not only not the same thing as a "spouse," but s/he is also a telltale sign of gayness. As such, revealing one's participation in a domestic partnership constitutes a mechanism by which one might be forced out of the closet against one's will. As Poirier argues, assigning LGB couples to domestic partnerships or civil unions works its

179. *See Perry*, Trial Transcript, 1/11/10: 38 (". . . the evidence will demonstrate that relegating gay men and lesbians to domestic partnerships is to inflict upon them badges of inferior [*sic*] that forever stigmatize their loving relationships as different, separate, unequal, and less worthy. . .").

180. *In Re Marriage Cases*, 43 Cal. 4th at 784. *See also Conaway*, 932 A.2d at 634, n.71 (noting that "Appellees here have expressly disavowed any present desire to obtain" relief other than marriage).

181. As quoted in Marx 1967/2007: 8.

own dignitary harm by forcing them to constantly and repeatedly remind others of their gayness.[182] This claim was readily
embraced by the California Supreme Court:

> Plaintiffs point out that one consequence of the coexistence
> of two parallel types of familial relationships is that—in
> numerous everyday social, employment, and governmental
> settings in which an individual is asked whether he or she is
> "married or single"—an individual who is a domestic partner
> and who accurately responds to the question by disclosing
> that status will (as a realistic matter) be disclosing his or her
> homosexual orientation, even if he or she would rather not
> do so under the circumstances and even if that information
> is totally irrelevant in the setting in question.[183]

We should not be surprised to see plaintiffs raising this claim,
nor the California Supreme Court accepting it. In this context,
it allows all of the relevant institutional actors to repair to the
familiar terrain of privacy jurisprudence in spite of the fact
that marriage is unintelligible except as a *public* mechanism for
distributing *public* goods (benefits, duties, rights, obligations,
and official "dignity"). The court continues:

> Because the constitutional right of privacy ordinarily would
> protect an individual from having to disclose his or her sexual
> orientation under circumstances in which that information is
> irrelevant, the existence of two separate family designations—
> one available only to opposite-sex couples and the other to
> same-sex couples—impinges upon this privacy interest, and

182. Poirier 2009: 1437.

183. *In Re Marriage Cases* at 847.

may expose gay individuals to detrimental treatment by those who continue to harbor prejudices that have been rejected by California society at large.[184]

If there is a better example of the institution-specific quality of juridical sexual discourse, I have not found it. This inverted privacy claim works on several levels, each a product of prior institutional commitments. First, it works as a kind of "don't ask, don't tell" strategy for marriage, intelligible only because the court (and plaintiffs) are able to hold in abeyance the central, pending claim for enjoyment of a legal status awarded to *couples* as they consider a subordinate claim to an *individual* right to "privacy." Privacy has its own constitutional demands, and one of these (in California) is that the state cannot require a person to disclose what sort of sexual being s/he is.

But in a practical sense, this seems at odds with the demand for marriage "recognition." How can I demand the right to keep my private life to myself as a condition of demanding public recognition of what I have already defined to be the essential fact of that private life? The California Supreme Court is able to rationalize this apparently incoherent formulation as a result of certain aspects of the juridical *habitus*, especially the compartmentalization of different sorts of doctrinal analysis within one overall adjudication, and the inevitable appearance of the discourse of privacy in the law of homosex. The court's discursis on the outing function of domestic partnership also perfectly condenses the relevancy and immutability discourses described above. Sexual orientation can stand separate and apart from same-sex marriage both because sexual orientation is a thing, a characteristic

184. *Ibid.*

of the self, distinguishable from and prior to sexual conduct, and because sexuality is (as we now know) irrelevant to marriage.

Finally, operating in the background are the institutional bracketing processes that have taken many policy alternatives off the table completely. The court never considers the possibility that domestic partnerships ought to be available to (non-aged) heterosexuals, nor does it consider the possibility that the state's sanctioning of intimate relationships might be troubling in a deeper sense, one that might suggest the wisdom of getting out of the marriage business altogether. And while it is the court that announces these rules of private being and public sanctioning, it is important to keep firmly in mind that it is doing so at plaintiffs' (or plaintiffs' counsels') urging. In responding to our desire for its discipline, the state invites us to submit to self-erasure and we gladly—and largely uncritically—offer our assent.

# 7

# Conclusion

It can be a peculiar sight: lawyers and judges pondering the nature of sexual attraction and antipathy, musing aloud (and in writing) about the things that turn people on or off, or about when and why sex matters. And it can seem odd when we repair to an institution that is as formal, traditional, and insular as law to address questions and conflicts that are so personal, current, and consequential. Quite frankly, it *is* odd—sometimes unintentionally comical—as we observe the juxtaposition of judicial reserve and a candid exposition of the erotic. Nonetheless, in contemporary American society, law is increasingly central to our most earnest explorations into the nature of sexuality.

This is so, in part, because many sexual progressives have expressly pursued legalism as a strategy, imagining the judiciary to be a relatively promising avenue of social change. Although they are hardly naïve about its shortcomings, many advocates believe that law's distance from majoritarian influences permits courts to act in ways that might advance the cause of sexual freedom, even as much of the public strenuously resists the prospect of changing sexual norms. For these social actors, litigation presents itself as an especially powerful instrument, one that can be wielded in conjunction with tactics emphasizing legislative change, administrative incrementalism, and grassroots cultural activism. Over time, however, these latter tactics have receded in importance, while litigation has become ever more central to LGB movement activism. The imprimatur of the juridical state is irresistibly seductive, in part because once engaged it cannot readily or freely be abjured. But the good graces of the state remain elusive, and the project of inclusion perpetually unfinished. And so we continue.

Yet, in this pursuit, we submit to a particular sort of disciplinary regime of self-governance. Whether or not the claims of LGB movement actors are successful—indeed, especially when they are successful—the outcome of litigation is always more (and less) than has been bargained for. Throughout this book, I have advanced the idea that law cannot be viewed primarily as an instrument held at one remove. Nor is it best understood as an arena, within which social actors deploy legal discourse as a tool or resource. Law does not merely respond to or take up such actors and groups but, rather, constitutes us in the first instance—a fact that many LGB activists and gaylegal advocates have acknowledged, but which has remained peripheral to their understanding of how the aims of sexual progress might be advanced. I think this is a mistake.

Because law is not merely an instrument or resource but, rather, a set of constitutive institutions and processes that exceed and subvert actors' instrumental designs, legalism is at best an unreliable and unpredictable mode of activism. At worst, it may be culpable in the construction of a sexually regressive social order. In reifying and authorizing categorical conceptions of sex, gender, and the body and in occluding and erasing gay specificity in the realm of the social, litigation as a set of institutional practices participates in the production of a sexual truth regime that grounds and ratifies social performances of domination and marginalization. And because sexuality is both an embodied and intersubjective phenomenon that is rendered possible by what the subject perceives, understands, and knows, law's production of knowledge about sex, gender, and the body radically reduces the field of sexual and social possibility in ways that can only frustrate the larger project of sexual freedom.

## I. States of Passion: The Social Construction of Desire in the Law of Homosex

My examination of the law of homosex has emphasized four institutional processes that help shape the production of juridical discourses of sex, gender, and the body. First, legal discourse produces *justificatory narratives* that authorize and invite law's regulatory enactments. These narratives draw force and shape from preexisting accounts of law's power to "intervene" in social relations. For example, hate crime discourse draws from retributivist, utilitarian, and expressivist frameworks; same-sex harassment discourse is embedded in an anti-discrimination narrative; and the marriage campaign depends in great measure on stories about immutability as a precondition for claiming fundamental rights. These justificatory narratives, in turn, limit the possibilities for how courts and advocates may represent the nature of sex, passion, love, power, and dominance.

Second, law is a rationalizing project. Legal procedures, rules, and professional practices reduce the complexity of social claims by *bracketing* the most expansive, multifaceted, and uncertain dimensions of those claims and by disarticulating compound questions and demands into discrete, singular, disconnected issues. For example, bracketing has significantly shaped the development of anti-gay hate crime law. In both the theory and the application of anti-gay hate crime prosecution, the complex, unruly, and murky phenomena that constitute the objects of law's intervention are regularly and repeatedly disaggregated *ex ante* into a series of elemental inquiries concerning the identities of victims and defendants. Framing an anti-gay hate crime inquiry as a series of questions about sexual orientation both draws from and reinscribes the predictive binary matrix of sex, gender, and the body. Courts adjudicating anti-gay hate crime prosecutions thus can and do engage in a process that is simultaneously interpolative (inserting motive forces between categorically identified victims and defendants) and interpellative (yoking disparate beings and performances together within the ambit of the binary model).

In same-sex harassment cases, as well, courts and litigants bracket contextual interrogations into the perversity of work itself or the possibility of fluid or labile sexual dynamics that exceed the categories of "attraction" or "repulsion." And same-sex marriage litigation brackets any number of difficult and complex issues (including the very wisdom of the state's involvement in sanctioning sexual and romantic relationships), even as it imagines itself to be tackling the big questions posed by the prospect of same-sex marriage: What is marriage? What does it do? What does it mean to be married?

Third, law *disciplines evidentiary boundaries*. Professional practices and habits, formal rules and procedures, and other aspects of law's *habitus* mark off the limits of what counts as relevant evidence bearing upon the questions reduced through juridical bracketing. Here, the preexisting policy environment is particularly important. Prior doctrine structures and constrains the kinds of evidence that can be deployed, further reducing and delimiting the terrain upon which specific legal discourses may be strategically invoked, circulated, and then ratified, amended, or dismissed. Armed with this evidence (such as it is) the analytical and doctrinal environment of the law of homosex then encourages courts to engage in a bad sort of social science. In collecting, examining, and analyzing the "material facts" of a particular issue or dispute, legal decision makers frequently and consistently produce and rely upon proxy measures in lieu of the unruly empirical data that they would otherwise have to contend with. In the anti-gay hate crime and sexual harassment contexts, for example, extant cultural and political discourses of desire, animus, fear, and identity are incorporated into legal practice as a way of domesticating and rationalizing the process of deciding which facts count and which do not. Ultimately, law's institutional mandates and practices encourage reductivism. The *Oncale* court's observation that evidence of an alleged sexual harasser's homosexual orientation would all but establish desire and therefore legal causation directed litigants to gather evidence and construct narratives designed to fix and locate sexual identity as either heterosexual or homosexual *being*. By repairing to categorical sexual identity, the Court both assumed and demanded that desire be understood as a univocal drive emerging from prediscursive bodies arrayed near and around one another, drawn to or repelled from one another in predictable ways based on the primary sex organs possessed by each of them. The evidentiary field (thus configured) precludes consideration of sexual performances that exceed or trouble the predictive capacities of the binary matrix.

Even where courts imagine themselves to be engaged in expansive social inquiries, as in the marriage cases, they fail to see the ways in which their investigations are drastically and specifically reduced before they begin. They sacrifice the complexity of desire, animus, love, and longing in service of an invisible pragmatics that encourages legal actors to resort to predictive and reconstructive maxims about sexual status and identity that have the ring of truth to them, but which necessarily lack social scientific rigor. This makes sense within law as a specific institutional location, but once these discourses exceed the bounds of this location, they inscribe an unduly limiting conception of sexuality upon the social body.

Finally, legal discourse is *polysemic,* subject to multiple meanings across multiple social fields. The power of law to do things with words amplifies itself through the homonymic nature of many of the core terms of art that figure in the law of homosex. The notion of causation operates in doctrinally specific ways in hate crime and harassment adjudications. Courts deploy "but for" causation or "substantial factor" tests and conceive of causation as a cognitive operation of discrimination in harassment cases or as an element of *mens rea* in hate crime cases. These are narrow and fairly technical understandings of causation. Beyond the judicial realm, however, the word "because" invokes a broader and different notion of attribution, one that sounds in empirical fact, not a normative judgment about liability. Similarly, while the legal notion of immutability is specifically contextualized in the marriage cases (given a precise meaning—one linked to a doctrinally relevant question about political vulnerability) its social and cultural counterpart is given meaning by a different set of concerns having to do with inclusion, willfulness, and the nature of individual identity.

Each of these aspects of law's institutional functioning—justificatory storytelling, bracketing, the disciplining of evidentiary boundaries, and the polysemic quality of legal discourse—serves to construct legal categories as social categories (and vice versa), to elaborate and authorize rules of prohibition and mandate, and to naturalize law's operations. We are left with the appearance of a comprehensive resolution of complex social questions, while law has merely tinkered at the edges of a technical subset of legally relevant disputes. Yet it is this naturalizing force of law's intervention that makes it a particularly powerful source of social construction. Discourse matters, not only because it establishes material rules of regulation, but because it is integral to the production of public representations of the possible. As De Lauretis, Grosz, Butler, and Bersani (among others) have demonstrated, the quality and scope of such representations are profoundly important in shaping experiences of sexual identity and practice. In setting out rules of desire, identity, and the body, law authorizes expressions and experiences that are profoundly limiting and narrowly constructed, yet which appear to be the very substance of freedom (if they appear at all).

All of this is made more troubling by the fact that the law engages in these practices increasingly at our bidding. LGB movement activists are pursuing a path that invites ever greater juridification of the social and cultural fields, and an increasingly prominent voice for the judiciary to describe who we are, what we do, and what we may become. Perhaps nowhere is this more evident than in the marriage cases. There, what began as a straightforward and nakedly instrumental effort to obtain access to a bundle of rights and benefits has, over time, metamorphosed into an urgent and irrevocable demand for cultural recognition by the state on the state's terms. The legal pursuit of same-sex marriage now stands for the proposition that only state-sanctioned marriage has the power to render our relationships real, valuable, and important. Moreover, the doctrinal demands of claims-making in the marriage context threaten the erasure of gayness itself; only a desexualized and un-gay version of same-sex relationship can be rendered compatible with the legal discourse of contemporary marriage. The playfulness, subversiveness, and cultural *differance* of gay and lesbian specificity is foreclosed and repudiated by the marriage project. Instead, gayness must be confined to a functional residuum marking social location, a sign of ontological identity rather than a modality of desire.

Advocates of marriage frequently claim that they are merely pursuing the right of gay couples to have the option of civil marriage, but this contention is unintelligible on its own terms. In their pursuit of marriage, advocates repeatedly argue that marriage is important because the state possesses unmatched constitutive power—and it does. As Bourdieu has demonstrated, the state enjoys a privileged position with respect to the power to enforce its own symbolic vision. When we submit to the state in this way, withdrawing our libidinal politics from other realms, other fields, and other sites of contestation and performance, that power can swiftly become monopolistic. Having made their arguments for the uniquely constitutive power of the word "marriage"—some of them strategic, but many of them simply the product of their professional training—gaylegal advocates cannot in the next breath assert that it may be embraced or ignored at will. Nor can they credibly argue that the word is infinitely malleable and subject to reinvention by gay couples; the power of the word "marriage" to constitute is utterly dependent upon its consistency as a cultural referent.

## II. Longing for a Different Longing

As seductive as it is, I think there are good reasons to question the wisdom of approaching the project of sexual freedom and equality via state-centric, juridical strategies. As Wendy Brown has argued in *States of Injury: Power and Freedom in Late Modernity*, progressive politics in late modern capitalist democracies demands an interrogation of the relationship between rights-based tactics and the structures of domination they are imagined to subvert. Late modern identity strategies, grounded in a politics of what Brown terms *ressentiment* (notions of injury and the fantasy of redress) feed from, and into, systems of oppression based on articulated statuses. She writes:

> While the effort to replace liberalism's abstract formulation of equality with legal recognition of injurious social stratifications is understandable, what such arguments do not query is whether legal "protection" for a certain injury-forming identity discursively entrenches the injury-identity connection it denounces. Might such protection codify within the law the very powerlessness it aims to redress? Might it discursively collude with the conversion of attribute

into identity, of a historical effect of power into a presumed cause of victimization?[1]

The problem, as Brown describes it, is not simply that law disables subjectivity through protectionist interventions. It is, rather, that injury claims become constitutive of identity through the disciplinary effects of state action. I would go further and say that it is not simply the injury predicate that is problematic, but the classification and categorization gestures that are the *modus vivendi* of the institutions comprising modern statehood. At best, reformation of the law of homosex will fail to move the project of sexual freedom forward. At worst, it may serve more deeply to inscribe the terms of sexual oppression by willingly submitting the articulation of sexual identities, practices, and communities to the disciplinary capacity of the state. If freedom inheres in the "struggle against what will otherwise be done to and for us,"[2] this willing submission to law's denominative and generative apparatus—an apparatus that serves to delimit the possibilities of existence—amounts to a forfeiture of freedom's defining praxis.

Having offered these critiques, I must at the same time concede that, even were they to be found persuasive by many gaylegal activists, they would be unlikely to change the trajectory of LGB legalism. As Evan Wolfson has said with respect to marriage (but which applies just as well to any other domain of the law of homosex): that ship has sailed. The institutional features of law, particularly those that establish its adversarial nature, create a ratchet effect; once engaged in litigation, it is difficult to

1. Brown 1995: 21.

2. *Ibid*: 25.

withdraw without consequence. Imagine for a moment what disengagement from, say, the dozens of cases now considering same-sex marriage would look like. At a minimum and in the short term, it would look a lot like losing. More importantly, it would *feel* and *sound* like losing. And failure is (it seems evident) worse than never having engaged the courts in the first place. For example, a failure in the *Perry* case would almost certainly result in a judgment by a court (perhaps even the United States Supreme Court) that the proactive exclusion of gay and lesbian couples from a central social institution is rational, or protected as a political prerogative of the majority, or not especially harmful. Plainly, any one of these findings would inure to the detriment of LGB-identified people and to the cause of sexual freedom. Held up against a loss, a win in the *Perry* case is something that a sexual progressive simply must root for.

At the same time, we can and should reengage some of the larger debates that once centrally occupied the time and energy of feminist and LGB movement activists. What might real sexual equality or freedom look like? How might we create the conditions within which sex, gender, and sexual binaries might be destabilized, troubled, and rendered benign (or playful or inert)? Can we imagine a political and cultural project that moves beyond our "desire for the state's desire"? It may seem as though our investments in legalism are too deep, too intimate, too cathected to allow us to move beyond them, and perhaps they are. It may also seem premature to suggest moving away from a focus on law when law has not yet extended even formal equality to LGB-identified people and relationships. But as I have tried to demonstrate in this book, there is no linear course of sexual progress to be conferred by law. Instead, law's approval always comes at a price: in the requirement that we discipline ourselves, that we participate in the construction of a sexual truth regime that is antithetical to our interests as people who occupy sexual and social margins, and that we contribute to the erasure of our own cultural, social, and sexual specificity. Ultimately, we may wish to pay this price to ensure that we can retain access to the retributive power of anti-gay hate crime laws, or to the right to sue an employer for failing to protect us from sexual harassment in the workplace, or to the right to use the word "husband" or "wife" in a legally and culturally resonant way. Perhaps.

But perhaps not.

# References


## CASES CITED

United States v. Carolene Products, 304 144 (1938).

Griswold v. Connecticut, 381 U.S. 479 (1965).

Loving v. Virginia, 388 U.S. 1 (1967).

Stanley v. Georgia, 394 U.S. 557 (1969).

Kramer v. Union Free School District, 395 U.S. 621 (1969).

Roe v. Wade, 410 U.S. 113 (1973).

Frontiero v. Richardson, 411 U.S. 677 (1973).

Williams v. Saxbe, 413 F. Supp. 654, (D. D.C. 1976).

Barnes v. Costle, 561 F.2d 983, (D.C. Cir. 1977).

City of Cleburne v. Cleburne Living Center, 473 U.S. 432 (1985).

Meritor Savings Bank v. Vinson, 477 U.S. 57 (1986).

Lyng v. Castillo, 477 U.S. 635 (1986).

Elden v. Sheldon, 46 Cal.3d 267, (Calif. Sup. Ct. 1988).

Price Waterhouse v. Hopkins, 490 U.S. 228 (1989).

Bennett v. Texas, 831 S.W.2d 20 (Ct. App. Tex. 1992).

Dillon v. Frank, 952 F.2d 403 (6th Cir. 1992).

Wisconsin v. Mitchell, 508 U.S. 476 (1993).

Baehr v. Lewin, 852 P.2d 44 (Sup. Ct. Hawai'i 1993).

In re Joshua H., 13 Cal. App. 4th 1734 (Cal. Ct. App. 1993).

Commonwealth v. Pierce, 642 N.E.2d 579 (Sup. Jud. Ct. Mass. 1994).

In re MS, 10 Cal. 4th 698 (Cal. Sup. Ct. 1995).

Romer v. Evans, 517 U.S. 620 (1996).

Dean v. District of Columbia, 653 A.2d 307 (D.C. Ct. App. 1995).

McWilliams v. Fairfax County Supervisors, 72 4th Cir. 1191 (4th Cir. 1996).

Wrightson v. Pizza Hut of Am., Inc., 99 F.3d 138, (4th Cir. 1996).

Quick v. Donaldson Co., 90 F.3d 1372 (8th Cir. 1996).

Hopkins v. Baltimore Gas & Elec. Co., 77 F.3d 745 (4th Cir. 1996).

Wiggins v. State, 1997 12453 (Tenn. Ct. Crim. App. 1997).

Johnson v. Hondo, 125 F.3d 408 (7th Cir. 1997).

Oncale v. Sundowner Offshore Svcs, 523 U.S. 75 (1998).

Dawn D. v. Superior Court, 17 Cal. 4th 932 (Sup. Ct. Calif. 1998).

Broome v. State, 687 N.E.2d 590 (Ct. App. Ind. 1998).

Burlington v. Ellerth, 524 U.S. 742 (1998).

Smith v. U.S. Truck, Inc., 1998 U.S. Dist. LEXIS 3455 (W.D. Ark. 1998).

Baker v. State, 744 A.2d 864 (Sup. Ct. Vt. 1999).

Parsons v. Galetka, 57 F. Supp. 2d 1151 (Utah Dist. Ct. 1999).

Shepherd v. Slater Steels Corp., 168 F.3d 1001 (7th Cir.1999).

Breitenfeldt v. Long Prairie Packing Co., 48 F. Supp. 2d 1170 (D. Ct. Minn. 1999).

Higgins v. New Balance Shoe, 194 F.3d 252 (1st Cir. 1999).

Kelly v. Oakland, 198 F.3d 779 (9th Cir. 1999).

Merritt v. Del. River Port Auth., LEXSEE 1999 U.S. Dist. LEXIS 5896 (E.D. Penn. 1999).

Carney v. City of Shawnee, 38 F. Supp. 2d 905 (D. Kan. 1999).

Brewer v. Hillard, 15 S.W.3d 1 (Ky. Ct. App. 1999).

Cuevas v. State of Florida, 770 So. 2d 703 (Dist. Ct. App. Fla. 2000).

Hampel v. Food Ingredients Specialties, Inc., 729 N.E.2d 726 (Sup. Ct. Ohio 2000).

Simonton v. Runyon, 2000 U.S. App. LEXIS 21139 (2d Cir. 2000).

Hamner v. St. Vincent Hosp. and Health Care Ctr., Inc., 224 F.3d 701 (7th Cir. 2000).

State v. Timothy K., 27 P.3d 1263 (Ct. App. Wash. 2001).

People v. Diaz, 188 Misc. 2d 341 (N.Y. Sup. Ct. 2001).

Rene v. MGM Hotels, Inc., 243 F.3d 1206 (9th Cir. 2001).

La Day v. Catalyst Technology, 302 F.3d 474 (5th Cir. 2002).

English v. Pohanka of Chantilly, Inc., 190 F. Supp. 833 (E.D. Va. 2002).

Samborski v. West Valley Nuclear Svcs. Co., Inc., 2002 U.S. Dist. LEXIS 12745 (W.D.N.Y. 2002).

Lawrence v. Texas, 539 U.S. 558 (2003).

Goodridge v. Dept. of Public Health, 798 N.E.2d 941 (Sup. Jud. Ct. Mass. 2003).

Standhardt v. Superior Court, 77 P.3d 451 (Ariz. Ct. App. 2003).
Marcicky v. Renico, 2003 WL 22272142 (E.D. Mich. 2003).
Dick v. Phone Directories Comp., Inc., 265 F. Supp. 2d 1274 (W.D. Utah 2003).
Lockyer v. City and County of San Francisco, 33 Cal. 4th 1055 (Sup. Ct. Calif. 2004).
Yanowitz v. L'Oreal USA, Inc., 36 1028 (Calif. Sup. Ct. 2005).
Commonwealth v. Cutts, 831 N.E.2d 1279 (Sup. Jud. Ct. Mass. 2005).
Shafer v. Kal Kan Foods, Inc., 417 F.3d 665 (7th Cir. 2205).
Dawson v. Bumble & Bumble, 398 F.3d 211 (2nd Cir. 2005).
Hernandez v. Robles, 855 N.E.2d 1 (Ct. App. N.Y. 2006).
Andersen v. State of Washington, 138 P.3d 963 (Sup. Ct. Wash. 2006).
Lewis v. Harris, 908 A.2d 196 (Sup. Ct. N.J. 2006).
Vickers v. Fairfield Medical Center, 453 F.3d 757 (6th Cir. 2006).
Conaway v. Deane, 932 A.2d 571 (Ct. App. Md. 2007).
People v. Fox, 17 Misc. 3d 281 (Sup. Ct. N.Y. 2007).
Russell v. University of Texas of the Permian Basin, 234 Fed. Appx. 195 (5th Cir. 2007).
In re Marriage Cases, 43 Cal. 4th 757 (Sup. Ct. Calif. 2008).
Kerrigan v. Commissioner of Public Health, 957 A.2d 407 (Sup. Ct. Conn. 2008).
State v. Christian, 984 So.2d 132 (Ct. App. La. 2008).
Varnum v. O'Brien, 763 N.W.2d 862 (Sup. Ct. Iowa 2009).
Strauss v. Horton, 46 Cal. 4th 364 (Sup. Ct. Calif. 2009).
Love v. Motiva Enterprises LLC, 349 Fed. Appx. 900 (5th Cir. 2009).
Perry v. Schwarzenegger, 704 F. Supp. 2d 921 (N.D. Cal. 2010).


**LEGISLATIVE MATERIALS**

1988. Congressional Record, United States House of Representatives, "H.R. Rep. No. 100–575."
1989. Congressional Record, United States House of Representatives. "Hate Crime Statistics Act.".
1990. Congressional Record, United States House of Representatives. "Hate Crime Statistics Act."
2007. Congressional Record, United States House of Representatives "Matthew Shepard Local Law Enforcement Hate Crimes Prevention Act of 2007."
2009. Congressional Record, United States House of Representatives, "Employment Non-Discrimination Act of 2009." H.R. 3017.

2010. State of California, "California Fair Employment and Housing Act." Cal. Govt Code Sec 12900 *et seq.*

2010. 42 U.S.C. 1981 § 2000e, *et seq.*

## SECONDARY SOURCES

Abrams, Kathryn. 1998. "The New Jurisprudence of Sexual Harassment." *Cornell Law Review* 83:1169–1230.

Adam, Barry D. 1998. "Theorizing Homophobia." *Sexualities* 1: 387–404.

Althusser, Louis. 2001. *Lenin and philosophy, and other essays*. New York: Monthly Review Press.

Amenta, Edwin, Neal Caren, Elizabeth Chiarello, and Yang Su. 2010. "The Political Consequences of Social Movements." *Annual Review of Sociology* 36:287–307.

Amenta, Edwin, Bruce G. Carruthers, and Yvonne Zylan. 1992. "A Hero for the Aged? The Townsend Movement, the Political Mediation Model, and U.S. Old-Age Policy, 1934–1950." *American Journal of Sociology* 98:308.

American Civil Liberties Union, Gay and Lesbian Advocates and Defenders, Lambda Legal, National Center for Lesbian Rights, Equality Federation, Freedom to Marry, Gay and Lesbian Alliance Against Defamation, Human Rights Campaign, and National Gay and Lesbian Task Force. 2009. "Make Change, Not Lawsuits."

Andenæs, Johannes. 1974. *Punishment and deterrence*. Ann Arbor: University of Michigan Press.

Andersen, Ellen Ann. 2006. *Out of the closets & into the courts : legal opportunity structure and gay rights litigation*. Ann Arbor: University of Michigan Press.

Anderson, Eric. 2005. *In the game : gay athletes and the cult of masculinity*. Albany, NY: State University of New York Press.

Andriote, John-Manuel. 1999. *Victory deferred : how AIDS changed gay life in America*. Chicago: The University of Chicago Press.

APA Task Force on Appropriate Therapeutic Responses to Sexual Orientation. 2009. "Report of the Task Force on Appropriate Therapeutic Responses to Sexual Orientation." Washington, D.C.: American Psychological Association, Lesbian, Gay, Bisexual, and Transgender Concerns Office, Public Interest Directorate.

Aristotle. 1962. *The Politics*. Translated by E. Barker. New York: Oxford University Press.

Armstrong, Elizabeth A. 2002. *Forging gay identities : organizing sexuality in San Francisco, 1950–1994.* Chicago: University of Chicago Press.

Balkin, J.M. 1997. "The Constitution of Status." *Yale Law Journal* 106:2313.

Ball, Carlos A. 2006. "The Backlash Thesis and Same Sex Marriage: Learning from Brown v. Board and its Aftermath." *William and Mary Bill of Rights Journal* 14.

Bandes, Susan A. 1999. *The passions of law.* New York: New York University Press.

Barber, Sotirios A. 2005. *Welfare and the Constitution.* Princeton: Princeton University Press.

Barclay, Scott, Mary Bernstein, and Anna-Maria Marshall. 2009. *Queer mobilizations : LGBT activists confront the law.* New York: New York University Press.

Barclay, Scott and Shauna Fisher. 2008. "Said and Unsaid: State Legislative Signaling to State Courts over Same Sex Marriage 1990–2004." *Law & Policy* 30:254–275.

Barclay, Scott and Anna-Maria Marshall. 2003. "In Their Own Words: How Ordinary People Construct the Legal World." *Law & Social Inquiry* 28:617–28.

Barclay, Scott and Anna-Maria Marshall. 2005. "Supporting a Cause, Developing a Movement, and Consolidating a Practice: Cause Lawyers and Sexual Orientation Litigation in Vermont." Pp. 171–202 in *The Worlds Cause Lawyers Make*, edited by A. Sarat and S. A. Scheingold. Stanford: Stanford University Press.

Beale, Sara Sun. 2000. "Federalizing Hate Crimes: Symbolic Politics, Expressive Law, or Tool for Criminal Enforcement?" *Boston University Law Review* 80:1227–1272.

Beauvoir, Simone de. 1953. *The second sex.* New York,: Knopf.

Bell, Alan P., Martin S. Weinberg, and Institute for Sex Research. 1978. *Homosexualities : a study of diversity among men and women.* New York: Simon and Schuster.

Benjamin, Jessica. 1983. "Master and Slave: the fantasy of erotic domination." Pp. 280 – 299 in *Powers of Desire: the politics of sexuality*, edited by A. B. Snitow, C. Stansell, and S. Thompson. New York: Monthly Review Press.

Benjamin, Jessica. 1988. *The bonds of love : psychoanalysis, feminism, and the problem of domination.* New York: Pantheon Books.

Benjamin, Jessica. 1995. *Like subjects, love objects : essays on recognition and sexual difference*. New Haven: Yale University Press.

Benjamin, Jessica. 1998. *Shadow of the other : intersubjectivity and gender in psychoanalysis*. New York: Routledge.

Benjamin, Jessica. 2006. "Two-Way Streets: Recognition of Difference and the Intersubjective Third." *differences* 17:116–146.

Bentham, Jeremy. 1996. *An Introduction to the Principles of Morals and Legislation*, Edited by J. H. a. H. Burns, H.L.A. New York: Oxford.

Berger, Peter L. and Thomas Luckmann. 1990. *The social construction of reality : a treatise in the sociology of knowledge*. New York: Anchor Books.

Bernstein, Elizabeth. 2007. *Temporarily yours: intimacy, authenticity, and the commerce of sex*. Chicago: University of Chicago Press.

Bernstein, Elizabeth and Laurie Schaffner. 2005. *Regulating sex: the politics of intimacy and identity*. New York: Routledge.

Bernstein, Mary. 1997. "Celebration and Suppression: the Uses of Identity by the Lesbian and Gay Movement." *The American Journal of Sociology* 103:531–565.

Bernstein, Mary. 2003. "Nothing Ventured, Nothing Gained? Conceptualizing Social Movement 'Success' in the Lesbian and Gay Movement." *Sociological Perspectives* 46:353–379.

Bernstein, Mary. 2005. "Liberalism and Social Movement Success: The Case of United States Sodomy Statutes." Pp. 3–18 in *Regulating Sex: The Politics of Intimacy and Identity*, edited by E. Bernstein and L. Schaffner. New York: Routledge.

Bernstein, Mary and Renate Reimann. 2001. *Queer families, queer politics : challenging culture and the state*. New York: Columbia University Press.

Berrill, Kevin T. and Gregory M. Herek. 1992. "Primary and Secondary Victimization in anti-gay hate crimes." Pp. 289–305 in *Hate Crimes*, edited by G. M. Herek and K. T. Berrill. Thousand Oaks, CA: Sage.

Bersani, Leo. 1987. "Is the Rectum a Grave?" *October* 43:197–222.

Bersani, Leo. 1995. *Homos*. Cambridge: Harvard University Press.

Black, Donald J. 1976. *The behavior of law*. New York: Academic Press.

Block, Fred L. 1987. *Revising state theory : essays in politics and postindustrialism*. Philadelphia: Temple University Press.

Blumer, Herbert. 1969. *Symbolic interactionism; perspective and method*. Englewood Cliffs, N.J.,: Prentice-Hall.

Boso, Luke. 2009. "Disrupting Sexual Categories of Intimate Preference." *Hastings Women's Law Journal* 21:59–98.

Bourdieu, Pierre. 1984. *Distinction : a social critique of the judgement of taste*. Cambridge: Harvard University Press.

Bourdieu, Pierre. 1987. "The Force of Law: Toward a Sociology of the Juridical Field." *Hastings Law Journal* 38:805–853.

Bourdieu, Pierre and John B. Thompson. 1991. *Language and symbolic power*. Cambridge: Harvard University Press.

Boyd, Susan B. 1997. *Challenging the public/private divide : feminism, law, and public policy*. Toronto; Buffalo: University of Toronto Press.

Braidotti, Rosi. 1994. *Nomadic subjects : embodiment and sexual difference in contemporary feminist theory*. New York: Columbia University Press.

Braidotti, Rosi and Judith Butler. 1997. "Feminism by any other name. Interview." Pp. 31–67 in *Feminism meets queer theory*, edited by E. Weed and N. Schor. Bloomington, Ind.: Indiana University Press.

Brick, Michael. 2007. "To Commit a Hate Crime, Must the Criminal Truly Hate the Victim?," *The New York Times*, June 20, 2007.

Brigham, John. 1996. *The constitution of interests : beyond the politics of rights*. New York: New York University.

Brodin, Mark S. 1982. "The Standard of Causation in the Mixed-Motive Title VII Action: A Social Policy Perspective." *Columbia Law Review* 82:292–326.

Brower, Todd. 2009. "Social Cognition 'At Work': Schema Theory and Lesbian and Gay Identity in Title VII." *Law & Sexuality* 18:1–77.

Brown, Lyn Mikel and Carol Gilligan. 1992. *Meeting at the crossroads : women's psychology and girls' development*. Cambridge: Harvard University Press.

Brown, Wendy. 1995. *States of injury : power and freedom in late modernity*. Princeton, N.J.: Princeton University Press.

Brown, Wendy and Janet Halley. 2002. "Left Legalism/Left Critique." Durham, NC: Duke University Press.

Brush, Lisa. 2002. "Changing the Subject: Gender and Welfare Regime Studies." *Social Politics* 9:161–186.

Burke, Kenneth. 1969. *A grammar of motives*. Berkeley,: University of California Press.

Butler, Judith. 1990. *Gender trouble: feminism and the subversion of identity*. New York: Routledge.

Butler, Judith. 1997. *Excitable speech : a politics of the performative.* New York: Routledge.

Butler, Judith. 1999. *Subjects of desire : Hegelian reflections in twentieth-century France.* New York: Columbia University Press.

Butler, Judith. 2002. "Is Kinship Always Already Heterosexual?" *differences* 13:14–44.

Butler, Judith. 2004. *Undoing gender.* New York; London: Routledge.

Butler, Judith. 2005. *Giving an Account of Oneself.* New York: Fordham University Press.

Butler, Judith 2009. "Interview with Judith Butler: "Gender is Extramoral"." *MRZine,* May 16, 2009.

Calhoun, Craig. 1989. "Commentary: Social Theory And The Law: Systems Theory, Normative Justification, And Postmodernism." *Northwestern University Law Review* 83:398–460.

Chauncey, George. 2004. *Why marriage? : the history shaping today's debate over gay equality.* New York: Basic Books.

Cherlin, Andrew J. 1992. *Marriage, divorce, remarriage.* Cambridge: Harvard University Press.

Cherlin, Andrew J. 2009. *The marriage-go-round : the state of marriage and the family in America today.* New York: Alfred A. Knopf.

Chodorow, Nancy. 1978. *The reproduction of mothering : psychoanalysis and the sociology of gender.* Berkeley: University of California Press.

Cixous, Hélène and Marta Segarra. 2010. *The portable Cixous.* New York: Columbia University Press.

Cohen, Michael D., James G. March, and Johan P. Olsen. 1972. "A Garbage Can Model of Organizational Choice." *Administrative Science Quarterly* 17:1–25.

Comstock, Gary David. 1992. "Dismantling the Homosexual Panic Defense." *Law & Sexuality Review* 2:81–102.

Conley, John M. and William M. O'Barr. 2005. *Just words : law, language, and power.* Chicago: University of Chicago Press.

Connell, R. W. 1987. *Gender and power : society, the person, and sexual politics.* Stanford, Calif.: Stanford University Press.

Connell, R. W. 2005. *Masculinities.* Berkeley, Calif.: University of California Press.

Cossman, Brenda. 2007. *Sexual citizens : the legal and cultural regulation of sex and belonging.* Stanford, Calif.: Stanford University Press.

Cott, Nancy F. 2000. *Public vows : a history of marriage and the nation.* Cambridge: Harvard University Press.

Cotterrell, Roger. 1999. *Emile Durkheim : law in a moral domain*. Stanford, Calif.: Stanford University Press.

Cover, Susan M. 2009. "Fight Goes On Over Marriage, *The Portland Press Herald*, March 4, 2009.

Crenshaw, Kimberle. 1991. "Mapping the Margins: Intersectionality, Identity Politics, and Violence Against Women of Color." *Stanford Law Review* 43:1241–1299.

Crenshaw, Kimberlé. 1995. *Critical race theory : the key writings that formed the movement*. New York: New Press.

Cress, Daniel M. and David A. Snow. 2000. "The Outcomes of Homeless Mobilization: The Influence of Organization, Disruption, Political Mediation, and Framing." *The American Journal of Sociology* 105:1063–1104.

Crimp, Douglas. 2002. *Melancholia and moralism : essays on AIDS and queer politics*. Cambridge: MIT Press.

D'Emilio, John. 1983. *Sexual Politics, Sexual Communities*. Chicago: University of Chicago Press.

D'Emilio, John and Estelle B. Freedman. 1997. *Intimate matters : a history of sexuality in America*. Chicago: University of Chicago Press.

De Lauretis, Teresa. 1984. *Alice doesn't : feminism, semiotics, cinema*. Bloomington: Indiana University Press.

De Lauretis, Teresa. 1994. *The practice of love : lesbian sexuality and perverse desire*. Bloomington: Indiana University Press.

De Lauretis, Teresa and Patricia White. 2007. *Figures of resistance : essays in feminist theory*. Urbana: University of Illinois Press.

Deflem, Mathieu. 2008. *Sociology of law : visions of a scholarly tradition*. Cambridge, UK; New York: Cambridge University Press.

Delgado, Richard and Jean Stefancic. 2000. *Critical race theory : the cutting edge*. Philadelphia: Temple University Press.

Delgado, Richard and Jean Stefancic. 2001. *Critical race theory : an introduction*. New York: New York University Press.

Diefenbach, Clare. 2007. "Article: Same-Sex Sexual Harassment After Oncale: Meeting the "Because of . . . Sex" Requirement." *Berkeley J. Gender L. & Just.* 22.

Dillof, Anthony M. 1997. "Punishing Bias: An Examination Of The Theoretical Foundations Of Bias Crime Statutes." *Northwestern University Law Review* 91:1015.

DiMaggio, Paul and Walter W. Powell. 1983. "The Iron Cage Revisited: Institutional Isomorphism and Collective Rationality in Organizational Fields." *American Sociological Review* 48: 147–160.

Dong, Arthur. 2005. "Licensed to Kill." Deep Focus Productions, Inc.

Douglas, Mary. 1986. *How institutions think*. Syracuse, N.Y.: Syracuse University Press.

Dressler, Joshua. 1995. "When 'Heterosexual' Men Kill 'Homosexual' Men: Reflections on Provocation Law, Sexual Advances, and the 'Reasonable Man' Standard." *Journal of Criminal Law & Criminology* 85:726–763.

Durkheim, Emile. 1952. *Suicide, a study in sociology*. London,: Routledge & K. Paul.

Durkheim, Emile. 1982. "What is a Social Fact?" Pp. 50–59 in *The Rules of the Sociological Method*, edited by S. Lukes. New York: Free Press.

Durkheim, Emile and W. D. Halls. 1984. *The division of labor in society*. New York: Free Press.

Dworkin, Andrea. 1987. *Intercourse*. New York: Free Press.

Dworkin, Ronald. 1977. *Taking rights seriously*. Cambridge: Harvard University Press.

Edelman, Lauren B. 2002. "Legality and the Endogeneity of Law." Pp. 187–202 in *Legality and Community*, edited by L. B. Edelman. Lanham, MD: Rowman & Littlefield.

Ehrenreich, Rosa. 1999. "Dignity and Discrimination: Toward a Pluralistic Understanding of Workplace Harassment." *Georgetown Law Journal* 88:1–64.

Ehrlich, Howard 1992. "The Ecology of Anti-Gay Violence." Pp. 105–110 in *Hate Crimes: confronting violence against lesbians and gay men*, edited by G. M. Herek and K. T. Berrill. Thousand Oaks, CA: Sage.

Elder-Vass, Dave. 2008. "Integrating Institutional, Relational and Embodied Structure: An Emergentist Perspective." *British Journal of Sociology* 59:281–299.

Emirbayer, Mustafa. 1997. "Manifesto for a Relational Sociology." *The American Journal of Sociology* 103:281–317.

Eribon, Didier and Michael Lucey. 2004. *Insult and the making of the gay self*. Durham, NC: Duke University Press.

Eskridge, William N. 1999. *Gaylaw : challenging the apartheid of the closet*. Cambridge: Harvard University Press.

Eskridge, William N. 2002. *Equality practice : civil unions and the future of gay rights*. New York: Routledge.

Eskridge, William N. 2008. *Dishonorable passions : sodomy laws in America, 1861–2003*. New York: Viking.

Ewick, Patrick and Susan S. Silbey. 1995. "Subversive Stories and Hegemonic Tales: Toward a Sociology of Narrative." *Law & Society Review* 29:197–226.

Ewick, Patricia and Susan S. Silbey. 1998. *The common place of law: stories from everyday life*. Chicago: University of Chicago Press.

Ewick, Patricia and Susan S. Silbey. 1999. "Common Knowledge and Ideological Critique: the Significance of Knowing That the 'Haves' Have Come Out Ahead." *Law & Society Review* 33:1025–1041.

Fausto-Sterling, Anne. 2000. *Sexing the body : gender politics and the construction of sexuality*. New York, NY: Basic Books.

Fee, Elizabeth and Daniel M. Fox. 1992. *AIDS : the making of a chronic disease*. Berkeley: University of California Press.

Felstiner, William L. F., Richard L. Abel, and Austin Sarat. 1980. "The Emergence and Transformation of Disputes: Naming, Blaming, Claiming." *Law & Society Review* 15:631–654.

Fetner, Tina. 2008. *How the religious right shaped lesbian and gay activism*. Minneapolis: University of Minnesota Press.

Fineman, Martha. 1991. *The illusion of equality : the rhetoric and reality of divorce reform*. Chicago: University of Chicago Press.

Fineman, Martha. 1995. *The neutered mother, the sexual family, and other twentieth century tragedies*. New York: Routledge.

Fineman, Martha. 2004. *The autonomy myth : a theory of dependency*. New York: New Press.

Fineman, Martha and Terence Dougherty. 2005. *Feminism confronts homo economicus : gender, law, and society*. Ithaca, N.Y.: Cornell University Press.

Fineman, Martha, Jack E. Jackson, and Adam P. Romero. 2009. *Feminist and queer legal theory : intimate encounters, uncomfortable conversations*. Burlington, VT: Ashgate.

Fineman, Martha and Nancy Sweet Thomadsen. 1991. *At the boundaries of law : feminism and legal theory*. New York: Routledge.

Foner, Eric. 2002. *Reconstruction : America's unfinished revolution, 1863–1877*. New York: Perennial Classics.

Foucault, Michel. 1972. *The archaeology of knowledge*. New York,: Pantheon Books.

Foucault, Michel. 1990. *The History of Sexuality, Vol. I*. Translated by R. Hurley. New York: Vintage Books.

Foucault, Michel. 1995. *Discipline and punish : the birth of the prison*. New York: Vintage Books.

Foucault, Michel, Graham Burchell, Colin Gordon, and Peter Miller. 1991. *The Foucault effect : studies in governmentality : with two lectures by and an interview with Michel Foucault*. Chicago: University of Chicago Press.

Foucault, Michel and Colin Gordon. 1980. *Power/knowledge : selected interviews and other writings, 1972–1977*. New York: Pantheon Books.

Foucault, Michel and David Couzens Hoy. 1986. *Foucault : a critical reader*. Oxford, UK; New York, NY, USA: B. Blackwell.

Foucault, Michel, Michel Senellart, and Arnold Ira Davidson. 2007. *Security, territory, population : lectures at the Collège de France, 1977–1978*. Houndmills, Basingstoke, Hampshire; New York: Palgrave Macmillan.

Franke, Katherine. 2006. "Sexuality and Marriage: the Politics of Same-Sex Marriage Politics." *Columbia Journal of Gender and Law* 15:236–248.

Franke, Katherine M. 1997. "What's Wrong With Sexual Harassment?" *Stanford Law Review* 49:691–772.

Franke, Katherine M. 2004. "The Domesticated Liberty of Lawrence v. Texas." *Columbia Law Review* 104:1399.

Franke, Katherine M. 2006. "The Politics of Same-Sex Marriage Politics." *Columbia Journal of Gender and Law* 15:236.

Fraser, Nancy and Linda Gordon. 1994. "A Genealogy of Dependency: Tracing a Keyword of the U.S. Welfare State." *Signs* 19: 309–336.

Freeman, Jo. 1975. *The Politics of Women's Liberation: a case study of an emerging social movement and its relation to the policy process*. New York: Longman.

Freeman, Jo. 2008. *We will be heard : women's struggles for political power in the United States*. Lanham, Md.: Rowman & Littlefield Publishers.

Freud, Sigmund and James Strachey. 2005. *Civilization and its discontents*. New York: Norton.

Friedman, Lawrence M. 1994. *Total Justice*. New York: Russell Sage Foundation.

Friedman, Lawrence M. 2005. *A History of American Law*. New York: Simon & Schuster.

Fuss, Diana. 1991. *Inside/out : lesbian theories, gay theories*. New York: Routledge.

Gabel, Peter. 1980. "Reification in Legal Reasoning." *Research in Law and Sociology* 3:25–51.

Gabilondo, Jose. 2006. "Asking the Straight Question: How to Come to Speech in Spite of Conceptual Liquidation as a Homosexual." *Wisconsin Women's Law Journal* 21:1–45.

Gamson, Joshua. 1998. *Freaks talk back : tabloid talk shows and sexual nonconformity*. Chicago: University of Chicago Press.

Gamson, William A. 1990. *The strategy of social protest*. Belmont, Calif.: Wadsworth Pub.

Garfinkel, Harold. 1967. *Studies in ethnomethodology*. Englewood Cliffs, N.J.,: Prentice-Hall.

Gay and Lesbian Alliance Against Defamation. 1998. "GLAAD and National Coalition of Anti-Violence Programs Express Sorrow and Horror at Attack on Gay Man in Wyoming."

Gay and Lesbian Alliance Against Defamation. 2007. "Covering Hate Crimes."

Ghaziani, Amin. 2008. *The dividends of dissent : how conflict and culture work in lesbian and gay marches on Washington*. Chicago: University of Chicago Press.

Gibbs, Jack P. 1975. *Crime, punishment, and deterrence*. New York: Elsevier.

Giddens, Anthony. 1984. *The constitution of society : outline of the theory of structuration*. Berkeley: University of California Press.

Giddens, Anthony. 1992. *The transformation of intimacy : sexuality, love, and eroticism in modern societies*. Stanford, Calif.: Stanford University Press.

Gilligan, Carol, Nona Lyons, Trudy J. Hanmer, and Emma Willard School (Troy N.Y.). 1990. *Making connections : the relational worlds of adolescent girls at Emma Willard School*. Cambridge: Harvard University Press.

Glendon, Mary Ann. 1991. *Rights talk : the impoverishment of political discourse*. New York: Free Press.

Glendon, Mary Ann. 1994. *A nation under lawyers : how the crisis in the legal profession is transforming American society*. New York: Farrar, Straus, and Giroux.

Goffman, Erving. 1961/2007. *Asylums : essays on the social situation of mental patients and other inmates*. New Brunswick, NJ: Aldine Transaction.

Goffman, Erving. 1969. *The presentation of self in everyday life*. London,: Allen Lane.

Gray, John. 1992. *Men are from Mars, women are from Venus : a practical guide for improving communication and getting what you want in your relationships*. New York, NY: Harper Collins.

Greenberg, David F. 1988. *The construction of homosexuality*. Chicago: University of Chicago Press.

Grosz, Elizabeth. 1994a. "Experimental Desire: Rethinking Queer Subjectivity." Pp. 133–157 in *Supposing the Subject*, edited by J. Copjec. London: Verso.

Grosz, E. A. 1994b. *Volatile bodies : toward a corporeal feminism*. Bloomington: Indiana University Press.

Grosz, Elizabeth A. 1997. "The Labors of Love: Analyzing Perverse Desire: An Interrogation of Teresa De Lauretis's *The Practice of Love*." Pp. 292–314 in *Feminism meets queer theory*, edited by E. Weed and N. Schor. Bloomington, Ind.: Indiana University Press.

Habermas, Jurgen. 1973. *Legitimation Crisis*. Boston: Beacon Press.

Habermas, Jürgen. 1996. *Between facts and norms : contributions to a discourse theory of law and democracy*. Cambridge: MIT Press.

Hacker, Jacob S. 2004. "Privatizing Risk Without Privatizing the Welfare State: the Hidden Politics of Social Policy Retrenchment in the United States." *American Political Science Review* 98:243–260.

Halley, Janet. 1993. "The Construction of Heterosexuality." Pp. 82–102 in *Fear of a Queer Planet: Queer Politics and Social Theory*, edited by M. Warner. Minneapolis: University of Minnesota Press.

Halley, Janet. 1994. "Sexual Orientation and the Politics of Biology." *Stanford Law Review* 46.

Halley, Janet. 1998. "Gay Rights and Identity Imitation: Issues in the Ethics of Representation." Pp. 115–146 in *The Politics of Law: a Progressive Critique*, edited by D. Kairys. New York: Basic Books.

Halley, Janet. 2002. "Sexuality Harassment." Pp. 80–104 in *Left Legalism/Left Critique*, edited by W. Brown and J. Halley. Durham, NC: Duke University Press.

Halley, Janet. 2006. *Split decisions : how and why to take a break from feminism*. Princeton, N.J.: Princeton University Press.

Handler, Joel F. 1990. *Law and the search for community*. Philadelphia: University of Pennsylvania Press.

Haney-López, Ian. 1996. *White by law : the legal construction of race*. New York: New York University Press.

Harel, Alon and Gideon Parchomovsky. 1999. "On Hate and Equality." *Yale Law Journal* 109.

Harney, Diane M. 1999. "Lesbians on the Frontline: Battling AIDS, Gays, and the Myth of Community." Pp. 167–179 in *Power in the Blood: a handbook on AIDS, politics, and communication*, edited by W. N. Elwood. New York: Routledge.

Harrison, Cynthia. 1988. *On Account of Sex: the politics of women's issues, 1945–1968*. Berkeley: University of California Press.

Hart, H. L. A. 1968. *Punishment and responsibility: essays in the philosophy of law*. Oxford: Clarendon P.

Hart, H. L. A. and Tony Honoré. 1985. *Causation in the law*. New York:Oxford University Press.

Harvard Law Review. 1990. *Sexual orientation and the law*. Cambridge: Harvard University Press.

Heimer, Carol A. 1996. "Explaining Variation in the Impact of Law: Organizations, Institutions, and Professions." *Studies in Law, Politics, and Society* 15:29–59.

Heimer, Carol A. 2001. "Cases and Biographies: An Essay on Routinization and the Nature of Comparison." *Annual Review of Sociology* 27:47–76.

Herek, Gregory M. 1992. "The Social Context of Hate Crimes: Notes on Cultural Heterosexism." in *Hate Crimes: Confronting Violence Against Lesbians and Gay Men*, edited by G. M. Herek and K. T. Berrill. New York: Sage.

Herek, Gregory M. and Kevin T. Berrill. 1992. *Hate Crimes: confronting violence against lesbians and gay men*. New York: Sage Publications.

Heydebrand, Wolf V. and Carroll Seron. 1990. *Rationalizing justice : the political economy of federal district courts*. Albany: State University of New York Press.

Hilderbrand, Lucas. 2006. "Retroactivism." *GLQ: A Journal of Lesbian and Gay Studies* 12:303–317.

Hill Collins, Patricia. 2004. *Black sexual politics : African Americans, gender, and the new racism*. New York: Routledge.

Hoff-Wilson, Joan. 1991. *Law, gender, and injustice : a legal history of U.S. women*. New York: New York University Press.

Holmes, Oliver W. 1897. "The Path of the Law." *Harvard Law Review* 10(8): 457–478.

Hooks, Bell. 2000. *Feminist theory : from margin to center*. Cambridge: South End Press.

Howe, Adrian. 2000. "Homosexual Advances in Law: Murderous Excuse, Pluralized Ignorance and the Privilege of Unknowing." Pp. 84–99 in *Sexuality in the Legal Arena*, edited by C. F. Stychin and D. Herman. London: The Athlone Press.

Hull, Kathleen. 2006. *Same-sex marriage : the cultural politics of love and law*. Cambridge, UK; New York: Cambridge University Press.

Hulse, Carl. 2009. "House Votes to Expand Hate Crimes Definition *The New York Times*, October 8, 2009.

Human Rights Campaign. 2000. "The State of the Workplace for Lesbian, Gay, Bisexual, and Transgendered Americans 2000." Human Rights Campaign, Washington, D.C.

Hunt, Alan. 1993. *Explorations in law and society : towards a constitutive theory of law*. New York: Routledge.

Hunt, Alan and Gary Wickham. 1994. *Foucault and law : towards a sociology of law as governance*. London; Boulder, Colo.: Pluto Press.

Hurd, Heidi M. 1994. "What in the World is Wrong?" *Journal of Conteporary Legal Issues* 5:157–216.

Hurd, Heidi M. 2001. "Why Liberals Should Hate Hate Crime Legislation." *Law and Philosophy* 20:215–232.

Hurd, Heidi M. and Michael S. Moore. 2004. "Punishing Hatred and Prejudice." *Stanford Law Review* 56:1081–1146.

Hyde, Alan. 1997. *Bodies of law*. Princeton, N.J.: Princeton University Press.

Iganski, Paul. 2001. "Hate Crimes Hurt More." *American Behavioral Scientist* 45:627–38.

Ingraham, Chrys. 2008. *White weddings : romancing heterosexuality in popular culture*. New York: Routledge.

Irigaray, Luce. 1985. *This sex which is not one*. Ithaca, N.Y.: Cornell University Press.

Jacob, Pierre. 2010. ""Intentionality"." in *The Stanford Encyclopedia of Philosophy*, edited by E. N. Zalta.

Jacobs, James B. and Kimberly Potter. 2000. *Hate Crimes: criminal law and identity politics*. New York: Oxford University Press.

Jenness, Valerie. 1999. "Managing differences and making legislation: social movements and the racialization, sexualization, and gendering of federal hate crime law in the U.S., 1985–1998." *Social Problems* 46:548–571.

Jenness, Valerie and Kendal Broad. 1997. *Hate Crimes: new social movements and the politics of violence*. New York: Aldine de Gruyter.

Jenness, Valerie and Ryken Grattet. 2004. *Making Hate a Crime: from social movement to law enforcement*. New York: Russell Sage.

Jessop, Bob. 1990. *State theory : putting the Capitalist state in its place*. Cambridge, U.K.: Polity Press.

Johnson, Cathryn, Timothy J. Dowd, and Cecilia L. Ridgeway. 2006. "Legitimacy as a Social Process." *Annual Review of Sociology* 32:53–77.

Jones, Owen D. and Timothy H. Goldsmith. 2005. "Law and Behavioral Biology." *Columbia Law Review* 105: 405–502.

Kahan, Dan M. 1996. "What Do Alternative Sanctions Mean?" *University of Chicago Law Review* 63:591–653.

Kahan, Dan M. 1998. "The Anatomy of Disgust in Criminal Law." *Michigan Law Review* 96:1621–1657.

Kahan, Dan M. and Martha G. Nussbaum. 1996. "Two Conceptions of Emotion in Criminal Law." *Columbia Law Review* 96: 269–374.

Kairys, David. 1998. *The politics of law : a progressive critique*. New York: Basic Books.

Katz, Leo, Michael S. Moore, and Stephen J. Morse. 1999. *Foundations of criminal law*. New York: Oxford University Press.

Kayal, Philip M. 1993. *Bearing witness : Gay Men's Health Crisis and the politics of AIDS*. Boulder: Westview Press.

Kennedy, Duncan. 1993. *Sexy dressing, etc.* Cambridge: Harvard University Press.

Kennedy, Duncan and Paul Carrington. 2004. *Legal education and the reproduction of hierarchy : a polemic against the system : a critical edition*. New York: New York University Press.

Kennedy, Elizabeth Lapovsky and Madeline D. Davis. 1994. *Boots of leather, slippers of gold : the history of a lesbian community*. New York: Penguin Books.

Kimmel, Michael S. 2007. *The gendered society*. Oxford; New York: Oxford University Press.

Kimmel, Michael S. and Michael A. Messner. 2007. *Men's lives*. Boston, MA: Pearson Allyn and Bacon.

Kinsey, Alfred C., Wardell Baxter Pomeroy, and Clyde E. Martin. 1948. *Sexual behavior in the human male*. Philadelphia,: W. B. Saunders Co.

Klein, Bennett and Daniel Redman. 2009. "From Separate to Equal: Litigating Marriage Equality in a Civil Union State." *Connecticut Law Review* 41:1381–1396.

Kmiec, Douglas W. 1989–1990. "Judicial Selection and the Pursuit of Justice: the Unsettled Relationship Between Law and Morality." *Catholic University Law Review* 19: 1–27.

Kmiec, Keenan D. 2004. "The Origin and Current Meanings of "Judicial Activism"." *California Law Review* 92:1441–47.

Koppelman, Andrew. 2004. "The Decline and Fall of the Case Against Same Sex Marriage." *University of St. Thomas Law Journal* 2: 5–32.

Kornhauser, Lewis A. 2004. "Governance Structures, Legal Systems, and the Concept of Law." *Chicago-Kent Law Review* 79:355–381.

Kotulski, Davina. 2004. *Why you should give a damn about gay marriage*. Los Angeles: Advocate Books.

Lacan, Jacques and Bruce Fink. 2006. *Ecrits : The first complete edition in English*. New York: W.W. Norton & Co.

Lacey, Nicola. 2006. "Analytical Jurisprudence Versus Descriptive Sociology Revisited." *Texas Law Review* 84:945–982.

Landsman, Stephan. 1984. *The adversary system : a description and defense*. Washington, D.C.: American Enterprise Institute for Public Policy Research.

Lawrence, Frederick. 1999. *Punishing Hate: bias crimes under American Law*. Cambridge: Harvard University Press.

Lawson, Joel. 2000. "Ex-Gay Leader Confronted in Gay Bar," *Southern Voice*, September 21, 2000.

Lee, Cynthia. 2003. *Murder and the reasonable man : passion and fear in the criminal courtroom*. New York: New York University Press.

Leeser, Jaimie. 2003. "The Causal Role of Sex in Sexual Harassment." *Cornell Law Review* 88:1750–1793.

Lehring, Gary L. 2003. *Officially gay : the political construction of sexuality by the U.S. military*. Philadelphia: Temple University Press.

Levin, Jack and Jack McDevitt. 2002. *Hate Crimes Revisited: America's War on Those Who Are Different*. Cambridge: Westview Press.

Levit, Nancy. 2010. "Theorizing and Litigating the Rights of Sexual Minorities." *Columbia Journal of Gender and Law* 19:21–63.

Levit, Nancy and Robert R. M. Verchick. 2006. *Feminist legal theory : a primer*. New York: New York University Press.

Lewis, C.S. 1987. "The Humanitarian Theory of Punishment." *The AMCAP Journal* 13:147–153.

Lind, E. Allan and Tom R. Tyler. 1988. *The social psychology of procedural justice*. New York: Plenum Press.

Lithwick, Dahlia. 2009. "Once More, Without Feeling: the GOP's Misguided and Confused Campaign Against Judicial Empathy." Slate.com: Jurisprudence, http://www.slate.com/id/2218103/

Lorber, Judith. 1994. *Paradoxes of gender*. New Haven: Yale University Press.

Lorber, Judith and Susan A. Farrell. 1991. *The Social construction of gender*. Newbury Park, Calif.: Sage Publications.

Luhmann, Niklas and Martin Albrow. 1985. *A sociological theory of law*. Boston: Routledge & Kegan Paul.

Luhmann, Niklas, Klaus A. Ziegert, and Fatima Kastner. 2004. *Law as a social system*. New York: Oxford University Press.

MacKinnon, Catharine A. 1979. *Sexual harassment of working women : a case of sex discrimination*. New Haven: Yale University Press.

MacKinnon, Catharine A. 1987. *Feminism unmodified : discourses on life and law*. Cambridge: Harvard University Press.

MacKinnon, Catharine A. 1989. *Toward a feminist theory of the state*. Cambridge: Harvard University Press.

MacKinnon, Catharine A. 1993. *Only words*. Cambridge: Harvard University Press.

Maltz, Earl M. 1992. "Slavery, Federalism, and the Structure of the Constitution." *The American Journal of Legal History* 36: 466–498.

Mansbridge, Jane J. 1986. *Why We Lost the ERA*. Chicago: University of Chicago Press.

March, James G. and Johan P. Olsen. 1984. "The New Institutionalism: Organizational Factors in Political Life." *The American Political Science Review* 78:734–749.

Marcus, Ruth. 1990. "Powell Regrets Backing Sodomy Law," *The Washington Post*, October 26, 1990.

Marcuse, Herbert. 1955. *Eros and civilization; a philosophical inquiry into Freud*. Boston: Beacon Press.

Marshall, Anna-Maria. 2005. *Confronting sexual harassment: the law and politics of everyday life*. Burlington, VT: Ashgate.

Marx, Groucho. 1967/2007. *The Groucho letters*. New York: Simon & Schuster.

McAdam, Doug. 1988. *Freedom Summer*. New York: Oxford University Press.

McAdam, Doug. 1995. ""Initiator" and "Spin-off" Movements: Diffusion Processes in Protest Cycles." Pp. 217–240 in *Repertoires and cycles of collective action*, edited by M. Traugott. Chapel Hill, NC: Duke University Press.

McAdam, Doug, John D. McCarthy, and Mayer N. Zald. 1996. *Comparative perspectives on social movements : political opportunities, mobilizing structures, and cultural framings*. New York: Cambridge University Press.

Parsons, Talcott. 1951. *The social system*. Glencoe, Ill.,: Free Press.

Parsons, Talcott. 1961. *Theories of society; foundations of modern sociological theory*. New York: Free Press of Glencoe.

Parsons, Talcott. 1977. *Social systems and the evolution of action theory*. New York: Free Press.

Pascoe, C. J. 2007. *Dude, you're a fag : masculinity and sexuality in high school*. Berkeley: University of California Press.

Patton, Cindy. 1993. "Tremble, Hetero Swine!" Pp. 143–177 in *Fear of a Queer Planet*, edited by M. Warner. Minneapolis: University of Minnesota Press.

Paul, Jay. 1984. "The Bisexual Identity: An Idea Without Social Recognition." *Journal of Homosexuality* 9:45–63.

Phelan, Shane. 2001. *Sexual strangers : gays, lesbians, and dilemmas of citizenship*. Philadelphia: Temple University Press.

Pickel, Andreas. 2007. "Rethinking Systems Theory." *Philosophy of the Social Sciences* 37:391–407.

Pinello, Daniel R. 2003. *Gay rights and American law*. New York: Cambridge University Press.

Pinello, Daniel R. 2006. *America's struggle for same-sex marriage*. New York: Cambridge University Press.

Piven, Frances Fox and Richard A. Cloward. 1979. *Poor people's movements : why they succeed, how they fail*. New York: Vintage books.

Piven, Frances Fox and Richard A. Cloward. 1993. *Regulating the poor : the functions of public welfare*. New York: Vintage Books.

Plato. 1998. *Symposium*, Edited by C. J. Rowe. Warminster, England: Aris & Phillips.

Poirier, Marc R. 2008a. "Microperformances of identity: Visible Same-Sex Couples and the Marriage Controversy." *Washington & Lee Journal of Civil Rights and Social Justice* 15:3–84.

Poirier, Marc R. 2008b. "Where is Same Sex Marriage?" *Florida International University Law Review* 3:307–339.

Poirier, Marc R. 2009. "Name Calling: Identifying Stigma in the "Civil Union"/"Marriage" Distinction." *Connecticut Law Review* 41: 1425–1494.

Polikoff, Nancy D. 2008. *Beyond straight and gay marriage : valuing all families under the law*. Boston: Beacon Press.

Posner, Richard. 1985. "An Economic Theory of the Criminal Law." *Columbia Law Review* 85:1193–1231.

Posner, Richard. 1992. *Sex and Reason*. Cambridge: Harvard University Press.

Poulantzas, Nicos Ar. 1969. "The Problem of the Capitalist State." *New Left Review* 1.

Poulantzas, Nicos Ar. 1978. *State, power, socialism*. London: NLB.

Pound, Roscoe. 1942. *Social control through law*. New Haven Yale University Press.

Powell, Walter W. 1996. "Fields of Practice: Connections Between Law and Organizations." *Law & Social Inquiry* 21:959–966.

Powell, Walter W. and Paul DiMaggio. 1991. *The New institutionalism in organizational analysis*. Chicago: University of Chicago Press.

Riley, Denise. 1988/2003. *Am I That Name?: Feminism and the Category of "Women" in History*. Minneapolis: University of Minnesota Press.

Robertson, Campbell and Clifford Krauss. 2010. "Robots Work to Stop Leak of Oil in the Gulf," *The New York Times*, April 26, 2010.

Robson, Ruthann. 2009. "Compulsory Matrimony." Pp. 313–328 in *Feminist and Queer Legal Theory: Intimate Encounters, Uncomfortable Conversations*, edited by M. Fineman, J. E. Jackson, and A. P. Romero. Burlington, VT: Ashgate.

Rosenberg, Gerald N. 1991. *The hollow hope : can courts bring about social change?* Chicago: University of Chicago.

Rubin, Gayle. 1975. "The Traffic in Women: Notes on the "Political Economy of Sex"." Pp. 157–210 in *Toward and Anthropology of Women*, edited by R. Reiter. New York: Monthly Review Press.

Rubin, Henry. 2003. *Self-made men : identity and embodiment among transsexual men*. Nashville: Vanderbilt University Press.

Saad, Lydia. 2007. "Tolerance for Gay Rights at High-Water Mark: Public Evenly Divided Over Whether Homosexuality is Morally Acceptable or Wrong." in *Gallup News Service*, May 29, 2007.

Saliers, Emily and Amy Ray. 1997. "Get out the map, Shaming of the Sun.

Sandalow, Marc. 2000. "Exuberant Gay March in D.C.: Hundreds of Thousands Join Call for Equality." in *The San Francisco Chronicle*, May 1, 2000.

Sarat, Austin and Stuart A. Scheingold. 2005. *The worlds cause lawyers make : structure and agency in legal practice*. Stanford, Calif.: Stanford Law and Politics.

Sarat, Austin and Stuart A. Scheingold. 2006. *Cause lawyers and social movements*. Stanford, CA: Stanford Law and Politics.

Sarat, Austin and Stuart A. Scheingold. 2008. *The cultural lives of cause lawyers*. Cambridge; New York: Cambridge University Press.

Sarat, Austin and Jonathan Simon. 2001. "Beyond Legal Realism?: Cultural Analysis, Cultural Studies, and The Situation of Legal Scholarship." *Yale Journal of Law and the Humanities* 1:3–34.

Savage, Dan. 2005. *The commitment : love, sex, marriage, and my family.* New York: Dutton.

Schacter, Jane S. 2009. "The Other Same-Sex Marriage Debate." *Chicago-Kent Law Review* 84: 379–402.

Scheingold, Stuart A. 1974. *The politics of rights : lawyers, public policy, and political change.* New Haven: Yale University Press.

Scheingold, Stuart A. and Austin Sarat. 1998. *Cause Lawyering: political commitments and professional responsibilities.* New York: Oxford University Press.

Schmeiser, Susan. 2009. "Changing the Immutable." *Connecticut Law Review* 41:1495–1522.

Schrock, Douglas, Lori Reid, and Emily M. Boyd. 2005. "Transsexuals' Embodiment of Womanhood." *Gender & Society* 19:317–335.

Schultz, Vicki. 1998. "Reconceptualizing Sexual Harassment." *Yale Law Journal* 107:1683–1805.

Schultz, Vicki. 2003. "The Sanitized Workplace." *Yale Law Journal* 112:2061–2193.

Sedgwick, Eve Kosofsky. 1990. *Epistemology of the closet.* Berkeley: University of California Press.

Sedgwick, Eve Kosofsky. 1993. *Tendencies.* Durham: Duke University Press.

Seidman, Steven. 1993. "Identity and Politics in a 'Postmodern' Gay Culture: Some Historical and Conceptual Notes." Pp. 105–142 in *Fear of a Queer Planet*, edited by M. Warner. Minneapolis: University of Minnesota Press.

Seidman, Steven. 1996. *Queer Theory/Sociology*, Edited by C. C. Lemert. Cambridge: Blackwell Publishers.

Seidman, Steven. 2010. *The social construction of sexuality.* New York: W. W. Norton.

Seron, Carroll and Frank Munger. 1996. "Law and Inequality: Race, Gender . . . and, of Course, Class." *Annual Review of Sociology* 22: 187–212.

Shaman, Jeffrey M. 1996. "The Impartial Judge: Detachment or Passion?" *DePaul Law Review* 45: 605–632.

Skocpol, Theda. 1992. *Protecting soldiers and mothers : the political origins of social policy in the United States.* Cambridge: Belknap Press of Harvard University Press.

Smith, Dorothy E. 1990. *The Conceptual Practices of Power: A Feminist Sociology of Knowledge*. Boston: Northeastern University Press.

Smythe, Michael A. 2006. "Queers and Provocateurs: Hegemony, Ideology, and the 'Homosexual Advance' Defense." *Law & Society Review* 40:903–927.

Socarides, Charles W. 1978. *Homosexuality*. New York: J. Aronson.

Soule, Sarah and Jennifer Earl. 2001. "The Enactment of State-Level Hate Crime Law in the United States: Intrastate and Interstate Factors." *Sociological Perspectives* 44:281–305.

Soule, Sarah A. and Yvonne Zylan. 1997. "Runaway Train? The Diffusion of State-Level Reform in ADC/AFDC Eligibility Requirements, 1950–1967." *The American Journal of Sociology* 103:733–762.

Spaulding, Pam. 2010. "Republican Sexual Hypocrites, 2010 Edition: Add Anti-Gay California State Senator Roy Ashburn." in *Pam's House Blend*, http://www.pamshouseblend.com/diary/15414/republican-sexual-hypocrites-2010-edition-add-antigay-california-state-senator-roy-ashburn.

Stein, Arlene and Kenneth Plummer. 1996. ""I Can't Even Think Straight":'Queer' Theory and the Missing Sexual Revolution in Sociology" Pp. 129–144 in *Queer Theory/Sociology*, edited by S. Seidman. Cambridge: Blackwell Publishers.

Storrow, Richard F. 1998. "Same-Sex Sexual Harassment Claims After Oncale: Defining the Boundaries of Actionable Conduct." *American University Law Review* 47: 677–745

Stryker, Robin. 2007. "Half Empty, Half Full, or Neither: Inequality, and Social Change in Capitalist Democracies." *Annual Review of Law and Social Science* 3:69–97.

Stychin, Carl F. 1998. *A nation by rights : national cultures, sexual identity politics, and the discourse of rights*. Philadelphia: Temple University Press.

Stychin, Carl F. 2003. *Governing sexuality : the changing politics of citizenship and law reform*. Portland: Hart Pub.

Stychin, Carl F. and Didi Herman. 2001. *Law and sexuality : the global arena*. Minneapolis: University of Minnesota Press.

Suchman, Mark C. and Lauren B. Edelman. 1996. "Legal Rational Myths: The New Institutionalism and the Law and Society Tradition." *Law & Social Inquiry* 21:903–941.

Sudnow, David. 1965. "Normal Crimes: Sociological Features of the Penal Code in a Public Defender Office." *Social Problems* 12: 255–276.

Suffredini, Kara S. 2001. "Pride and Prejudice: the homosexual panic defense." *B.C. Third World Law Journal* 21: 279–314.

Sullivan, Andrew. 1996. *Virtually normal : an argument about homosexuality*. New York: Vintage Books.

Sunstein, Cass R. 1989. "Sexual Orientation and the Constitution: A Note on the Relationship Between Due Process and Equal Protection." *University of Chicago Law Review* 55:1161–79.

Sunstein, Cass R. 1990. *After the Rights Revolution: Reconceiving the Regulatory State*. Cambridge: Harvard University Press.

Sunstein, Cass R. 1996. "On the Expressive Function of Law." *University of Pennsylvania Law Review* 144:2021–2053.

Sutton, John R. 1996. "Rethinking Social Control." *Law & Social Inquiry* 21:943–958.

Swartz, David. 1997. *Culture & power : the sociology of Pierre Bourdieu*. Chicago: University of Chicago Press.

Tamanaha, Brian Z. 2001. *A general jurisprudence of law and society*. New York: Oxford University Press.

Tamanaha, Brian Z. 2006. *Law as a means to an end : threat to the rule of law*. New York: Cambridge University Press.

Tarrow, Sidney G. 1998. *Power in movement : social movements and contentious politics*. New York: Cambridge University Press.

Taylor, Verta, Katrina Kimport, Nella Van Dyke, and Ellen Andersen. 2009. "Culture and Mobilization: Tactical Repertoires, Same-Sex Weddings, and the Impact on Gay Activism." *American Sociological Review* 74:865–890.

The New York Times. 2009. "Obama's Remarks on the Resignation of Justice Souter, in *The New York Times*, May 1, 2009.

Thorne, Barrie. 1993. *Gender play : girls and boys in school*. New Brunswick, N.J.: Rutgers University Press.

Thorne, Barrie and Marilyn Yalom. 1992. *Rethinking the family : some feminist questions*. Boston: Northeastern University Press.

Touraine, Alain. 1977. *The self-production of society*. Chicago: University of Chicago Press.

Touraine, Alain. 1981. *The voice and the eye : an analysis of social movements*. New York: Cambridge University Press.

Traugott, Mark. 1995. *Repertoires and cycles of collective action*. Durham: Duke University Press.

Tushnet, Mark. 1984. "A Critique of Rights." *Texas Law Review* 62: 1363–1403.

Tyler, Carole-Anne. 1997. "Passing: Narcissism, Identity, and Difference." in *feminism meets queer theory, Differences*, edited by E. Weed and N. Schor. Bloomington: Indiana University Press.

United States Department of Justice, Federal Bureau of Investigation. 2006. "Hate Crime Statistics, 2005." Washington, D.C: U.S. Government Printing Office.

United States Bureau of the Census. 2010. "2010 Statistical Abstracts, "Marital Status of the Population by Sex and Age, 2008"." Washington, D.C: U.S. Government Printing Office.

United States Department of Health and Human Services, National Center for Health Statistics. 2009. "Who Marries and When? Age at First Marriage in the United States, 2002." Washington, D.C: U.S. Government Printing Office.

Valocchi, Stephen. 2009. "The Importance of Being 'We': Collective Identity and the Mobilizing Work of Progressive Activists in Hartford, Connecticut." *Mobilization* 14:65–84.

Warner, Michael. 1991. "Introduction: Fear of a Queer Planet." *Social Text*:3–17.

Warner, Michael. 1999. *The trouble with normal : sex, politics, and the ethics of queer life*. New York: Free Press.

Warner, Michael and Social Text Collective. 1993. *Fear of a queer planet : queer politics and social theory*. Minneapolis: University of Minnesota Press.

Weber, Max. 1954. *Max Weber on law in economy and society*. Cambridge,: Harvard University Press.

Weber, Max. 1978. *Economy and Society: an outline of interpretive sociology*. Translated by G. Roth and C. Wittich. Berkeley: University of California Press.

Weed, Elizabeth and Naomi Schor. 1997. *Feminism meets queer theory*. Bloomington, Ind.: Indiana University Press.

Weeks, Jeffrey. 1985. *Sexuality and its discontents : meanings, myths, & modern sexualities*. Boston: Routledge & K. Paul.

Weisberg, D. Kelly. 1993. *Feminist legal theory : foundations*. Philadelphia: Temple University Press.

Wells, Michael L. 2007. "Sociological Legitimacy in Supreme Court Opinions." *Washington & Lee Law Review* 64:1011–1070.

West, Candace and Don H. Zimmerman. 1987. "Doing Gender." *Gender & Society* 1:125–151.

West, Robin. 2007. *Marriage, sexuality, and gender*. Boulder, CO: Paradigm Publishers.

Weston, Kath. 1991. *Families we choose : lesbians, gays, kinship*. New York: Columbia University Press.

Williams, Patricia J. 1991. *The alchemy of race and rights*. Cambridge: Harvard University Press.

Wilson, Edward O. 1978. *On human nature*. Cambridge: Harvard University Press.

Wittig, Monique. 1992. *The straight mind and other essays*. Boston: Beacon Press.

Wolfson, Evan. 1994. "Crossing the Threshold: Equal Marriage Rights for Lesbians and Gay Men and the Intra-Community Critique." *New York University Review of Law & Social Change* 21:567–615.

Yoshino, Kenji. 2006. *Covering : the hidden assault on our civil rights*. New York: Random House.

Yoshino, Kenji. 2007. "Marriage, Trademarked." in *Slate: Jurisprudence*, http://www.slate.com/id/2169615/.

Zald, Mayer N. and John D. McCarthy. 1987. *Social movements in an organizational society : collected essays*. New Brunswick: Transaction Books.

Zimring, Franklin E. and Gordon Hawkins. 1973. *Deterrence; the legal threat in crime control*. Chicago: University of Chicago Press.

Zylan, Yvonne. (in progress) "The Salacious State: Postmodern Patriarchy and the Enforcement of the Marriage Contract."

Zylan, Yvonne. 1995. "The Divided Female State: gender, citizenship, and U.S. social policy development, 1945–1990." New York University, Dept. of Sociology (Ph.D. Dissertation).

Zylan, Yvonne. 1996. "Comment on Fraser and Gordon's "A Genealogy of Dependency: Tracing a Keyword of the U.S. Welfare State"." *Signs* 21:515–530.

Zylan, Yvonne. 2000. "Maternalism Redefined: Gender, the State, and the Politics of Day Care, 1945–1962." *Gender & Society* 14:608–629

Zylan, Yvonne. 2006. "Finding the Sex in Sexual Harassment: How Title VII and Tort Schemes Miss the Point of Same-Sex Hostile Environment Harassment." *Michigan Journal of Law Reform* 39:391–431.

Zylan, Yvonne. 2009. "Passions We Like . . . And Those We Don't: Anti-Gay Hate Crime and the Discursive Construction of Sex, Gender, and the Body." *Michigan Journal of Gender & Law* 16:1–48.

Zylan, Yvonne and Sarah A. Soule. 2000. "Ending Welfare As We Know It (Again): Welfare State Retrenchment, 1989–1995." *Social Forces* 79:623–652.

# Index